ROMANS THROUGH REVELATION

THEOLOGY OF WORK BIBLE COMMENTARY

ROMANS THROUGH REVELATION
VOLUME 5

THEOLOGY OF WORK PROJECT

THEOLOGY OF WORK BIBLE COMMENTARY, VOLUME 5: ROMANS THROUGH REVELATION

Copyright © 2015 by the Theology of Work Project, Inc.

Print edition published by Hendrickson Publishers Marketing, LLC, P.O. Box 3473, Peabody, Massachusetts 01961-3473 under license from the Theology of Work Project, Inc. No part of the print edition may be reproduced or transmitted in any form or by any means, electronic or mechanical, including photocopying, recording, or by any information storage and retrieval system, without permission in writing from the publisher.

ISBN 978-1-61970-596-8

Printed in the United States of America

First Printing — March 2015

Library of Congress Cataloging-in-Publication Data

Theology of work Bible commentary / by the Theology of Work Project ;
    William Messenger, executive editor.
        volumes cm
    Includes bibliographical references and index.
        Contents: volume 4. Matthew through Acts — 1. Work—Religious aspects—
Christianity. 2. Work—Biblical teaching. I. Messenger, William, 1960- editor.
II. Theology of Work Project (Boston, Mass.)
    BT738.5.T45 2014
    220.8'331—dc23
                    2014022025

Table of Contents

Abbreviations	ix
Foreword	xi
Introduction to the Theology of Work	1

Romans and Work

Introduction to Romans	3
The Gospel of Salvation—Paul's Vocation (Romans 1:1–17)	4
Our Need for Salvation in Life and Work (Romans 1:18–1:32)	6
All Have Sinned (Romans 2–3)	8
Judgment, Justice, and Faith (Romans 3)	10
An Exemplary Faith: Abraham Trusted God's Promises (Romans 4)	15
Grace Reigns for Eternal Life through Jesus Christ (Romans 5)	16
Walking in Newness of Life (Romans 6)	18
The Invasive Power of "Sin" (Romans 7)	21
Living According to the Spirit (Romans 8)	22
God's Character Is to Have Mercy on Everyone (Romans 9–11)	28
The Community of Grace at Work (Romans 12)	30
Living under the Power of God (Romans 13)	36
Welcoming—Living Peacefully with Different Values and Opinions (Romans 14–15)	38
A Community of Leaders (Romans 16)	41
Conclusion to Romans	43

1 Corinthians and Work

Introduction to 1 Corinthians	45
All Are Called (1 Corinthians 1:1–3)	47
Spiritual Resources Available (1 Corinthians 1:4–9)	48
The Need for a Common Vision (1 Corinthians 1:10–17)	49
Friends in Low Places (1 Corinthians 1:18–31)	50
It Takes All Sorts (1 Corinthians 3:1–9)	51

Do Good Work (1 Corinthians 3:10–17)   52
Leadership as Service (1 Corinthians 4:1–4)   53
Working with Nonbelievers (1 Corinthians 5:9–10)   54
Bloom Where You Are Planted (1 Corinthians 7:20–24)   55
Maintain the Proper Perspective (1 Corinthians 7:29–31)   56
Everyone Gets Their Fair Share (1 Corinthians 9:7–10)   58
God's Glory Is the Ultimate Goal (1 Corinthians 10)   59
Gifted Communities (1 Corinthians 12:1–14:40)   61
Our Work Is Not in Vain (1 Corinthians 15:58)   63
We Share Our Resources with Those in Hardship
    (1 Corinthians 16:1–3)   64
Conclusion to 1 Corinthians   65

2 Corinthians and Work

Introduction to 2 Corinthians   67
Thank God for Relationships (2 Corinthians 1:1–11)   68
Transparency (2 Corinthians 1:12–23)   70
Working for the Joy of Others (2 Corinthians 1:24)   71
The Priority of Relationships (2 Corinthians 2:12–16)   72
Sincerity (2 Corinthians 2:17)   73
A Genuine Reputation (2 Corinthians 3)   74
Leading and Serving (2 Corinthians 4)   75
Performance and Accountability (2 Corinthians 5:1–15)   78
Reconciling the Whole World (2 Corinthians 5:16–21)   79
Transparency Revisited (2 Corinthians 6:11)   80
Working with Nonbelievers (2 Corinthians 6:14–18)   81
The Encouragement of Praise (2 Corinthians 7)   85
Generosity Is Not Optional (2 Corinthians 8:1–9)   85
Timely Fulfillment of Obligations (2 Corinthians 8:10–12)   87
Sharing the Wealth (2 Corinthians 8:13–15)   87
You Can't Out-Give God (2 Corinthians 9)   89
Assessing Performance (2 Corinthians 10–13)   91
Conclusion to 2 Corinthians   92

Galatians, Ephesians, Philippians, and Work

Galatians and Work   93
Ephesians and Work   99
Philippians and Work   107

Colossians & Philemon and Work

Introduction to Colossians and Philemon   119

Background on Colossae and the Colossians   119

God at Work, Jesus at Work (Colossians 1:15–20)   121

God Worked in Creation, Making Humans Workers
in His Image (Colossians 1:1–14)   122

Jesus, the Image of the Invisible God (Colossians 1:15–29)   123

"I'm Doing Alright by Myself" (Colossians 2:1–23)   125

Heavenly Living for Earthly Good: The Shape of our
Reorientation (Colossians 3:1–16)   126

Of Slaves and Masters, Ancient and Contemporary
(Colossians 3:18–4:1)   131

Philemon   134

Conclusion to Colossians and Philemon   135

1 & 2 Thessalonians and Work

Introduction to 1 & 2 Thessalonians   137

Working Faith, Finishing Up, and Keeping the Faith
(1 Thessalonians 1:1–4:8; 4:13–5:28;
2 Thessalonians 1:1–2:17)   139

Faithful Work (1 Thessalonians 4:9–12 and
2 Thessalonians 3:6–16)   140

Christians Are Expected to Work
(1 Thessalonians 4:9–12; 5:14)   143

Those Truly Unable to Work Should Receive Assistance
(1 Thessalonians 4:9–10)   146

Idleness (2 Thessalonians 3:6–15)   148

Conclusion to 1 & 2 Thessalonians   149

The Pastoral Epistles and Work

Introduction to the Pastoral Epistles   151

1 Timothy: Working for Order in God's Household   152

2 Timothy: Encouragement for a Faithful Worker   162

Titus: Working for Good Deeds   166

Conclusion to the Pastoral Epistles   170

Hebrews and Work

Introduction to Hebrews   173

Christ Created and Sustains the World (Hebrews 1:1–2:8)   173

The Creation Has Become Subject to Evil (Hebrews 2:14–3:6)   176
Life in the Wilderness: Journey to the New World
        (Hebrews 3:7–4:16)   177
Our Great High Priest (Hebrews 5:1–10:18)   179
Realizing the Faith (Hebrews 10–11)   183
Enduring Hardship, Pursuing Peace (Hebrews 12:1–16)   186
Shaking Things Up (Hebrews 12:18–29)   187
Hospitality (Hebrews 13:1–3)   188
Money Matters (Hebrews 13:5–6)   189
Working Outside the Camp (Hebrews 13:11–25)   190
Conclusion to Hebrews   191

The General Epistles and Work
Introduction to the General Epistles   193
James: Faith and Work   194
1 Peter: Serving the World as Resident Alien Priests   210
2 Peter: Work and New Creation   215
1 John: Walking in the Light   218
2 John and Work   221
3 John and Work   224
Jude   226
Conclusion to the General Epistles   227

Revelation and Work
Introduction to Revelation   231
The Time of God's Kingdom (Revelation 1)   231
Messages to the Churches (Revelation 2 and 3)   232
The Throne Room of God (Revelation 4 and 5)   233
The Strange Way Forward (Revelation 6–16)   233
A Tale of Two Cities (Revelation 17–22)   236
Conclusion to Revelation   239

Bibliography   241
Contributors   249
Index of Names and Subjects   255

Abbreviations

Old Testament

Gen.	Genesis	Eccl.	Ecclesiastes
Exod.	Exodus	Song	Song of Songs
Lev.	Leviticus	Isa.	Isaiah
Num.	Numbers	Jer.	Jeremiah
Deut.	Deuteronomy	Lam.	Lamentations
Josh.	Joshua	Ezek.	Ezekiel
Judg.	Judges	Dan.	Daniel
Ruth	Ruth	Hos.	Hosea
1 Sam.	1 Samuel	Joel	Joel
2 Sam.	2 Samuel	Amos	Amos
1 Kgs.	1 Kings	Obad.	Obadiah
2 Kgs.	2 Kings	Jonah	Jonah
1 Chr.	1 Chronicles	Mic.	Micah
2 Chr.	2 Chronicles	Nah.	Nahum
Ezra	Ezra	Hab.	Habakkuk
Neh.	Nehemiah	Zeph.	Zephaniah
Est.	Esther	Hag.	Haggai
Job	Job	Zech.	Zechariah
Ps(s).	Psalm(s)	Mal.	Malachi
Prov.	Proverbs		

New Testament

Matt.	Matthew	Rom.	Romans
Mark	Mark	1 Cor.	1 Corinthians
Luke	Luke	2 Cor.	2 Corinthians
John	John	Gal.	Galatians
Acts	Acts	Eph.	Ephesians

Phil.	Philippians	James	James
Col.	Colossians	1 Pet.	1 Peter
1 Thess.	1 Thessalonians	2 Pet.	2 Peter
2 Thess.	2 Thessalonians	1 John	1 John
1 Tim.	1 Timothy	2 John	2 John
2 Tim.	2 Timothy	3 John	3 John
Titus	Titus	Jude	Jude
Philem.	Philemon	Rev.	Revelation
Heb.	Hebrews		

Any commentary references not in this particular volume can be found at the Theology of Work website (www.theologyofwork.org), along with video interviews and sidebars on people in the work world.

Foreword

The *Theology of Work Bible Commentary* is unique in that it explores what the entire Bible says about work. It represents more than five years of research by 140 contributors from sixteen countries, guided by an international steering committee of twenty scholars, pastors, and Christians from a variety of workplaces. We are thankful to God for this opportunity to present it to you in this volume.

Why does anyone need a theology of work? When we talk about a "theology," it can sound as stuffy as a tomb. Theology is often considered the domain of scholars who are wrestling with questions that no one ever asks, or solving problems that have never really arisen. When we talk about theology, however, we are really talking about what we know or do not know about God. Everyone does theology. Atheists who say they don't believe in God are already dealing with theology. Wars are fought over theology by people who are convinced that they are doing God's will. Agree with them or not, everyone everywhere does theology. People in the workplace who may never attend church are dealing with theology in some way every day. Ultimately, the questions we ask about God are not merely religious, they are life altering. In fact, what you believe about God may be the most important thing you ever think about. That's theology!

When it comes to work, theology is seldom practiced out loud. During my early years as president at Denver Seminary, I hosted a morning Bible study for business people. After class, over breakfast, we discussed the myriad dilemmas these workers and leaders faced in the workplace. Again and again, I heard, "You're the first pastoral person to actively address how my faith relates to my work." It was then that I realized there was a great divide between the leadership of the church and the everyday lives of the people they are called to equip.

At its heart, the perceived distance between God and everyday work is a theological issue. Most Christians believe that God cares about how we relate to others, how we relate to him, and whether we cheat, steal, lie, or break the Ten Commandments. However, it would surprise a lot of us to learn that our work matters to God. God cares what we do for a living, how we do it, and how we use our resources. As it turns out, the Bible has much to say about work. In fact, work is a major topic in the Bible, beginning with the surprising statement in Genesis 2:15 that God created people to work—not as a punishment, but as a pleasure and a way of relating to God himself.

The Scriptures provide principles that both give *meaning* to work and tell us *how* to work. Unfortunately, there is not a book in the Bible called First and Second Executive or Letter to the Christian Plumbers. Instead, what the Bible teaches about God's view of work is embedded in the Scriptures. Only a few of the biblical writers speak directly about the work that people do. They simply assume it. For instance, one of the Ten Commandments declares, "Remember the sabbath day and keep it holy" (Exod. 20:8), as if the only day God cared about was the Sabbath. But the command also says, "Six days you shall labor and do all your work" (Exod. 20:9). So the command deals not only with a special day when we can rest, but with the other days of the week designed for work.

The *Theology of Work Bible Commentary* goes through the Bible book by book to bring to the surface what we might not have seen about work at first blush. For example, consider the last book of the Bible, Revelation. It is possible to be so caught up in the visions in Revelation and questions about when they will occur, that we do not see that the Scripture also tells us about work now and in the future. You might be surprised that the Song of Solomon, a love poem, has quite a bit to say about workers and work. This book attempts through a study of the Scriptures to answer the question, "Does the work we do matter to God?"

This commentary deals with the theology of *work*. In that sense, it is limited. And in another sense, it is very broad. It is limited to work, but work is as diverse as are the people in the world. One question that may come to mind is, "What is work?" The answer to that question seems obvious. Work is what we do to make a living. Saying that, however, implies that people work for forty or fifty hours a week in order to live for the other hours of the week. There is more to work than that. A farmer, for example, doesn't "work to make a living." Plowing a field, planting a crop, bringing in a harvest is really his life. Or when we say that people "work to make a living," we imply that they work to receive a salary or a wage. But what about volunteers who travel to another country at their own expense to help people who have suffered in an earthquake or a flood? What about the person who raises children, cooks meals, and takes care of the family home? Certainly these people work, and work hard, but do not receive a salary. What, then, do we mean when we talk about their "work"?

Others might insist that the opposite of work is play. These are the folks who say, "TGIF: Thank God, it's Friday and the weekend is coming!" The recreation we enjoy on the weekend stands in contrast to the labor we put in during the week. But what about the professional basketball or tennis player? Do they work? How does their "work" differ from recreation?

If you own a business, what responsibility do you have to the people who work for you and to the people who buy your products or services? If you're an employee, does God care about the products you make or the way your company advertises them? Is what you talk about when you're having coffee with co-workers important to God? Does God have anything to do with the work that consumes a major part of your life?

If you're a pastor reading this material on a theology of work, do you find yourself thinking about a woman in the eighth row, three seats from the end, who works in financial services, or the man behind her who is a nurse? Or a couple on the other side of the sanctuary who has recently invested everything they have to open a restaurant? Do you think about yourself as a pastor? Do you work? Perhaps you are tempted to respond, "Of course I do, but it's really not the same thing. I have a special calling from God." That leads to another question: What do you mean by a "call"? Is it reserved for missionaries, teachers at a Bible college or a seminary, or translators of the Bible? How about the executive, the vice president of an insurance company, or the bus driver who attends your church? Do they have a call from God? Does God call men and women in business, government, or nonprofit organizations to their positions? Can you imagine God "calling" a pastor to go back into the world of work? Is that whole way of thinking true to the Bible?

So you see, there is a flood of questions about the simple concept of work. In fact, we are barraged by questions about work that have to be answered. This commentary will not answer these sticky issues by providing a set of rules, but it will give you direction in coming to your own conclusions. After all, the Scriptures resemble a compass rather than a road map. But when you're on the journey, a compass can be very helpful. The *Theology of Work Bible Commentary* helps us plumb the depths of God's word, so that we can hear and respond to Jesus' voice in the calling of our everyday work.

Haddon W. Robinson
President
Theology of Work Project

Harold John Ockenga Distinguished Professor of Preaching
Gordon-Conwell Theological Seminary
Hamilton, Massachusetts, USA

Introduction to the Theology of Work

Work is not only a human calling, but also a divine one. "In the beginning God created the heavens and the earth." God worked to create us and created us to work. "The LORD God took the man and put him in the garden of Eden to till it and keep it" (Gen. 2:15). God also created work to be good, even if it's hard to see in a fallen world. To this day, God calls us to work to support ourselves and to serve others (Eph. 4:28).

Work can accomplish many of God's purposes for our lives—the basic necessities of food and shelter, as well as a sense of fulfillment and joy. Our work can create ways to help people thrive; it can discover the depths of God's creation; and it can bring us into wonderful relationships with co-workers and those who benefit from our work (customers, clients, patients, and so forth).

Yet many people face drudgery, boredom, or exploitation at work. We have bad bosses, hostile relationships, and unfriendly work environments. Our work seems useless, unappreciated, faulty, frustrating. We don't get paid enough. We get stuck in dead-end jobs or laid off or fired. We fail. Our skills become obsolete. It's a struggle just to make ends meet. But how can this be if God created work to be good—and what can we do about it? God's answers for these questions must be somewhere in the Bible, but where?

The Theology of Work Project's mission has been to study what the Bible says about work and to develop resources to apply the Christian faith to our work. It turns out that every book of the Bible gives practical, relevant guidance that can help us do our jobs better, improve our relationships at work, support ourselves, serve others more effectively, and find meaning and value in our work. The Bible shows us how to live all of life—including work—in Christ. Only in Jesus can we and our work be transformed to become the blessing it was always meant to be.

To put it another way, if we are not following Christ during the 100,000 hours of our lives that we spend at work, are we really following Christ? Our lives are more than just one day a week at church. The fact is that God cares about our life *every day of the week*. But how do we become equipped to follow Jesus at work? In the same ways we become equipped for every aspect of life in Christ—listening to sermons, modeling our lives on others' examples, praying for God's guidance, and most of all by studying the Bible and putting it into practice.

This Theology of Work series contains a variety of books to help you apply the Scriptures and Christian faith to your work. This book is one volume in the multivolume *Theology of Work Bible Commentary*, examining what the Gospels and the book of Acts say about work. These commentaries are intended to assist those with theological training or interest to conduct in-depth research into passages or books of Scripture.

Pastors will find these volumes helpful as they consider the Bible's perspective on work when teaching on particular passages or topics. Professors may use the commentary to help prepare classes or as a textbook for students. Laypeople may find practical help for workplace decisions (the topical index could be helpful in this regard), or they may read it as part of their personal or group Bible study. Other books in the Theology of Work series include Bible studies adapted from the *Theology of Work Commentary* and additional materials to help apply the Christian faith to daily work.

Christians today recognize God's calling to us in and through our work—for ourselves and for those whom we serve. May God use this book to help you follow Christ in every sphere of life and work.

Will Messenger, Executive Editor
Theology of Work Project

ROMANS AND WORK

Introduction to Romans

Paul's letter to the Romans is best known for its vision of God's gracious actions toward humanity through the cross and resurrection of Christ. "It is the power of God for salvation to everyone who has faith" (Rom. 1:16). There is something deeply wrong with us individually, and with the world as a whole, from which we need to be saved, and Romans tells us how God is saving us from it.

Romans is deeply theological, but it is not abstract. God's salvation is not a concept for analytical discourse in Romans, but a call to action (Rom. 6:22). Paul tells how God's salvation affects our wisdom, our honesty, our relationships, our judgment, our ability to endure setbacks, our character, and our ethical reasoning, all of which are essential to our work. Here, in the nitty-gritty of human relationships and the desire to do good work, is where God's salvation takes hold in our world.

Written sometime during the reign of the Roman Emperor Nero (AD 54–68), the letter to the Romans hints of darkness and danger surrounding the Roman house churches, which comprised both Jewish and Gentile converts to Christ. Some of the Jewish members of the congregations had been exiled by an edict of Emperor Claudius in 49 and had only recently returned, probably having lost their property and financial stability in the meantime (Acts 18:2). Anti-Jewish sentiment in the wider Roman culture surely exerted pressures upon the Christian churches. Paul's extended reflection on God's faithfulness to both Jew and Gentile in this letter was not an abstract pondering of the ways of God, but a skillful theological reflection on these historical events and their consequences. The result is a set of practical tools for making moral decisions leading to a new quality of life in every place where people live and work.

The letter to the Romans has been exceptionally important in the development of Christian theology. To give just two examples, Martin

Luther broke with Pope Leo X largely because of his disagreement with what he perceived to be the Roman Catholic understanding of Romans. And Karl Barth's *Epistle to the Romans* was arguably the most influential theological work of the twentieth century.[1] In the past twenty-five or thirty years, a major theological debate concerning the relationship between salvation and good works has arisen about Romans and the rest of Paul's letters, often called the New Perspective on Paul. The general commentaries on Romans explore these issues at length. We will focus specifically on what the letter contributes to the theology of work. Of course, we need to have a basic understanding of Paul's general points before applying them to work, so we will do a certain amount of general theological exploration as needed.

The Gospel of Salvation—Paul's Vocation (Romans 1:1–17)

The opening verse of Romans announces Paul's own vocation, the work that God has called him to do: proclaiming the gospel of God in word and deed. So what is the gospel of God? Paul says that it is "the power of God for salvation to everyone who has faith, to the Jew first and also to the Greek. For in it the righteousness of God is revealed through faith for faith; as it is written, 'The one who is righteous will live by faith'" (Rom. 1:16–17, NRSV). For Paul, the gospel is more than words—it is the power of God for salvation. He emphasizes that this salvation is not for one group of people only but is intended to help anyone on earth to be among the people of God, by faith. Romans, then, is above all about God's salvation.

What is salvation? Salvation is the work of God that sets human beings in right relationship with God and with one another. As we will see momentarily, what we are being saved from are broken relationships—with God and with other people—that unleash the evil forces of sin and death in the world. Therefore, salvation is first of all the healing of broken relationships, beginning with the healing that reconciles the

---

[1] See, for example, Ian A. McFarland, *Creation and Humanity: The Sources of Christian Theology* (Louisville: Westminster John Knox Press, 2009), 138.

Creator and the created, God and us. Our reconciliation with God leads to freedom from sin and a newness of life that is not limited by death.

Christians have sometimes reduced Paul's gospel of salvation to something like, "Believe in Jesus so that you personally can go to heaven when you die." This is true, as far as it goes, but grossly inadequate. To begin with, a statement like that says nothing about relationships other than between the individual and God, yet Paul never ceases talking about relationships among people and between people and the rest of God's creation. And Paul has much more to say about faith, about life in Jesus, about God's kingdom, and about the quality of life both before and after death than could ever be encapsulated in a single slogan.

Likewise salvation cannot be reduced to a single moment in time. Paul says both that we "were saved" (Rom. 8:24) and that we "will be saved" (e.g., Rom. 5:9). Salvation is an ongoing process rather than a one-time event. God interacts with each person in a dance of divine grace and human faithfulness over time. There are decisive moments in the process of being saved, of course. The central moments are Christ's death on the cross and resurrection from the dead. "We were reconciled to God through the death of his Son," Paul tells us (Rom. 5:10), and "He who raised Christ from the dead will give life to your mortal bodies also" (Rom. 8:11).

Each of us might also regard the first time we said we believe in Christ as a decisive moment in our salvation. Romans, however, never speaks of a moment of personal salvation, as if salvation happened to us in the past and is now in storage until Christ comes again. Paul uses the past tense of salvation only to speak of Christ's death and resurrection, the moment when Christ brought salvation to the world. When it comes to each believer, Paul speaks of an ongoing process of salvation, always in the present or future tenses. "One believes with the heart and so is justified, and one confesses with the mouth and so is saved" (Rom. 10:10). Not "believed" and "confessed," past tense, but "believes" and "confesses," present tense. This leads directly to, "Everyone who calls on the name of the Lord shall be saved," future tense (Rom. 10:13). Salvation is not something that was given to us. It is always being given to us.

We take the trouble to emphasize the ongoing action of salvation because work is one of the preeminent places where we act in life. If salvation were something that happened to us only in the past, then what we do at work (or anywhere in life) would be irrelevant. But if salvation is something going on in our lives, then it bears fruit in our work. To be more precise, since salvation is the reconciliation of broken relationships, then our relationships with God, with other people, and with the created world at work (as everywhere in life) will be getting better as the process of salvation takes hold. Just to give a few examples, our salvation is evident when we take courage to speak an unpopular truth, listen to others' views with compassion, help colleagues attain their goals, and produce work products that help other people thrive.

Does this mean that we must work—and keep working—to be saved? Absolutely not! Salvation comes solely through "the grace of God and the free gift in the grace of one man, Jesus Christ" (Rom. 5:15). It "depends on faith" (Rom 4:16) and nothing else. As N. T. Wright puts it, "Whatever language or terminology we use to talk about the great gift that the one true God has given to his people in and through Jesus Christ, it remains precisely a gift. It never is something we can earn. We can never put God into our debt; we always remain in his."[2] We do not work to be saved. But because we are being saved we do work that bears fruit for God (Rom. 7:4). We will return to the question of how salvation is given to us in "Judgment, Justice, and Faith" below in Romans 3.

In sum, salvation is the ultimate work of Christ in the world, the goal toward which believers always "press on," as Paul puts it (Phil. 3:12). Salvation underlies everything Paul and everything believers do in work and life.

Our Need for Salvation in Life and Work (Romans 1:18–1:32)

We saw in Romans 1:1–17 that salvation begins with reconciliation to God. People have become estranged from God because of their "godlessness and wickedness" (Rom. 1:18). "Although they knew God, they neither glorified him as God nor gave thanks to him" (Rom. 1:21). We were created to walk in intimacy with God among the creatures of the

---

[2] N. T. Wright, *After You Believe: Why Christian Character Matters* (New York: HarperOne, 2010), 69.

Garden of Eden (Gen. 1–2), but our relationship with God has become so broken that we no longer recognize God. Paul calls this state a "debased mind" (Rom. 1:28).

Lacking the presence of mind to remain in the presence of the real God, we try to make our own gods. We have "exchanged the glory of the immortal God for images made to look like mortal man and birds and four-footed animals or reptiles" (Rom. 1:23). Our relationship with God is so thoroughly damaged that we cannot tell the difference between walking with God and carving an idol. When our real relationship with the true God is broken, we create fake relationships with false gods. Idolatry, then, is not merely one sin among others, but the essence of a broken relationship with God. (For more on idolatry, see "You Shall Not Make for Yourself an Idol," Exodus 20:4, at www.theologyofwork.org.)

When our relationship with God is broken, our relationships with other people also break down. Paul lists some of the broken aspects of human relationships that ensue.

> They were filled with every kind of wickedness, evil, covetousness, malice. Full of envy, murder, strife, deceit, craftiness, they are gossips, slanderers, God-haters, insolent, haughty, boastful, inventors of evil, rebellious toward parents, foolish, faithless, heartless, ruthless. (Rom. 1:29–31)

We experience nearly all these forms of broken relationships at work. Covetousness, strife, and envy over others' positions or paychecks, malice and rebellion toward those in authority, gossip and slander of co-workers and competitors, deceit and faithlessness in communications and commitments, insolence, haughtiness, and boastfulness of those who experience success, foolishness in decisions, heartlessness and ruthlessness by those in power. Not all the time of course. Some workplaces are better and some worse. But every workplace knows the consequences of broken relationships. All of us suffer from them. All of us contribute to causing them.

We may even compound the problem by making an idol of work itself, devoting ourselves to work in the vain hope that it alone will bring us meaning, purpose, security, or happiness. Perhaps this seems to work for a time, until we are passed over for promotion or are fired or laid off or retire. Then we discover that work comes to an end, and meanwhile we have become strangers to our family and friends. Like "mortal men and birds and four-footed animals and reptiles," work was created by God (Gen. 2:15) and is inherently good, yet it becomes evil when elevated to the place of God.

All Have Sinned (Romans 2–3)

Sadly, this brokenness extends even to Paul's own workplace, the Christian church, and in particular the Christians in Rome. Despite being God's own people (Rom. 9:25), "called to be saints" (Rom. 1:7), the Christians in Rome are experiencing a breakdown in their relationships with one another. Specifically, Jewish Christians are judging Gentile Christians for not conforming to their own peculiar expectations, and vice versa. "You say, 'We know that God's judgment on those who do such things is in accordance with the truth,'" Paul notes (Rom. 2:2). Each side claims that they know God's judgments and speak for God. Claiming to speak for God makes their own words into idols, illustrating in miniature how idolatry (breaking relationship with God) leads to judgment (breaking relationship with other people).

Both sides are wrong. The truth is that both Gentiles and Jews have strayed from God. Gentiles, who should have recognized the sovereignty of God in the creation itself, have given themselves over to the worship of idols and to all the destructive behavior that follows from this basic mistake (Rom. 1:18–32). Jews, on the other hand, have become judgmental, hypocritical, and boastful that they are the people of the Torah. Paul summarizes both situations by saying, "All who have sinned apart from the law will also perish apart from the law, and all who have sinned under the law will be judged by the law" (Rom. 2:12).

But the crux of the problem is not that each side misunderstands God's expectations. It is that each side judges the other, destroying the relationships that God had brought into being. It is crucial to recognize the role of judgment in Paul's argument. Judgment causes broken relationships. The specific sins noted in Romans 1:29–31 are not the causes of our broken relationships, but the results. The causes of our broken relationships are idolatry (toward God) and judgment (toward people). In fact, idolatry can be understood as a form of judgment, the judgment that God is not adequate and that we can create better gods on our own. Therefore, Paul's overarching concern in chapters 2 and 3 is our judgment of others.

> You have no excuse, whoever you are, when you judge others; for in passing judgment on another you condemn yourself, because you, the judge, are doing the very same things. You say, "We know that God's judgment on those who do such things is in accordance with truth." Do you imagine, whoever you are, that when you judge those who do such things and yet do them yourself, you will escape the judgment of God? (Rom. 2:1–3)

If we wonder what we have done that puts us in need of salvation, the answer above all is judgment and idolatry, according to Paul. We judge others, though we have no right to do so, and thus we bring God's judgment on ourselves as he works to restore true justice. To use a modern metaphor, it is like the Supreme Court overturning a corrupt judge in a lower court who didn't even have jurisdiction in the first place.

Does this mean that Christians are never to assess people's actions or to oppose people at work? No. Because we work as God's agents, we have a duty to assess whether the things happening in our workplaces serve or hinder God's purposes and to act accordingly (see Rom. 12:9–13:7 for some examples from Paul). A supervisor may need to discipline or fire an employee who is not doing his or her job satisfactorily. A worker may need to go over a supervisor's head to report an ethical or policy violation. A teacher may need to give a low grade. A voter or politician may need to oppose a candidate. An activist may need to protest a corporate or government injustice. A student may need to report cheating by another student. A victim of abuse or discrimination may need to cut off contact with the abuser.

Because we are responsible to God for the outcomes of our work and the integrity of our workplaces, we do need to assess people's actions and intentions and to take action to prevent injustice and do good work. But this does not mean that we judge others' worthiness as human beings or set ourselves up as morally superior. Even when we oppose others' actions, we do not judge them.

It can be difficult to tell the difference sometimes, but Paul gives us some surprisingly practical guidance. Respect the other person's conscience. God has created all people in such a way that "what the law requires is written on their hearts, to which their own conscience also bears witness" (Rom. 2:15). If others are genuinely following their own conscience, then it is not your job to judge them. But if you are setting up yourself as morally superior, condemning others for following their own moral compass, you are probably passing judgment in a way for which "you have no excuse" (Rom. 2:1).

Judgment, Justice, and Faith (Romans 3)

Judgment, the Source of Broken Relationships (Romans 3:1–20)

What can be done with a world of people separated from God by idolatry and from one another by judgment? God's true justice is the answer. In Romans 3, as Paul describes what happens in salvation, he puts it in terms of God's justice. "Our injustice serves to confirm the justice of God" (Rom. 3:5).

Before proceeding, we need to say a bit about the terminology of justice and righteousness. Paul uses the Greek word for justice, *dikaiosyne* and its various forms, thirty-six times in Romans. It is translated as "righteousness" most often and as "justice" (or "justification") less frequently. But the two are the same in Paul's language. The primary use of *dikaiosyne* is in courts of law, where people are seeking justice to restore a situation that is not right. Therefore, salvation means being made right with God (righteousness) and with other people and all of creation (justice). A full exploration of the relationship between the words *salvation, justification, righteousness,* and *salvation* is beyond the scope of this chapter but will be addressed in any general commentary on Romans.[3]

If this seems abstract, ask yourself whether you can see concrete implications at work. Is it the case that the (false) judgments people make about one another are the root of broken relationships and injustice where you work? For example, if a manager and employee disagree over the employee's performance review, which of these causes greater

---

[3] See, for example, N. T. Wright, "*The Letter to the Romans,*" vol. 10, *The New Interpreter's Bible* (Nashville: Abingdon Press, 1994).

damage—the performance gap itself or the hostility arising from their judgment? Or if someone gossips about another person at work, which causes greater damage—embarrassment over the item that was gossiped about or resentment over the judgment revealed by the gossiper's tone and the listeners' snickers?

If our false judgment is the root of our broken relationships with God, other people, and the creation, how can we possibly find salvation? The thing we need—justice/righteousness—is the one thing we are most incapable of. Even if we want to be put back into right relationships, our inability to judge rightly means that the harder we try, the worse we make the problem. "Who will rescue me?" Paul cries (Rom. 7:24).

We cannot hope to be rescued by anyone else, for they are in the same boat we're in. "Everyone is a liar," Paul tell us (Rom. 3:4). "There is no one who is righteous, not even one; there is no one who seeks God. All have turned aside, together they have become worthless; there is no one who shows kindness, there is not even one" (Rom. 3:10–12). "All have sinned and fall short of the glory of God" (Rom 3:23).

Yet there is hope—not in humanity, but in God's faithfulness. "Will their unfaithfulness nullify the faithfulness of God?" Paul asks. "By no means!" he replies (Rom 3:3–4). On the contrary, "injustice serves to confirm the justice of God." This means our workplaces are settings for grace just as much as our churches or families. If we feel that our workplace is too secular, too unethical, too hostile to faith, too full of greedy, soulless people, then it is exactly the place where the cross of Christ is effective! God's grace can bring reconciliation and justice in a factory, office block, or petrol station just as fully as in a cathedral, abbey, or church. Paul's gospel is not only for the church, but for the whole world.

God's Justice, the Solution to Our False Judgments (Romans 3:21–26)

Given that our judgment is false and hypocritical, how can we ever find righteousness and justice? This is the question that leads into the dramatic crux of Romans 3. God's response is the cross of Christ. God gives his justice/righteousness to us because we are unable to bring justice/righteousness ourselves. God accomplishes this through the cross of Jesus, in which he demonstrates that "he himself is righteous and that he justifies the one who has faith in Jesus" (Rom. 3:26).

God's means of accomplishing this is through the death and resurrection of Jesus. "God proves his love for us in that while we still were sinners Christ died for us" (Rom. 5:8). God freely chose to accept the cross of Christ as though it were a holy sacrifice of atonement in the Jewish temple (Rom. 3:25). As on the Day of Atonement, God chose to pass over people's wrongdoing in order to establish a kind of new beginning for all who believe. And although Jesus was a Jew, God regards the cross as an offer of salvation to all people. Through the cross, everyone can be restored to a right relationship with God.

Although we lack righteousness/justice, God has both in infinite supply. Through the cross of Jesus, God gives us the righteousness/justice that restores our broken relationships with God, other people, and all creation. When God gives us salvation, he gives us righteousness/justice.

> The *righteousness* of God has been disclosed, and is attested by the law and the prophets, the *righteousness* of God through faith in Jesus Christ for all who believe. For there is no distinction, since all have sinned and fall short of the glory of God; they are now *justified* by his grace as a gift, through the redemption that is in Christ Jesus, whom God put forward as a sacrifice of atonement by his blood, effective through faith. He did this to show his *righteousness*, because in his divine forbearance he had passed over the sins previously committed; it was to prove at the present time that he himself is *righteous* and that he *justifies* the one who has faith in Jesus. (Rom. 3:21–26; emphasis added)

The cross is God's surprising justice—surprising because although God is not the sinner, God makes the sacrifice. Does this mean anything in today's secular workplaces? It could be a very hopeful note. In situations where the problems in our workplaces are caused by our own errors or injustice, we can count on God's righteousness/justice to overcome our failings. Even though we can't make ourselves right, God can work his righteousness/justice in us and through us. In situations where others' errors and injustice cause the problems, we may be able to set things right by sacrificing something of ourselves—in imitation of our Savior—even though we did not cause the problem.

For example, consider a work group that operates in a culture of blame. Rather than working together to fix problems, people spend all their time trying to blame others whenever problems arise. If your workplace is a culture of blame, it may not be your fault. Perhaps your boss is the blamer-in-chief. Even so, could a sacrifice by you bring reconciliation and justice? The next time the boss starts to blame someone, imagine if you stood up and said, "I remember that I supported this idea the last time we talked about it, so you'd better blame me too." What if the time after that, two or three other people did the same thing along with you? Would that begin to make the blame game fall apart? You might end up sacrificing your reputation, your friendship with the boss, even your future job prospects. But is it possible that it could also break the hold of blame and judgment in your work group? Could you expect God's grace to take an active role through your sacrifice?

Faith/Faithfulness, the Entry to God's Justice (Romans 3:27–31)

In the previous section we looked at Romans 3:22–26 and highlighted the righteousness/justice that God gives us in salvation. Now let us look again at the passage to highlight the role of faith.

> The righteousness of God has been disclosed, and is attested by the law and the prophets, the righteousness of God through *faith* in Jesus Christ for all who *believe*. For there is no distinction, since all have sinned and fall short of the glory of God; they are now justified by his grace as a gift, through the redemption that is in Christ Jesus, whom God put forward as a sacrifice of atonement by his blood, effective through *faith*. He did this to show his righteousness, because in his divine forbearance he had passed over the sins previously committed; it was to prove at the present time that he himself is righteous and that he justifies the one who has *faith* in Jesus. (Rom. 3:21–26; emphasis added)

Clearly, God's gift of righteousness/justice is intimately tied up in faith and belief. This brings us to one of the most famous themes in Romans, the role of faith in salvation. In many ways, the Protestant Reformation was founded on paying attention to this and similar passages in Romans, and their importance remains central to Christians of virtually every kind today. While there are many ways of describing it, the central idea is that people are restored to a right relationship with God by faith.

The Greek root-word *pistis* is translated as "faith" (or sometimes "believe," as in one instance above), but also as "faithfulness" as in Romans 3:3. The English language distinguishes between faith (mental assent, trust, or commitment) and faithfulness (actions consistent with one's faith). But in Greek there is only the single word *pistis* for both faith and faithfulness. There is no separating what a person believes from the evidence of that belief in the person's actions. If you have faith, you will act in faithfulness. Given that in most workplaces our faithfulness (what we do) will be more directly evident than our faith (what we believe), the relationship between these two aspects of *pistis* takes on a particular significance for work.

Paul speaks of "the *pistis* of Jesus" twice here, in Romans 3:22 and 3:26. If translated literally, the Greek says "*pistis* of Jesus," not "*pistis* in Jesus." The literal wording of Romans 3:22 is thus that we are saved by *Jesus'* faithfulness to God (the *pistis* of Jesus). In other passages, *pistis* clearly refers to *our* faith in Jesus, such as Romans 10:9, "If you confess with your lips that Jesus is Lord and believe in your heart that God raised him from the dead, you will be saved." In truth, our faith in Jesus cannot be separated from Jesus' faithfulness to God. Our faith in Jesus comes about because of Jesus' faithfulness to God on the cross, and we respond by living faithfully to him and placing our trust in him. Remembering that our salvation flows from Jesus' faithfulness, not merely our state of belief, keeps us from turning the possession of faith into a new form of works-righteousness, as if our act of saying "I believe in Jesus" is what brings us salvation.

The full meaning of faith/faithfulness in Paul's writing has two important implications for work. First of all, it puts to rest any fear that by taking our work seriously we might waver in recognizing that salvation comes solely by God's gift of faith. When we remember that Christ's faithfulness on the cross has already accomplished the work of salvation, and that our faith in Christ comes solely by God's grace, then we recognize that our faithfulness to God in our work is simply a response to God's grace. We are faithful in our work because God has given us faith as a free gift.

Second, the faithfulness of Christ impels us to become more and more faithful ourselves. Again, this is not because we think that our faithful actions earn us salvation, but because having been given faith in Christ, we earnestly desire to become more like him. Paul speaks of this as the "obedience of faith" (Rom. 1:5, 26). Without faith, it is impossible to be obedient to God. But if God gives us faith, then we can respond in obedience. In fact, much of the latter half of Romans is devoted to showing us how to be more obedient to God as a result of the grace God has given us through faith.

An Exemplary Faith: Abraham Trusted God's Promises (Romans 4)

As we have seen in Romans 1–3, the cross of Christ brings salvation to all people—Jews and Gentiles alike. In Christ, God puts all people back into right relationship with God and one another without regard to the provisions of the Jewish law. For this reason, Paul's principal focus throughout Romans is helping the divided and quarreling Christians in Rome to reconcile their broken relationships in order to live faithfully into what God has accomplished in Christ.

This interpretation of Christ's death raises a problem for Paul, however, since he is writing not only to uncircumcised Gentiles but also to circumcised Jews, for whom the law still matters. Further, Paul's interpretation seems to ignore the story of Abraham, understood to be "father" of the Jews, who was in fact circumcised as a sign of his covenant with God (Gen. 17:11). Doesn't the story of Abraham suggest that entering the covenant of God requires male circumcision for all peoples, whether Jewish or Gentile?

"No," argues Paul in Romans 4. Interpreting the story of Abraham from Genesis 12:1–3, 15:6, and 17:1–14, Paul concludes that Abraham had faith that God would honor his word and make the childless Abraham the father of many nations through his barren wife Sarah. Consequently, God reckoned Abraham's faith as righteousness (Rom. 4:3, 9, 22). Paul reminds his readers that God's acknowledgment of Abraham's righteousness took place long *before* Abraham was circumcised, which came *later* as a *sign* of his already-existing faith in God (Rom. 4:10–11).

In other words, at the time God reckoned Abraham's faith as putting him in right relationship with God, Abraham shared the same status as an uncircumcised Gentile in Paul's world. Thus, concludes Paul, Abraham became the father of both Jews and Gentiles through the righteousness of faith rather than righteousness under the Jewish law (Rom. 4:11–15).

The example of Abraham in Romans 4 provides Christians with great hope for our work and workplaces. Abraham's example of trusting God's promises—despite adverse circumstances and seemingly impossible odds—emboldens us not to waver in trust when we face challenges at work or when God does not seem to be present (see Rom. 4:19). God did not immediately fulfill the promise to Abraham, which further encourages us to be patient in waiting for God to renew or redeem our circumstances in life.

Grace Reigns for Eternal Life through Jesus Christ (Romans 5)

In Romans 5 Paul links this divine gift of righteousness to the obedience of Christ and the grace that now flows into the world through him. Several important features of this chapter illuminate our experiences of work.

Grace Transforms Suffering in Our Life in Christ (Romans 5:1–11)

In Romans 5:1–11 Paul offers more encouragement by reminding the Romans that *through* Christ we have *already* "gained access" to God's "grace in which we stand" (Rom. 5:2). Grace signifies God's life-giving power that raised Jesus from the dead. Grace continues to bring new and more abundant life into the world to and through Christ's followers. By living *Christ's* obedient life of faith and faithfulness in our own circumstances, we experience God's life-giving grace that can bring us joy and peace at work, at home, and in every context of life.

Nevertheless, trusting the grace of God often calls for steadfast patience in the face of many challenges. Just as Christ suffered in the course of his obedience to God, we too may experience suffering when we embody Christ's life of faith and faithfulness. Paul even says he "boasts" in his suffering (Rom. 5:3), knowing that his suffering is a participation

in the suffering Jesus experienced in his mission to reconcile the world
to God (Rom. 8:17–18). Moreover, suffering often brings growth.

> Suffering produces endurance, and endurance produces character, and
> character produces hope, and hope does not disappoint us, because God's
> love has been poured into our hearts. (Rom. 5:3–5)

Therefore God does not promise that life and work will be happy for
believers all the time. Many people suffer at work. Work can be boring,
degrading, humiliating, exhausting, and heartless. We can be underpaid,
endangered, and discriminated against. We can be pressured to violate
our consciences and God's principles. We can be fired, laid off, made
redundant, downsized, terminated, unemployed or underemployed for
long periods. We can bring suffering on ourselves by our own arrogance,
carelessness, incompetence, greed, or malice against others. We can suffer even in good jobs. We should never be content with abuse or mistreatment at work, but when we have to endure suffering at work, all is
not lost. God's grace is poured out on us when we suffer, and it makes
us stronger if we remain faithful.

To give an example, preparing the soil and caring for crops cannot
guarantee that the grain will grow tall or the vegetables will ripen. Poor
weather, drought, insects, and blight can ruin the harvest. Yet, through
grace, farmers may come to accept all these aspects of nature, while
trusting God's care. This in turn shapes the patient, faithful character
of farmers who come to care deeply for all of God's creation. A deep appreciation of nature, in turn, can be a great asset for the work of farming.

Similarly, grace empowers us to remain faithful and hopeful even
when the employer for whom we work closes their doors during hard
economic times. So, too, God's life-giving power sustains many highly
educated young adults who still have trouble finding meaningful employment. Grace also inspires a team to persevere in developing a new
product, even after repeated failures, knowing that what they learn by
failing is what makes the product better.

God's love sustains us through all kinds of suffering in life and work.
"Hope does not disappoint us, because God's love has been poured into
our hearts." Even when suffering threatens to harden our hearts, God's

love makes us agents of his reconciliation, which we have received in Christ (Rom. 10–11).

Grace and Righteousness Lead to Eternal Life through Christ (Romans 5:12–21)

Romans 5:12–21 reflects a dense and complex theological argument involving a number of different contrasts between the disobedient Adam and the obedient Christ, through whom we are made righteous and promised eternal life. The passage gives us assurance that Christ's obedient act of self-giving for others puts all who come to him into right relationship with God and one another. As participants in Christ's faith and faithfulness, we receive a share of the divine gifts of righteousness and eternal life promised by God through Christ. Therefore, we no longer participate in Adam's disobedience but find eternal life by participating in Christ's obedience to God.

Paul speaks of God's grace operating in both the present time and eternity. Reconciliation has already been given through Christ (Rom. 5:11), so that we are already able to live God-honoring lives. Yet God's reconciliation is not yet complete and is still in the process of "*leading* to eternal life" (Rom. 12:21). If we have received Christ's reconciliation, then our work now is an opportunity to contribute to the better future where Christ is leading. Innovators gain new possibilities to create, design, and build products that improve the common good. Service workers have new opportunities to make other lives better. Artists or musicians can create aesthetic beauty that enhances human life for God's glory. None of these are means to eternal life. But every time we work to make the world more as God intends it to be, we receive a foretaste of eternal life. When we remain obedient to Christ's pattern of faith and faithfulness in our workplace settings, no matter what the circumstances, we can trust that our life is eternally secure in the hands of our faithful God.

Walking in Newness of Life (Romans 6)

Although God's grace has come into the world to bring reconciliation and justice, there are still evil spiritual powers at work opposing the life-giving power of God's grace (Rom. 6:14). Paul often personifies these evil spiritual forces, calling them such names as "sin" (Rom. 6:2), "flesh" (Rom. 7:5), "death" (Rom. 6:9), or "this world" (Rom. 12:2). Human beings must choose whether, through their actions in daily life, to partner with God through Christ or with these evil forces. Paul calls choosing to partner with God "walking in newness of life" (Rom. 6:4). He compares walking in newness of life to Christ's new life after being raised from the dead. "Just as Christ was raised from the dead by the glory of the father, so we too might walk in newness of life" (Rom. 6:4). In our lives here and now, we can begin to live—or "walk"—in reconciliation and justice just as Christ now lives.

To walk in newness of life requires us to abandon our judgmentalism and to do God's justice rather than continuing in our self-serving habits (Rom. 6:12–13). As instruments of God's justice, believers act in ways *through which* the life-giving power of God's grace builds up people and communities in Christ. This is far more active than merely refraining from bad behavior. Our calling is to become instruments of justice and reconciliation, working to root out the effects of sin in a troubled world.

For example, workers may have fallen into a habit of judging management as evil or unfair, and vice versa. This may have become a convenient pretext for workers to cheat the company, use paid time for personal activities, or fail to do excellent work. Conversely, it may be a convenient excuse for managers to discriminate against workers they don't personally like, or to evade safety or workplace fairness regulations, or to withhold information from workers. Merely following the regulations or refraining from cheating would not be walking in newness of life. Instead, walking in newness of life would require us first of all to give up our judgments of the other side. Once we no longer regard them as unworthy of our respect, then we can begin to discern specific ways to restore good relationships, reestablish just and fair dealings with one another, and build up one another and our organizations.

Making this kind of change in our life and work is exceedingly difficult. Paul says that sin continually seeks to "exercise dominion in your mortal bodies, to make you obey their passions." However good our intentions, we soon fall back into our broken ways. Only God's grace, made real in Christ's death, has the power to pry us free from our habits of judgment (Rom. 6:6).

Therefore God's grace does not cast us "free" to wander aimlessly back into our old ills. Instead he offers to strap us into new life in Christ. The bindings will chafe whenever we begin to wander off course, and Paul admits that walking in newness of life will feel a lot like slavery at first. Our choice, then, is *which kind* of slavery to accept—slavery to newness of life or slavery to our old sins. "You are slaves of the one you obey, either of sin, which leads to death, or of obedience, which leads to righteousness [justice]" (Rom. 6:25). "But now that you have been freed from sin and enslaved to God, the advantage you get is sanctification [newness of life]. The end is eternal life" (Rom. 6:22). The advantage of walking in newness of life is not that it feels freer than slavery to sin, but that it results in justice and life, rather than shame and death.

Walking in Newness of Life in the Workplace (Romans 6)

What does it mean to be a "slave" of God's grace in our places of work? It means that we do not make decisions at work based on how things affect us, but about how they affect our master, God. We make decisions as God's stewards or agents. This is actually a familiar concept in both Christian faith and the secular workplace. In the Christian faith, Christ himself is the model steward, who gave up his own life in order to fulfill God's purposes. Similarly, many people in the workplace have a duty to serve the interests of others, rather than their own. Among them are attorneys, corporate officers, agents, trustees and boards of directors, judges, and many others. Not many workplace stewards or agents are as committed as Jesus was—willing to give their lives to fulfill their duties—but the concept of agency is an everyday reality in the workplace.

The difference for Christians is that our duty ultimately is to God, not the state or shareholders or anyone else. Our overarching mission must be God's justice and reconciliation, not merely obeying the law, making a profit, or satisfying human expectations. Unlike Albert Carr's claim that business is just a game in which normal rules of ethics don't apply,[4]

---

[4] Albert Z. Carr, "Is Business Bluffing Ethical?" *Harvard Business Review* 46 (January/February 1968).

walking in newness of life means integrating justice and reconciliation into our lives at work.

For instance, walking in newness of life for a high school teacher might mean repeatedly forgiving a rebellious and troublesome student, while also seeking new ways to reach that student in the classroom. For a politician, walking in newness of life might mean drafting new legislation that includes input from a number of different ideological perspectives. For a manager, it might mean asking the forgiveness of an employee in front of everyone who is aware of the manager's transgression against the employee.

Walking in newness of life requires us to look deeply into our patterns of work. Bakers or chefs might easily see how their work helps feed hungry people, which in itself is a form of justice. The same bakers and chefs might also need to look more deeply at their personal interactions in the kitchen. Do they treat people with dignity, help others succeed, bring glory to God? Walking in newness of life affects both the ends we try to accomplish and the means we use to do so.

The Invasive Power of "Sin" (Romans 7)

In chapter 7, Paul continues to emphasize that newness of life in Christ frees us from being "captive" to the "old written code" of the law (Rom. 7:6). Nonetheless, the law itself is not the problem with human existence, for "the law is holy, and the commandment is holy and just and good" (Rom. 7:12). Instead, concludes Paul, the problem is the God-opposing power he calls "sin" taking up residence in human beings (Rom. 7:13). Sin has taken advantage of the law's commandments by using them as tools to deceive people (Rom. 7:11), thus preventing each person from being able to obey the law as God intended (Rom. 7:14, 17, 23).

Sin's power is not merely making bad choices or doing things we know we shouldn't. It is as if an evil power has invaded the territory of each person's spirit and taken control, "sold into slavery under sin," as Paul puts it (Rom. 7:14). Under this slavery to sin, we are unable to do the good called for in the commandments and known in our hearts (Rom. 7:15–20). This occurs despite our good intentions to do what God desires (Rom. 7:15–16, 22).

In other words, knowledge of what is good is not enough to overcome the power of sin that has invaded us! "For I do not do the good I want, but the evil I do not want is what I do" (Rom. 7:19). We can be rescued from this plight only by the intervention of another, more powerful spiritual force—the Holy Spirit who becomes the focus in Romans 8.

We are well aware that knowing what God wants is not enough to keep us on the right track in workplace situations. For instance, even when we know in our minds that God wants us to treat everyone with respect, we sometimes fall prey to the false perception that we could get ahead by speaking poorly about a co-worker. Likewise, in the work of parenting, mothers and fathers know that shouting in anger at a young child is not good. But sometimes the power of sin overtakes them and they do so anyway. A lawyer who charges clients for services by the hour knows he should keep scrupulous time records, but may nevertheless be overpowered by sin to pad his hours to increase his income.

Alone, we are especially vulnerable to the power of sin within us. Wherever we work, we would do well to seek out others (Rom. 12:5) and help one another resist this power that tries to overcome our will to do what is right and good. For example, a small but growing number of Christians are joining small peer groups of people who work in similar situations. Peer groups meet anywhere from an hour once a week, often at work locations, to half a day once a month. Members commit to telling each other the details of situations they face at work and to discussing them from a faith perspective, developing options and committing to action plans. A member might describe a conflict with a co-worker, an ethical lapse, a feeling of meaninglessness, a company policy that seems unfair. After gaining the others' insights, the member would commit to a course of action in response and report to the group about results at future meetings. (For more on this, see "Equipping Churches Connect Daily Work to Worship" at www.theologyofwork.org.)

Living According to the Spirit (Romans 8)

Living According to the Spirit Leads to a New Quality of Life (Romans 8:1–14)

Believers are free from the law, but walking in newness of life is based on a firm moral structure (hence, "the *law* of the Spirit," Rom. 8:2). Paul calls this moral structure "living according to the Spirit" or "setting our minds on the Spirit" (Rom. 8:5). Both terms refer to the process of moral reasoning that guides us as we walk in newness of life.

This kind of moral compass does not work by listing specific acts that are right or wrong. Instead it consists of following the "law of the Spirit of life in Christ Jesus" that has freed believers "from the law of sin and death" (Rom. 8:1–2). The words *life* and *death* are the keys. As discussed earlier in Romans 6, Paul understands "sin," "death," and the "flesh" as spiritual forces in the world that lead people to act in ways that are contrary to God's will and produce chaos, despair, conflict, and destruction in their lives and in their communities. By contrast, living according to the Spirit means doing whatever brings life instead of death. "To set the mind on the flesh [our old patterns of judgment] is death but to set the mind on the Spirit is life and peace" (Rom. 8:6). Setting the mind on the Spirit means looking for whatever will bring more life to each situation.

For example, the Jewish law taught that "you shall not murder" (Exod. 20:13). But living according to the Spirit goes far beyond not literally murdering anyone. It actively seeks opportunities to bring better life to people. It can mean cleaning a hotel room so that guests remain healthy. It can mean clearing the ice from a neighbor's sidewalk (or pavement) so pedestrians can walk safely. It can mean studying for years to earn a Ph.D. in order to develop new treatments for cancer.

Another way to put it is that living according to the Spirit means living a *new quality of life* in Christ. This comes from setting aside our judgments of what another person deserves and seeking instead what would bring them a better quality of life, deserved or not. When making assignments, a manager could assign a task that stretches subordinates' abilities, rather than limiting them to what they are already capable of, then inviting them to check in every day for guidance. When asked to lend a replacement tool, a skilled tradesperson could instead show a junior worker a new technique that will prevent breaking the tool the next time around. When asked "Why did our dog die?" a parent could ask a child "Are you afraid someone you love might die?" instead of only explaining the pet's immediate cause of death. In each of these situations, the moral goal is to bring a better quality of life to the other person, rather than to fulfill a demand of the law.

Bringing life, rather than fulfilling the law, is the moral compass of those who are being saved by God's grace. We are free to live according to the Spirit rather than to enslave ourselves to the law because "there is now no condemnation for those who are in Christ Jesus" (Rom. 8:1).

Paul's inclusion of "peace" as an aspect of setting our minds on the Spirit (Rom. 13:6, as above) points out the social aspects of living according to the Spirit because peace is a social phenomenon.[5] When we follow Christ, we try to bring a new quality of life to our society, not just to ourselves. This means paying attention to the social conditions that diminish life at work and elsewhere. We do what we can to make life better for people we work among. At the same time, we work to bring justice/righteousness to the social systems that shape the conditions of work and workers.

Christians can be a positive force for improvement—even survival—if we can help our organizations set their minds on the need for a new quality of life. We probably can't change our organizations much on our own. But if we can build relationships with others, earn people's trust, listen to the people nobody else listens to, we may help the organization break out of its ruts. Plus, we bring the secret ingredient—our faith that God's grace can use us to bring life to even the deadest situation.

Conversely, if we do not set our minds on the Spirit at work, we can be arrogant and destructive, whether in our relationships with fellow workers, competitors, clients, or others. Setting our minds on the Spirit requires constantly evaluating the *consequences* or *fruit* of our work, always asking whether our work enhances the quality of life for other people. If we are honest in our assessments, no doubt it also requires daily repentance and the grace to change.

---

[5] Robert Jewett, *Romans: A Commentary* (Minneapolis: Fortress Press, 2007), 487.

Suffering with Christ in Order to Be Glorified with Christ (Romans 8:15–17)

Paul contrasts life in the Spirit with life under the Jewish law. Paul says believers have received a "spirit of adoption" as children of God, rather than "a spirit of slavery to fall back into fear" (Rom. 8:15). Everyone who "belongs to" Christ (Rom. 8:9–10) is now an adopted child of God. In contrast, those under the law live in slavery to the power of sin and also in fear—presumably fear of the law's threats of punishment for disobedience. Believers are free of this fear, since there is now "no condemnation for those who are in Christ Jesus" (Rom. 8:1). When we live faithfully in Christ, we do not face the law's threats of punishment, even when we get things wrong in our daily life and work. Hardships and failures may still mar our work, but God's response is not condemnation but redemption. God will bring something worthwhile out of our faithful work, no matter how bad it seems at present.

At least two aspects of these verses inform our approach to work or life in our workplaces. First, as adopted children of God, we are never alone in our work. No matter what our dissatisfaction or frustrations with the people we work among, or the work, or even a lack of support for the work from our families, the Spirit of God in Christ abides with us. God is always looking for an opportunity to redeem our suffering and turn it into something good and satisfying in our lives. As we observed earlier in connection with Romans 5, faithfully enduring hardship and suffering in our work can lead to the formation of our character and ground our hope for the future. (See "Grace Transforms Suffering in Our Life in Christ," above in Romans 5:1–11.)

Second, at one time or another, most people encounter failures, frustrations, and hardships in their work. Our work places obligations on us that we wouldn't otherwise have, even obligations as simple as showing up on time every day. Faithfully engaging these challenges can actually make the work more rewarding and satisfying. Over time these experiences give us greater confidence in God's redeeming presence and greater experience of his motivating and energizing Spirit.

In some situations you may be welcomed and promoted for bringing reconciliation and justice to your place of work. In other situations you may be resisted, threatened, punished, or terminated. For example, bad relationships are an unfortunate feature of many workplaces. One department may habitually sabotage another department's accomplishments. Strife between managers and workers may have become institutionalized. People may be terrorized by an office bully, an academic clique, a shop floor gang, a racial dividing line, or an abusive boss. If you bring reconciliation in situations like these, productivity may increase, turnover may be reduced, morale may soar, customer service may rebound, and you may be praised or promoted. On the other hand, the bullies, cliques, gangs, racial divides, and abusive bosses are almost certain to oppose you.

Eagerly Awaiting Bodily Redemption for Ourselves and God's Creation (Romans 8:18–30)

Being "glorified" with Christ (Rom. 8:17) is our hope for the future. But according to Paul that hope is part of a *process* already underway. We are to engage patiently in it, with the expectation that at some point it will be completed (Rom. 8:18–25). The gift of the Holy Spirit already received as "first fruits" of this process (Rom. 8:23) signifies our adoption as children of God (Rom. 8:14–17, 23). This constitutes proof that the process is underway.

This process culminates in "the redemption of our bodies" (Rom. 8:23). This is not a rescue of our souls out of our physical bodies, but the transformation of our bodies along with the entire creation (Rom. 8:21). This process has already begun, and we experience its "first fruits" (Rom. 8:24) in our life and work today. But far more and better is yet to come, and at present the "whole creation" groans in "labor pains" as it eagerly anticipates being set free from its own "bondage to decay" (Rom. 8:19–23). Paul is clearly drawing on imagery from Genesis 2–3, where not only Adam but also creation itself was subjected to decay and death, no longer able to live into what God created them to be. This reminds us to consider the impact of our work on all of God's creation, not only on people. (For more on this topic, see "Dominion" in Genesis 1:26 and 2:5 at www.theologyofwork.org.)

The process is slow and sometimes painful. We "groan" while we wait for it to be accomplished, Paul says, and not only us individually but "the whole creation has been groaning in labor pains" (Rom. 8:22–23). This echoes the groaning of Israel while enslaved in Egypt (Exod. 6:5) and reminds us that nearly 30 million people are still enslaved in the world today.[6] We can never be content with merely our own release from the evil forces in the world, but we must serve God faithfully until he completes his salvation in every part of the world.

Nonetheless, the salvation of the world is sure, for "all things work together for good for those who love God and are called according to his purpose" (Rom. 8:28). God is at work in us now, and the time is coming when God's salvation will be complete in the world. God's original verdict "It is very good" (Gen. 1:31) is vindicated by the transformation at work in us now, to be fulfilled in God's time.

Because the transformation is not yet complete, we have to be prepared for difficulties along the way. Sometimes we do good work, only to see it wasted or destroyed by the evil that is presently in the world. Even if we do good work, our work may be vandalized. Our recommendations may be watered down. We may run out of capital, lose the election to a scoundrel, drown in red tape, fail to engage a student's interest. Or we may succeed for a time, and then find our results undone by later events. Health workers, for example, have been on the verge of eradicating polio on several occasions, only to face new outbreaks due to political opposition, ignorance, vaccine-related transmission, and the swift pace of modern travel.[7]

Nothing Can Come Between Us and the Love of God (Romans 8:31–39)

God is for us, says Paul, having given his own Son for "all of us" (Rom. 8:31–32). Nothing is able to come between us and the love of God in Christ Jesus our Lord (Rom. 8:35–39). "Neither death, nor life, nor angels, nor rulers, nor things present, nor things to come, nor powers, nor height, nor depth, nor anything else in all creation, will be able

---

[6] "Inaugural Global Slavery Index Reveals More Than 29 Million People Living in Slavery," *Global Slavery Index 2013*, October 4, 2013, http://www.globalslaveryindex.org/category/press-release.

[7] "Poliomyelitis Eradication," in *Wikipedia,* http://en.wikipedia.org/wiki/Poliomyelitis_eradication.

to separate us from the love of God in Christ Jesus our Lord" (Rom. 8:38–39). Many of these things seem to threaten us in the sphere of work. We face menacing or incompetent bosses (rulers). We get stuck in dead-end jobs (things present). We make sacrifices now—working long hours, taking classes after work, serving in low-paid internships, moving to another country looking for work—that we hope will pay off later but may never pan out (things to come). We lose our jobs because of economic cycles or regulations or unscrupulous actions by power-ful people we never even see (powers). We are forced by circumstance, folly, or the crimes of others into degrading or dangerous work. All these things can do us real hurt. But they cannot triumph over us.

Christ's faithfulness—and ours, by God's grace—overcomes the worst that life and work can do to us. If career progress, income, or prestige is our highest goal at work, we may end up disappointed. But if salvation—that is, reconciliation with God and people, faithfulness, and justice—is our chief hope, then we will find it amid both the good and bad in work. Paul's affirmations mean that no matter what the difficulties we encounter with our work, or the complexities and challenges we face with co-workers or superiors in our workplaces, the love of God in Christ always abides with us. The love of God in Christ is the steadying force in the midst of adversity now, as well as our hope for bodily redemption in the future.

God's Character Is to Have Mercy on Everyone (Romans 9–11)

In Romans 9–11, Paul returns to the immediate problem the letter is meant to address—the conflict between Jewish and Gentile Christians. Since this is not our primary concern in the theology of work, we will summarize quickly.

Paul discusses God's history with Israel, with special attention to God's mercy (Rom. 9:14–18). He explains how God's salvation comes also to the Gentiles. Jews experienced God's salvation first, beginning with Abraham (Rom. 9:4–7). But many have fallen away, and at present it seems as if the Gentiles are more faithful (Rom. 9:30–33). But the

Gentiles should not become judgmental, for their salvation is interwoven with the Jews (Rom. 11:11–16). God has preserved a "remnant" of his people (Rom. 9:27, 11:5) whose faithfulness—by the grace of God—leads to the reconciliation of the world.

For Jews and Gentiles alike, then, salvation is an act of God's mercy, not a reward for human obedience (Rom. 9:6–13). With this in mind, Paul takes on a number of arguments on both sides, always concluding that "God has mercy on whomever he chooses" (Rom. 9:18). Neither Jews nor Gentiles are saved by their own actions, but by God's mercy.

Salvation from God, says Paul, comes by confessing Jesus as Lord and believing that God raised him from the dead (Rom. 10:9–10). In other words, salvation comes to everyone who trusts in the life-giving power of God that enriches the lives of both Jews and Gentiles who follow Jesus as Lord (see Rom. 10:12–13). Disobedience—whether of Gentiles or Jews—provides God with the opportunity to show the world the mercy of God toward everyone (Rom. 11:33). Paul's concern in this letter is to *reconcile* broken relationships between Jewish and Gentile followers of Jesus.

Romans 9–11 offers hope to all of us in our work and in our workplaces. First, Paul emphasizes God's desire to have mercy on the disobedient. All of us, at one point or another in our working lives, have failed to embody Christ's faith and faithfulness in some aspect of our work. If God has mercy on us (Rom. 11:30), we are called to have mercy on others in our work. This does not mean ignoring poor performance or keeping quiet in the face of harassment or discrimination. Mercy is not the enablement of oppression. Instead, it means not letting a person's failures lead us to condemn the person in their entirety. When someone we work with makes a mistake, we are not to judge them as incompetent but to assist them in recovering from the error and learning how not to repeat it. When someone violates our trust, we are to hold that person accountable, while at the same time offering forgiveness that, if met with repentance, creates a path for reestablishing trust.

Second, this section of the letter reminds us of our responsibility to persevere as faithful Christians so that we might be the faithful "remnant" (Rom. 11:5) on behalf of those who have temporarily stumbled in their obedience of faith. When we see those around us fail, our task is not to judge them but to stand in for them. Perhaps our faithfulness can mitigate the damage done to others and even deliver those who caused it from harsh punishment. If we see a colleague mistreat a customer or a subordinate, for example, perhaps we can intervene to correct the situation before it becomes a firing offense. When we remember how close we have come to stumbling or how many times we have failed, our response to others' failings is mercy, as was Christ's. This does not mean we allow people to abuse others. It does mean we put ourselves at risk, as did Christ, for the redemption of people who have erred under the power of sin.

Third, these chapters remind us to demonstrate for the rest of our colleagues what the obedience of faith looks like in daily life and work. If we actually walk in newness of life (see "Walking in Newness of Life" in Romans 6) and set our minds on how our actions can bring a new quality of life to those around us (see "Living According to the Spirit Leads a New Quality of Life" in Romans 8), won't others be attracted to do the same? Our actions at work may be the loudest praise we can ever offer to God and the most attractive witness our co-workers ever see. God's desire is for everyone in the world to be reconciled to God and to one another. So every aspect of our work and life becomes an opportunity to bear witness for Christ—to be one of God's reconciling agents in the world.

Fourth, we need to remain humble. When we, like the factions to whom Paul was writing, judge our own position as superior to those around us, we imagine that we have the inside track to God. Paul speaks directly against this arrogance. We don't know everything about how God is at work in others. As General Peter Pace, retired chairman of the joint chiefs of staff of the U.S. Armed Forces, puts it, "You should always tell the truth as you know it, and you should understand that there is a whole lot that you don't know."[8]

The specific ways we embody this ministry of reconciliation in the world are as diverse as our work and workplaces. Thus we turn to Romans 12 for further direction from Paul on how to discern ways to carry out God's reconciling love in our work.

---

[8] Peter Pace, "General Peter Pace: The Truth as I Know It," *Ethix* 61 (September/October 2008), http://ethix.org/2008/10/10/the-truth-as-i-know-it.

The Community of Grace at Work (Romans 12)

Romans 12 highlights the social and community aspects of salvation. Paul was not writing to an individual but to the community of Christians in Rome, and his constant concern is their life together—with a special emphasis on their work. As we saw in Romans 1–3, salvation in Christ comprises reconciliation, righteousness and justice, and faith and faithfulness. Each of these has a communal aspect—reconciliation *with others*, justice *among people*, faithfulness *to others*.

Be Transformed by the Renewing of Your Minds (Romans 12:1–3)

To bring the communal aspect of salvation to life means a reorientation of our minds and wills from self-serving to community-serving.

> Do not be conformed to this world, but be transformed by the renewing of your minds, so that you may discern what is the will of God—what is good and acceptable and perfect. For by the grace given to me I say to everyone among you not to think of yourself more highly than you ought to think, but to think with sober judgment, each according to the measure of faith that God has assigned. (Rom. 12:2–3)

Let's begin with the second half of this passage, where Paul makes the communal aspect explicit. "I say to everyone among you not to think of yourself more highly than you ought to think." In other words, think less about yourself and more about others, more about the community. Later in chapter 12 Paul amplifies this by adding, "Love one another with mutual affection" (Rom. 12:10), "Contribute to the needs of the saints," "Extend hospitality to strangers" (Rom. 12:13), "Live in harmony with one another" (Rom. 12:17), and "Live peaceably with all" (Rom. 12:18).

The first part of this passage reminds us that we are unable to put others first without God's saving grace. As Paul points out in Romans 1, people are enslaved to a "debased mind" (Rom. 1:28), "futile in their thinking," darkened by "senseless minds" (Rom. 1:21), which results in doing every kind of evil to one another (Rom. 1:22–32). Salvation is liberation from this slavery of the mind, "so that you may discern what is the will of God—what is good and acceptable and perfect." Only if our minds are transformed from self-centeredness to other-centeredness—

imitating Christ, who sacrificed himself for others—can we put reconciliation, justice, and faithfulness ahead of self-serving aims.

With transformed minds, our purpose shifts from justifying our self-centered actions to bringing new life to others. For example, imagine that you are a shift supervisor at a restaurant and you become a candidate for promotion to manager. If your mind is not transformed, your chief goal will be to beat the other candidates. It will not seem hard to justify (to yourself) actions such as withholding information from the other candidates about supplier problems, ignoring sanitation issues that will become visible only in the others' shifts, spreading dissent among their workers, or avoiding collaboration on improving customer service. This will harm not only the other candidates but also their shift workers, the restaurant as a whole, and its customers. On the other hand, if your mind is transformed to care first about others, then you will help the other candidates perform well, not only for their sake but also for the benefit of the restaurant and its workers and customers.

Sacrificing for the Sake of the Community (Romans 12:1–3)

Needless to say, putting others ahead of ourselves requires sacrifice. "Present your bodies as a living sacrifice," Paul exhorts (Rom. 12:1). The words *bodies* and *living* emphasize that Paul means practical actions in the world of daily life and work. All believers become living sacrifices by offering their time, talent, and energy in work that benefits other people and/or God's entire creation.

We can offer a living sacrifice to God every waking moment of our lives. We do it when we forgive someone who transgresses against us in our workplace or when we take the risk to help heal a dispute between others. We offer a living sacrifice when we forego unsustainable use of the earth's resources in pursuit of our own comfort. We offer a living sacrifice when we take on less-than-satisfying work because supporting our family matters more to us than finding the perfect job. We become a living sacrifice when we leave a rewarding position so our spouse can accept a dream job in another city. We become a living sacrifice when, as a boss, we take the blame for a mistake a subordinate makes in his or her work.

Involving the Community in Your Decisions (Romans 12:1–3)

The transformation of the mind "so that you may discern what is the will of God" (Rom. 12:2) comes hand in hand with involving the community of faith in our decisions. As those in the process of being saved, we bring others into our decision-making processes. The word Paul uses for "discern" is literally "to test" or "to approve" in Greek (*dokimazein*). Our decisions must be tested and approved by other believers before we can have confidence that we have discerned the will of God. Paul's warning "not to think of yourself more highly than you ought to think" (Rom. 12:3) applies to our decision-making capability. Don't think you have the wisdom, the moral stature, the breadth of knowledge, or anything else needed to discern God's will by yourself. "Do not claim to be wiser than you are" (Rom. 12:6). Only by involving other members of the faithful community, with its diversity of gifts and wisdom (Rom. 12:4–8) living in harmony with one another (Rom. 12:16), can we develop, test, and approve reliable decisions.

This is more challenging than we might like to admit. We may gather to receive moral teaching as a community, but how often do we actually talk to one another when making moral decisions? Often decisions are made by the person in charge deliberating individually, perhaps after receiving input from a few advisors. We tend to operate this way because moral discussions are uncomfortable, or "hot" as Ronald Heifetz puts it. People don't like to have heated conversations because "most people want to maintain the status quo, avoiding the tough issues."[9] In addition, we often feel that community decision making is a threat to whatever power we possess. But making decisions on our own usually just means following preconceived biases, in other words, being "conformed to this world" (Rom. 12:2).

This raises a difficulty in the sphere of work. What if we don't work in a community of faith, but in a secular company, government, academic institution, or other setting? We could assess our actions communally with our co-workers, but they may not be attuned to the will of God. We could assess our actions communally with our small group

---

[9] Martin Linsky and Ronald A. Heifetz, *Leadership on the Line: Staying Alive Through the Dangers of Leading* (Boston: Harvard Business Review Press, 2002), 114.

or others from our church, but they probably will not understand our work very well. Either—or both—of these practices is better than nothing. But better still would be to gather a group of believers from our own workplace—or at least believers who work in similar situations—and reflect on our actions with them. If we want to assess how well our actions as programmers, fire fighters, civil servants, or school teachers (for example) implement reconciliation, justice, and faithfulness, who better to reflect with than other Christian programmers, fire fighters, civil servants, or school teachers? (See "Equipping Churches Encourage Everyone to Take Responsibility" in *The Equipping Church* at www .theologyofwork.org for more on this topic.)

Work as Members of One Another (Romans 12:4–8)

One essential practical application of walking in newness of life is to recognize how much we all depend on one another's work. "For as in the body we have many members, and not all of the members have the same function, so we, who are many, are one body in Christ, and individually we are members one of another" (Rom. 12:4–5). This interdependence is not a weakness, but a gift from God. As we are being saved by God, we become more integrated with one another.

Paul applies this to the work that each of us does in our particular role. "We have gifts that differ" (Rom. 12:6a) he notes, and when he names a few of them, we see that they are forms of work: prophecy, ministry, teaching, exhortation, generosity, leadership, and compassion. Each of them is a "grace given to us" (Rom. 12:6b) that enables us to work for the good of the community.

Paul develops this process in the context of a specific community—the church. This is fitting because the entire letter revolves around a problem in the church—the conflict between Jewish and Gentile believers. But the list is not particularly "churchy." All of them are equally applicable to work outside the church. Prophecy—"to proclaim a divinely imparted message" or "to bring light to something that is hidden"[10]—is the ability to apply God's word to dark situations, something desperately needed

---

[10] Gerhard Kittel, Gerhard Friedrich, and Geoffrey William Bromiley, eds., *Theological Dictionary of the New Testament* (Grand Rapids: Eerdmans, 1985), 960.

in every workplace. Ministry—with its cognate "administration"—is the ability to organize work so that it does in fact serve those it's supposed to serve, e.g., customers, citizens, or students. Another term for it is "management." Teaching, exhortation (or "encouragement"), and leadership are obviously as applicable to secular settings as to church. So is generosity, when we remember that giving our time, our skills, our patience, or our expertise to assist others at work are all forms of generosity.

Compassion is a vastly underrated element of work. While we might be tempted to view compassion as a hindrance in the competitive world of work, it is actually essential for doing our work well. The value of our work comes not merely from putting in hours, but from caring about how our goods or services serve others—in other words, by compassion. Autoworkers who do not *care* whether their parts are put on properly are of no use to the company, customers, or co-workers, and will sooner or later be candidates for dismissal. Or if the auto *company* doesn't care whether its workers care about its customers, the customers will soon enough switch to another brand. The exceptions to this are products and services that intentionally profit from customers' weaknesses—addictive substances, pornography, products that play on fears about body image and the like. To make money in cases like this, it may be necessary *not* to have compassion for customers. The very fact that it's possible to make money from harming customers in these fields suggests that Christians should try to avoid those workplaces in which compassion is not essential to success. Legitimate occupations make money from meeting people's true needs, not from exploiting their weaknesses.

With all these gifts, the life-giving power of God is experienced in particular *acts* and ways of *doing* things. In other words, the power of God that enriches people's lives comes through concrete *actions* taken by the followers of Jesus. God's grace produces action in God's people for the good of others.

Specific Behavioral Principles to Guide Moral Discernment (Romans 12:9–21)

Paul identifies specific guiding principles to help us serve as conduits to others for God's life-giving power. He introduces this section with his overarching concern to let love be genuine—or, literally, "unhypocritical" (Rom. 12:9). The rest of Romans 12:9–13 elaborates on genuine love, including honor, patience in suffering, perseverance in prayer, generosity to those in need, and hospitality to everyone.

Of particular note is Romans 12:16–18, where Paul encourages the Romans to "live in harmony with one another." Specifically, he says, this means associating with the least powerful in the community, resisting the urge to repay evil for evil, and, whenever possible, living peaceably with everyone.

If we have genuine love, then we care about the people we work for and among. By definition, when we work, we do so at least partly as a means to an end. But we can never treat the people we work among as a means to an end. Each is inherently valuable in his or her own right, so much so that Christ died for each one. This is genuine love, to treat each person as one for whom Christ died and rose again to bring new life.

We show genuine love when we honor the people with whom we work, calling everyone by name regardless of their status, and respecting their families, cultures, languages, aspirations, and the work they do. We show genuine love when we are patient with a subordinate who makes a mistake, a student who learns slowly, a co-worker whose disability makes us uncomfortable. We show genuine love through hospitality to the new employee, the late-night arrival, the disoriented patient, the stranded passenger, the just-promoted boss. Every day we face the possibility someone will do us some evil, small or great. But our protection is not to do evil to others in self-defense, nor to be worn down into despair, but to "overcome evil with good" (Rom. 12:21). We cannot do this by our own power, but only by living in the Spirit of Christ.

Living under the Power of God (Romans 13)

"Let every person be subject to the governing authorities," says Paul. "Those authorities that exist have been instituted by God" (Rom. 13:1). Knowing that the systems of Rome's rule were not in line with God's justice, this counsel must have been hard for some in the Roman churches to hear. How could obeying the idolatrous, ruthless Roman emperor be a way of living in the Spirit? Paul's answer is that God is sovereign over every earthly authority and that God will deal with the authorities at the right time. Even Rome, powerful though it might have been, was ultimately subject to the power of God.

In the workplace, it is often true that "rulers are not a terror to good conduct, but to bad" (Rom. 13:3). Bosses often organize work effectively and create a fair environment for ironing out disputes. Courts regularly settle cases involving patents, land title, labor relations, and contracts equitably. Regulators often serve to protect the environment, prevent fraud, enforce workplace safety, and ensure equal access to housing opportunities. Police generally apprehend criminals and assist the innocent. The fact that even nonbelieving authorities so often get things right is a mark of God's grace in the world.

But authorities in business, government, and every workplace can get things devastatingly wrong and sometimes abuse power for selfish ends. When this happens, it helps to distinguish between human-generated powers (even if they are significant) and the power of God that lies over, behind, and through all of creation. Often the human powers are so much closer to us that they can tend to block out our sense of God's movement in our lives. This passage serves as an encouragement to discern where God is active and to join our lives to those activities of God that will foster true fullness of life for us and for all.

People who worked at Tyco International when Dennis Kozlowski was CEO must have wondered why he was allowed to get away with raiding the company's coffers to pay for his outrageous personal lifestyle. We can imagine that those who tried to work with integrity may have felt afraid for their jobs. Some otherwise ethical people may have succumbed to the pressure to participate in Kozlowski's schemes. But eventually Kozlowski was found out, charged, and convicted of grand larceny, conspiracy, and fraud.[11] Those who trusted that justice would eventually be restored ended up on the right side of the story.

Paul offers practical advice to the Roman Christians, who were living in the center of the most powerful human authorities the Western world had ever known. Obey the law, pay your taxes and commercial

---

[11] Michael J. De La Merced, "Released from Prison," *New York Times,* December 4, 2013, B6.

fees, give respect and honor to those in positions of authority (Rom. 12:7). Perhaps some had thought that, as Christians, they should rebel against Roman injustice. But Paul seems to see self-centeredness in their attitude, rather than God-centeredness. Self-serving rebelliousness will not prepare them for God's "day" (Rom. 13:12) that is coming.

For example, in some countries tax evasion is so commonplace that needed services cannot be provided, bribery (to enable the evasion) corrupts officials at every level, and the tax burden is unfairly distributed. The government loses legitimacy in the eyes of both the taxpayers and the tax evaders. Civil instability slows economic growth and human development. No doubt, much of the money that is collected is used for purposes inconsistent with Christian values, and many Christians may respond by evading taxes along with everyone else. But what would happen if Christians committed, in an organized fashion, to pay their taxes *and* to monitor the government's use of funds? It could take decades to reform government in this manner, but would it eventually work? Paul's argument in Romans 12 suggests it would.

Many Christians live in democracies today, which gives the additional responsibility to vote for wise laws that express God's justice as best we can. Once the votes are counted, we have a responsibility to obey the laws and the authorities, even if we disagree with them. Paul's words imply that we are to obey the legitimate authorities, even while we may be working to change unjust ones through democratic means.

In every sphere of life, we have an ongoing responsibility to resist and to transform all unjust systems, always putting the common good above self-interest. Even so, we are to show respect to the authorities, whether at work, school, church, government, or civic life. We believe that change will occur not because we express outrage, but because God is sovereign over all.

Paul completes chapter 13 noting that by loving other people, we fulfill the commandments. Living in the Spirit inherently fulfills the Jewish law, even by those who don't know it. He reiterates that this comes not by human striving, but by the power of Christ in us. "Put on the Lord Jesus Christ," he concludes (Rom. 13:14).

Welcoming—Living Peacefully with Different Values and Opinions (Romans 14–15)

At this point in the letter, Paul has finished developing his method of moral reasoning. Now he pauses to give some implications arising from it in the unique context of the Roman churches, namely, in the disputes among believers.

The chief implication for the Roman churches is welcome. The Roman Christians are to welcome one another. It's not hard to see how Paul derives this implication. The goal of moral reasoning, according to Romans 6, is to "walk in newness of life," meaning to bring a *new quality of life* to those around us. If you are in a broken relationship with someone, welcome is inherently a new quality of life. Welcome is reconciliation in practice. Quarrels seek to exclude others, but welcome seeks to include them, even when it means respecting areas of disagreement.

Welcoming Overcomes Quarrels over Differing Opinions (Romans 14:1–23)

"Welcome those who are weak in faith, but not for the purpose of quarreling over opinions," begins Paul (Rom. 14:1). The "weak in faith" may be those who lack confidence in their own convictions on disputed issues (see Rom. 14:23) and rely on strict rules to govern their actions. Specifically, some of the Jewish Christians kept the strictures of Jewish dietary laws and were offended by other Christians consuming non-kosher meat and drink. Apparently they refused even to eat with those who did not keep kosher.[12] Although they regarded their strictness as a strength, Paul says it becomes a weakness when it causes them to judge those who do not share their conviction. Paul says that those who keep kosher "must not pass judgment on those who eat [non-kosher meat]."

Nonetheless, Paul's response to their weakness is not to argue with them, nor to ignore their beliefs, but to do whatever will make them feel welcome. He tells those who do not keep kosher not to flaunt their freedom to eat anything, because doing so would require the kosher-keepers

---

[12] Wright, "The Letter to the *Romans*," 735.

either to break fellowship with them or to violate their consciences. If there is no kosher meat to be found, then the non-kosher should join with the kosher and eat only vegetables, rather than demanding that the kosher-keepers violate their consciences. "It is wrong for you to make others fall by what you eat," Paul says (Rom. 14:20).

Both groups feel strongly that their views are morally important. The strong believe that for Gentiles to keep kosher is a refusal of God's grace in Christ Jesus. The weak believe that not keeping kosher—and the merely eating with people who don't keep kosher—is an affront to God and a violation of the Jewish law. The argument is heated because freedom in Christ and obedience to God's covenants are truly important moral and religious issues. But relationships in the community are even more important. Living in Christ is not about being right or wrong on any particular issue. It is about being in right relationship with God and with one another, about "peace and joy in the Holy Spirit" (Rom. 14:17).

Moral disagreements can be even more difficult at work, where there is less common ground. An interesting aspect in this regard is Paul's special concern for the weak. Although he tells both groups not to judge each other, he places a greater practical burden on the strong. "We who are strong ought to put up with the failings of the weak, and not to please ourselves" (Rom. 15:1). Our model for this is Jesus, "who did not please himself" (Rom. 15:3). This means that those who are in the right, or in the majority, or who otherwise have the most power are called to voluntarily refrain from violating the consciences of others. In most workplaces, the opposite occurs. The weak must accommodate themselves to the dictates of the strong, even if doing so violates their conscience.

Imagine, for example, that someone in your workplace has religious or moral convictions that require a particular modesty of dress, say covering the hair or the shoulders or legs. These convictions could be a form of weakness, to use Paul's terminology, if they make that person uncomfortable around others who do not conform to their idea of modest dress. Probably you would not object to the person wearing such modest dress themselves. But Paul's argument implies that *you* and all your co-workers should also dress modestly according to the other person's standards, at least if you want to make your workplace a place of welcome and reconciliation. The strong (those not hampered by legalism about dress codes) are to welcome the weak (those offended by others' dress) by accommodating to their weakness.

Remember that Paul does not want us to demand that others accommodate to our compunctions. That would turn us into the weak, whereas Paul wants us to become strong in faith. We should not be the ones tsk-tsk-ing about others' dress, language, or taste in music on the job. Imagine instead that Christians had a reputation for making everyone feel welcome, rather than for judging others' tastes and habits. Would that help or hinder Christ's mission in the world of work?

Welcoming Builds up the Community (Romans 14:19–15:33)

Another aspect of welcoming is that it strengthens the community. "Each of us must please the neighbor for the good purpose of building up the neighbor" (Rom. 15:3) in much the same way that a welcoming host makes sure that a visit strengthens the guest. The "neighbor" here is another member of the community. "Let us then pursue what makes for peace and *mutual* upbuilding," Paul says (Rom. 14:19). Mutual up-building means working together in community.

From chapters 14 and 15, we see that welcoming is a powerful practice. Paul is not talking about simply saying hello with smiles on our faces. He is talking about engaging in deep moral discernment as a community, yet remaining in warm relationship with those who come to different moral conclusions, even on important matters. As far as Paul is concerned, the continuing relationships in the community are more important than the particular moral conclusions. Relationships bring a quality of life to the community that far exceeds any possible satisfaction from being right about an issue or judging another to be wrong. It also is a more attractive witness to the world around us. "Welcome one another, therefore, just as Christ has welcomed you, *for the glory of God*" (Rom. 17:7). When we welcome one another, the final result by God's mercy (Rom. 15:9) is that "all the peoples praise him" (Rom. 15:12).

A Community of Leaders (Romans 16)

Chapter 16 of Romans belies many people's common assumptions about the nature of Paul's work—namely, that he was a solitary, heroic figure, enduring hardships to carry out his lonely and exalted calling to spread the gospel among the Gentiles. In Romans 16, however, Paul makes it clear that his work was a community effort. Paul mentions twenty-nine co-workers by name, plus many more by terms such as "the church in their house" and "the brothers and sisters who are with them." Paul's list sets equal value upon the work of both women and men, without distinct roles for either, and seems to include people of various social stations. Several are clearly wealthy, and some of those may be freedmen and freedwomen. Others may well be slaves. Paul praises the particular work of many, such as those who "risked their necks" (Rom. 16:3), "worked very hard" (Rom. 16:6), "were in prison with me" (Rom. 16:7), "worked hard in the Lord" (Rom. 16:12), or acted "as a mother to me" (Rom. 16:13). He mentions the work of Tertius "the writer [scribe] of this letter" (Rom. 16:22) and Erastus "the city treasurer" (Rom. 16:23).

Observing Paul within such a wide circle of co-workers undercuts the modern Western emphasis on individuality, especially in the workplace. Like everyone he names, Paul worked *in* community *for the good of* community. This final section of the letter lets us know that the gospel is *everyone's* work. Not all are apostles. We are not all called to leave our jobs and travel around preaching. Paul's list of the varied gifts of service in Romans 12:6–8 makes that clear. No matter what kind of work occupies our time, we are called to act as servants of the good news of God's salvation for all people. (See "Work as Members of One Another," in Romans 12:4–8.)

These greetings also remind us that church leaders are workers. It is sometimes tempting to see Paul's work as somehow distinct from other kinds of work. But Paul's repeated reference to the *work* of those he names reminds us that what is true of Paul's ministry is true of all workplaces. Here, where we spend much of our time each week, is where we will either learn to walk in newness of life (Rom. 6:4)—or remain mired in the power of death. In our workplace relationships we are invited to seek the good of the other, according to the model of Christ. In the often mundane work of our minds and hearts and hands is where we are offered the chance to become channels of God's grace for others.

In the final verses of Romans, it is apparent that no one's work stands in isolation; it is interwoven with the work of others. Paul recognizes those who have gone before him, passing on their faith to him, those who have worked beside him, and those who have risked their lives for him and for their common work. This point of view calls each of us to look at the whole fabric of community that constitutes our places of work, to consider all the lives intertwined with ours, supporting and enhancing what we are able to do, all who give up something that they might want for themselves in order to benefit us and to benefit the work that goes beyond us into God's world.

Conclusion to Romans

Paul's dominant concern in Romans is salvation—God's reconciliation of the world through the cross of Jesus Christ. In Christ, God is working to reconcile all people to himself, to reconcile people to one another, and to redeem the created order from the evil forces of sin, death, and decay. Paul's concern is not abstract but practical. His aim is to heal the divisions among Christians in Rome and to enable them to work together to accomplish God's will for their lives and work.

In this setting, Paul shows how salvation comes to us as a free gift bought by God's faithfulness in the cross of Christ and by God's grace in bringing us to faith in Christ. In no way does this free gift imply that God does not care about the work we do and the way we work. Instead, Paul shows how receiving God's grace transforms both the work we do and the way we do it. Although we don't work to earn salvation, as God is saving us, he gives us the amazing diversity of gifts needed to serve one another and build up our communities. As a result, we walk in a new way of life, bringing life in Christ to those around us and, in God's time, to the fullness of creation.

1 CORINTHIANS AND WORK

Introduction to 1 Corinthians

No other letter in the New Testament gives us a more practical picture of applying the Christian faith to the day-to-day issues of life and work than 1 Corinthians. Topics such as career and calling, the lasting value of work, overcoming individual limitations, leadership and service, the development of skills and abilities (or "gifts"), fair wages, environmental stewardship, and the use of money and possessions are prominent in the letter. The unifying perspective on all these topics is love. Love is the purpose, means, motivation, gift, and glory behind all work done in Christ.

The City of Corinth (1 Corinthians)

The Apostle Paul's first letter to the church in Corinth, which he founded on his second missionary journey (AD 48–51), is a treasure trove of practical theology for Christians facing everyday challenges. It provides Paul's instruction to Christians grappling with real-life issues, including conflicts of loyalty, class differences, conflicts between personal freedom and the common good, and the difficulty of leading a diverse group of people to accomplish a shared mission.

In Paul's time, Corinth was the most important city in Greece. Sitting astride the isthmus that joins the Peloponnesian Peninsula to mainland Greece, Corinth controlled both the Saronic Gulf to the east and the Gulf of Corinth to the north. Merchants wanted to avoid the difficult, dangerous sea journey around the fingers of the Peloponnese, so a great deal of the goods flowing between Rome and the western empire and the rich ports of the eastern Mediterranean were hauled across this isthmus. Almost all of it passed through Corinth, making it one of the empire's great commercial centers. Strabo, an older contemporary of Paul, noted that

"Corinth is called 'wealthy' because of its commerce, since it is situated on the Isthmus and is master of two harbors, of which the one leads straight to Asia, and the other to Italy; and it makes easy the exchange of merchandise from both countries that are so far distant from each other."[1]

The city had something of a boomtown atmosphere during the middle of the first century as freed slaves, veterans, merchants, and tradesmen streamed into the city. Though what we might now call "upward mobility" was elusive in the ancient world, Corinth was one place where it might be possible, with a little luck and a lot of hard work, to establish oneself and enjoy a reasonably good life.[2] This contributed to the unique ethos of Corinth, which viewed itself as prosperous and self-sufficient, a city whose core value was "entrepreneurial pragmatism in the pursuit of success."[3] Many cities in today's world aspire to this very ethos.

The Church in Corinth and Paul's Letters (1 Corinthians)

Paul arrived in Corinth in the winter of AD 49/50[4] and lived there for a year and a half. While there he supported himself by working in tentmaking—or perhaps leatherworking[5] (Acts 18:2), the trade he had learned as a boy—in the workshop of Aquila and Priscilla (see 1 Cor. 4:12). He lays out his reasons for following this course in 1 Corinthians 9 (see below), even though he could have taken advantage of full-time support as a missionary from the start, as indeed he later does (Acts 18:4 and 2 Cor. 11:9).

In any case, his Sabbath-day preaching in the synagogue soon bore fruit, and the church in Corinth was born. The church seems to have been made up of not more than a hundred people when Paul wrote 1 Corinthians. Some were Jews, while most were Gentiles. They met in

---

[1] Strabo, *Geographica* 8.6.20.

[2] Donald Engels, *Roman Corinth: An Alternative Model for the Classical City* (Chicago: University of Chicago Press, 1990), 49.

[3] Anthony C. Thiselton, *The First Epistle to the Corinthians: A Commentary on the Greek Text, New International Greek Testament Commentary* (Grand Rapids: Eerdmans, 2000), 4.

[4] Gordon Fee, *The First Epistle to the Corinthians* (Grand Rapids: Eerdmans, 1987), 5.

[5] Ronald F. Hock, *The Social Context of Paul's Ministry: Tentmaking and Apostleship* (Philadelphia: Fortress Press, 1980), 21–22.

the houses of two or three wealthier members, but most belonged to the large underclass that populated all urban centers.[6]

Paul continued to be keenly interested in the development of the church even after he left Corinth. Paul had written the congregation at least one letter prior to 1 Corinthians (1 Cor. 5:9) in order to address a problem that had come up after his departure. Members of the house of Chloe, who may have had business interests to attend to in Ephesus, visited Paul there and reported that the church in Corinth was in danger of coming apart at the seams over various divisions of opinion (1:11). In entrepreneurial Corinthian style, competing groups were creating parties around their favorite apostles in order to gain status for themselves (chs. 1–4). Many were up in arms due to serious differences over the sexual behavior and business ethics of some of their members (chs. 5–6). Then another group of representatives from the church arrived with a letter in hand (7:1, 16:17) querying Paul on a number of important issues, such as sex and marriage (ch. 7), the propriety of eating meat that had been previously offered to idols (chs. 8–10) and worship (chs. 11–14). Finally, Paul had also learned from one of these sources, or perhaps Apollos (see 16:12), that some in the Corinthian church were denying the future resurrection of believers (ch. 15).

These questions hardly grew out of academic discussions. The Corinthians wanted to know how as followers of Christ they should act in matters of daily life and work. Paul gives answers throughout 1 Corinthians, making it one of the most practical books of the New Testament.

All Are Called (1 Corinthians 1:1–3)

In the opening paragraph of 1 Corinthians, Paul lays out themes that he will address in more detail in the body of his letter. It is no coincidence that the concept of calling is front and center in the introduction. Paul states in the very first verse that he was "called to be an apostle of Christ Jesus by the will of God" (1:1). A strong conviction that he was called directly by God pervades Paul's letters (see e.g. Gal. 1:1) and is

---

[6]Wayne A. Meeks, *The First Urban Christians: The Social World of the Apostle Paul,* 2nd ed. (New Haven: Yale University Press, 2003), 51–73.

fundamental to his mission (see Acts 9:14–15). It lent him remarkable fortitude in the face of enormous challenges. Likewise, the Corinthian believers are "called" along with "all those who in every place call on the name of our Lord Jesus Christ" (1 Cor. 1:2). We will soon see that the basis of our calling is not individual satisfaction but community development. Although Paul doesn't develop this point until later in the letter (see 7:17–24), even at this juncture it is clear he thinks all believers are meant to pursue the calling designed for them by God.

Spiritual Resources Available (1 Corinthians 1:4–9)

According to the conventions of ancient letter writing, a greeting was followed by a section in which the author praised the recipient.[7] In most of his letters, Paul modifies this literary form by offering thanksgiving rather than praise and by using a standard phrase much like we have here: "I give thanks to my God always for you . . ." (see 1:4, as well as Rom. 1:8; Phil. 1:3; Col. 1:3; 1 Thess. 1:2; and 2 Thess. 1:3). In this case, Paul expresses his thanks that the Corinthian believers have experienced the grace of God in Christ. This is more than some vague piety. Rather, Paul has something quite specific in mind. The believers in Corinth have been "enriched in [Christ]" (1 Cor. 1:5) so that they "are not lacking in any spiritual gift as you wait for the revealing of our Lord Jesus Christ" (1:7). Paul specifically names two gifts, speech and knowledge, that the Corinthian church enjoyed in abundance.

For our purposes, it is especially important to note that Paul is convinced that the believers in Corinth have received the spiritual resources they need to fulfill their calling. God has called them, and he has given them gifts that will enable them to be "blameless on the day of our Lord Jesus Christ" (1:8). Although the day of perfection has not arrived yet, whether at work or anywhere else, Christians already have access to the gifts that will come to complete fruition on that day.

---

[7] Peter T. O'Brien, *Introductory Thanksgivings in the Letters of Paul*, in vol. 49 of *Novum Testamentum* (Leiden: Brill, 1977), 11.

It is hard to imagine that all Corinthian Christians felt as if their work was a special occupation designed individually for them by God. Most of them were slaves or common laborers, as we will see. What Paul must mean is that whether or not each person's occupation seems special, God gives the gifts needed to make everyone's work contribute to God's plan for the world. No matter how insignificant our work seems, no matter how much we long to have a different job, the work we do now is important to God.

The Need for a Common Vision (1 Corinthians 1:10–17)

Paul states in thesis-like fashion what he is trying to accomplish by writing 1 Corinthians.[8] "I appeal to you, brothers and sisters, by the name of our Lord Jesus Christ, that all of you be in agreement and that there be no divisions among you, but that you be united in the same mind and the same purpose" (1 Cor. 1:10). The verb he uses in this final phrase is a metaphor that connotes mending of human relationships. Thus Paul is urging the Corinthians to overcome the factionalism that has damaged the unity of the church.

Modern Western culture highly values diversity, so we are in danger of construing Paul's injunctions negatively. He is not arguing for conformity of thought (as other passages make clear), but he understands quite clearly that a sense of common purpose and vision is essential. If there is continual strife and disagreement about basic values and convictions and no cohesion among its members, any organization is doomed to failure. Although Paul is writing to a church, we know he also thought Christians should contribute to the workings of society at large. "Be subject to rulers and authorities, to be obedient, to *be ready for every good work*" (Titus 3:1; emphasis added). Therefore, we should seek common purpose not only in church but also in the places we work. Our role as Christians is to do good work in unity and harmony with both believers and nonbelievers. This does not mean we acquiesce to immorality

---

[8] Margaret M. Mitchell, *Paul and the Rhetoric of Reconciliation* (Louisville: Westminster John Knox Press, 1993).

or injustice. It does mean that we develop good relationships, support co-workers, and care to do our work excellently. If we cannot in good conscience do our work wholeheartedly, we need to find someplace else to work, rather than grumble or shirk.

Friends in Low Places (1 Corinthians 1:18–31)

Paul reminds the congregation in Corinth that most of them do not come from the ranks of the privileged classes. "Not many of you were wise by human standards, not many were powerful, not many were of noble birth" (1 Cor. 1:26). But the effectiveness of the church did not depend on having people with all the connections, educations, or fortunes. God accomplishes his purposes with ordinary people. We have already seen that the value of our work is based on God's gifts, not on our credentials. But Paul draws a further point. Because we are nobody special by nature, we can never treat other people as insignificant.

> God chose what is foolish in the world to shame the wise; God chose what is weak in the world to shame the strong; God chose what is low and despised in the world, things that are not, to reduce to nothing things that are, *so that no one might boast in the presence of God.* (1 Cor. 1:27–29; emphasis added)

Since Paul's day, many Christians have attained positions of power, wealth, and status. His words remind us that we insult God if we allow these things to make us arrogant, disrespectful, or abusive toward people in lower-status positions. Many workplaces still accord special privileges to higher-ranking workers, bearing no relevance to the actual work at hand. Aside from pay differences, high-status workers may enjoy fancier offices, first-class travel, executive dining rooms, reserved parking, better benefits packages, company-paid club memberships, residences, drivers, personal services, and other perquisites. They may receive special deference—for example, being called "Mr." or "Ms." or "Professor"—when others in the organization are called by first names only. In some cases, special treatment may be appropriate, based on the nature of the work performed and organizational responsibilities. But in other cases, such privileges may create unwarranted gradations of human worth and dignity. Paul's point is that such distinctions have no place among the people of God. If we enjoy—or suffer—such distinctions at work, we might ask ourselves whether they contradict the equal dignity of persons in the presence of God and, if so, what we might do to remedy them.

It Takes All Sorts (1 Corinthians 3:1–9)

We noted above that the main problem in the Corinthian church was that of factionalism. Cliques were forming under the banner of Paul's name versus the name of Apollos, another missionary to the Corinthian church. Paul will have none of this. He and Apollos are simply servants. Although they have different roles, neither of them is more valuable than the other. The planter (Paul) and the irrigator (Apollos)—to use an agricultural metaphor—are equally vital to the success of the harvest, and neither is responsible for the growth of the crop. That is entirely God's doing. The various workers have a common goal in mind (a bounteous harvest), but they have different tasks in line with their abilities and calling. All are necessary and no one can do every necessary task.

Paul, in other words, is aware of the importance of diversification and specialization. In his famous 1958 essay, "I, Pencil," economist Leonard Read followed the course of the manufacture of a common pencil, making the point that no single person knows how to make one. It is actually the product of several sophisticated processes, only one of which a given individual can master. By the grace of God, different people are able to play different roles in the world's workplaces. But specialization at times leads to interpersonal or interdepartmental factionalism, poor lines of communication, and even personal vilification. If Christians believe what Paul says about the God-given nature of different roles, perhaps we can take the lead in bridging dysfunctional divides in our organizations. If we are able simply to treat others with respect and value the work of people different from ourselves, we may be making significant contributions to our workplaces.

An important application of this is the value of investing in worker development, whether our own or that of people around us. In Paul's letters, including 1 Corinthians, it sometimes seems that Paul never does anything himself (see, for example, 14–15) but instructs others how to do it. This is not arrogance or laziness, but mentoring. He would far rather invest in training effective workers and leaders than in calling all the shots himself. As we mature in serving Christ in our places of work, perhaps we will find ourselves doing more to equip others and less to make ourselves look good.

Do Good Work (1 Corinthians 3:10–17)

Paul introduces the metaphor of a building under construction in order to make a new point—do good work. This point is so important to understanding the value of work that it is worth including the passage in its entirety here.

> According to the grace of God given to me, like a skilled master builder I laid a foundation, and someone else is building on it. Each builder must choose with care how to build on it. For no one can lay any foundation other than the one that has been laid; that foundation is Jesus Christ. Now if anyone builds on the foundation with gold, silver, precious stones, wood, hay, straw—the work of each builder will become visible, for the Day will disclose it, because it will be revealed with fire, and the fire will test what sort of work each has done. If what has been built on the foundation survives, the builder will receive a reward. If the work is burned up, the builder will suffer loss; the builder will be saved, but only as through fire. (1 Cor. 3:10–15)

This may be the most direct statement of the eternal value of earthly work in all of Scripture. The work we do on earth—to the extent we do it according to the ways of Christ—survives into eternity. Paul is speaking specifically of the work done by the community of the church, which he likens to a temple. Paul compares himself to a "skilled master builder" who has laid the foundation, which is, of course, Christ himself. Others build on top of this foundation, and each one is responsible for his own work. Paul likens good work to gold, silver, and precious stones, and shabby work to wood, hay, and straw. Though some have tried to assign specific meanings to each of these materials, it is more likely that the difference is simply that some materials have the ability to withstand testing by fire while others do not.

Paul is not making any judgment about any individual's salvation, for even if anyone's work fails the test, "the builder will be saved." This passage is not about the relationship between a believer's "good works" and his heavenly reward, though it has often been read in that way. Instead, Paul is concerned with the church as a whole and how its leaders work within the church. If they contribute to the unity of the church, they will be commended. If, however, their ministry results in strife and factionalism, they are actually provoking God's wrath, because he passionately protects his living temple from those who would destroy it (vv. 16–17).

Although Paul is writing about the work of building a Christian community, his words apply to all kinds of work. As we have seen, Paul regards Christian work to include the work believers do under secular authority as well as in the church. Whatever our work, it will be evaluated impartially by God. The final assize will be better than any performance review, since God judges with perfect justice—unlike human bosses, however just or unjust they may be—and he is able to factor in our intent, our limitations, our motives, our compassion, and his mercy. God has called all believers to work in whatever circumstances they find themselves, and he has given us specific gifts to fulfill that calling. He expects us to use them responsibly for his purposes, and he will inspect our work. And to the degree that our work is done in excellence, by his gifts and grace, it will become part of God's eternal kingdom. That should motivate us—even more than our employer's approval or our paycheck—to do as good a job as we possibly can.

Leadership as Service (1 Corinthians 4:1–4)

In this passage, Paul offers a definitive statement of what it means to be a leader: "Think of us in this way, as servants of Christ and stewards of God's mysteries" (1 Cor. 4:1). "Us" refers to the apostolic leaders through whom the Corinthians had come to faith and to whom the various factions in the church claimed allegiance (1 Cor. 4:6). Paul uses two words in this verse to elaborate what he means. The first, *hypēretēs* ("servants"), denotes an attendant, a servant who waits on or assists someone. In this sense, leaders attend personally to the needs of the people they lead. Leaders are not exalted, but humbled, by accepting leadership. The job requires patience, personal engagement, and individual attention to the needs of followers. The second is *oikonomos* ("stewards"), which describes a servant or slave who manages the affairs of a household or estate. The chief distinction in this position is trust. The steward is trusted to manage the affairs of the household for the benefit of the owner. Likewise, the leader is trusted to manage the group for the benefit of all its members, rather than the leader's personal benefit. This quality is explicitly ascribed to Timothy (2 Cor. 4:17), Tychicus (Eph. 6:21; Col. 4:7), Paul (1 Tim. 1:12), Antipas (Rev. 2:13), and, above all, Christ (2 Tim. 2:13; Heb. 2:17). These are the kinds of people God relies on to carry out his plan for his kingdom.

Modern workplaces often set up systems to reward leaders for using their teams to accomplish the organization's objectives. This is probably a wise practice, unless it encourages leaders to attain such rewards at the expense of the people they lead. Leaders are indeed responsible to accomplish—or better yet, exceed—the work their teams are assigned to do. But it is not legitimate to sacrifice the needs of the group in order to obtain the leader's personal rewards. Instead, leaders are called to accomplish the group's goals *by meeting the needs* of the group.

Working with Nonbelievers (1 Corinthians 5:9–10)

In chapter 5, Paul introduces the question of working with nonbelievers, a question he will explore more fully in chapter 10 and ultimately in 2 Corinthians 6 (see "Working with Nonbelievers" in 2 Corinthians). At this point, he says simply that Christians are not called to withdraw from the world because of fears about ethics. "I wrote to you in my letter not to associate with sexually immoral persons—not at all meaning the immoral of this world, or the greedy and robbers, or idolaters, since you would then need to go out of the world" (1 Cor. 5:9–10). By mentioning the greedy, robbers, and idolaters, he explicitly indicates he is including the work world in his instructions. Although we are to avoid immorality ourselves, and we are not to associate with immoral *Christians*, Paul expects us to work with nonbelievers, even those who do not observe God's ethical principles. Needless to say, this is a difficult proposition, although he defers getting into specifics until chapter 10. The point he makes here is simply that Christians are forbidden from trying to create some kind of Christian-only economy and leaving the world to fend for itself. Instead, we are called to take our place in the work of the world alongside the people of the world.

Bloom Where You Are Planted (1 Corinthians 7:20–24)

In the middle of a chapter that deals primarily with issues relating to marriage and singleness, Paul makes an important statement about calling and work. Other things being equal, believers should remain in the life situation in which they found themselves when they were converted (7:20). The specific question that Paul is dealing with does not directly impinge upon most people in the Western world, though it is critical in many parts of the globe today. What should believers who are slaves do if they have the chance to gain freedom?

Slavery in the ancient world was a complex phenomenon that is by no means identical to its modern manifestations, neither that of the pre-Civil War American South, nor debt bondage in contemporary South Asia, nor sex trafficking in virtually every country on earth. Certainly, it was equally heinous in many cases, but some slaves, particularly the household slaves Paul probably has in mind here, were better off, at least economically, than many free people. Many educated people, including doctors and accountants, actually chose slavery for precisely that reason. Thus, for Paul, it was a genuinely open question whether slavery or freedom would be the better lot in any given situation. Modern forms of slavery, on the other hand, always severely diminish the lives of those enslaved.

The question then is not whether slavery should be abolished, but whether slaves should seek to become free. It is difficult to determine the precise nature of Paul's instruction here because the Greek of 1 Corinthians 7:21 is ambiguous, so much so that it is open to two divergent interpretations. As the NRSV and a number of commentators understand it, it should be rendered as follows: "Were you a slave when called? Do not be concerned about it. Even if you can gain your freedom, make use of your present condition now more than ever." Equally possible (and more likely, in our opinion), however, is the sense given in the NIV, NASB, and KJV, which is, "Were you a slave when you were called? Don't let it trouble you—although if you can gain your freedom, do so" (NIV). Whatever Paul's advice, his underlying belief is that, compared to the difference between in Christ and not in Christ, the difference between being a slave and a free person is relatively minor. "For whoever was called in the Lord as a slave is a freed person belonging to the Lord, just as whoever was free when called is a slave of Christ" (7:22). Thus, if there are no compelling reasons to change your status, it is probably best to remain in the situation in which you were called.

Paul's teaching here has important application for the workplace. While we may feel that getting the right job is the most important factor in serving God or experiencing the life he intends for us, God is much more concerned that we make the most of every job we have over the course of our lives. In a given instance, there may be good reasons to change jobs or even professions. Fine, go ahead and do so. Yet any morally legitimate job can fulfill God's calling, so don't make finding your life's work *into* your life's work. There is no hierarchy of more godly and less godly professions. Certainly this cautions us against believing that God calls the most serious Christians into church jobs.

Maintain the Proper Perspective (1 Corinthians 7:29–31)

Paul addresses the question of whether the promised return of the Lord implies that Christians should abandon ordinary daily life, including work.

> I mean, brothers and sisters, the appointed time has grown short; from now on . . . let those who buy [be] as though they had no possessions, and those who deal with the world as though they had no dealings with it. For the present form of this world is passing away. (1 Cor. 7:29–31)

Apparently some believers neglected family duties and ceased working, in the same way you might neglect to sweep the floor before moving to a new house. Paul had previously dealt with this situation in the church in Thessalonica and given unambiguous instructions.

> Anyone unwilling to work should not eat. For we hear that some of you are living in idleness, mere busybodies, not doing any work. Now such persons we command and exhort in the Lord Jesus Christ to do their work quietly and to earn their own living. (2 Thess. 3:10–12)

Paul's logic will be easier to understand if we recognize that verse 29 does not indicate merely that "the time is short" in the sense that Jesus' second coming is almost here. Paul uses a verb here that describes how an object is pushed together (*synestalmenos*), so that it becomes shorter or smaller as a whole. "Time has been compressed" might be a better translation, as suggested by the NASB rendering, or "Time has been shortened." What Paul apparently means is that since Christ has come, the end of the vast expanse of time has at last become visible. "The future outcome of this world has become crystal clear," writes scholar David E. Garland.[9] Verse 31 explains that "the present form of this world is passing away." The "present form" has the sense of "the way things are" in our fallen world of damaged social and economic relationships. Paul wants his readers to understand that Christ's coming has already effected a change in the very fabric of life. The values and aspirations that are simply taken for granted in the present way of doing things are no longer operative for believers.

The proper response to the compression of time is not to cease working but to work differently. The old attitudes toward everyday life and its affairs must be replaced. This brings us back to the paradoxical statements in 1 Corinthians 7:29–31. We should buy, yet be as though we have no possessions. We should deal with the world as though not dealing with the world as we know it. That is, we may make use of the things this world has to offer, but we shouldn't accept the world's values and principles when they get in the way of God's kingdom. The things we buy, we should

---

[9] David E. Garland, *1 Corinthians*, Baker Exegetical Commentary on the New Testament (Grand Rapids: Baker, 2003), 329.

employ for the good of others instead of holding tightly to them. When we bargain in the market, we should seek the good of the person from whom we buy, not just our own interests. In other words, Paul is calling believers to "a radically new understanding of their relationship to the world."[10]

Our old attitude is that we work to make life more comfortable and satisfying for ourselves and those close to us. We seek to gather things into our possession that we think will bring us status, security, and advantage over others. We compartmentalize worship of our gods first, then attention to our marriage second, then work third, and then civic engagement fourth, if we have any time and energy left. The new attitude is that we work to benefit ourselves, those close to us, *and all those for whom Jesus worked and died.* We seek to release the things in our possession for use where they will make the world more as God desires it. We integrate our lives of worship, family, work, and society and seek to invest in—rather than shuffle around—physical, intellectual, cultural, moral, and spiritual capital. In this we emulate the forefather of the people of God, Abraham, to whom God said, "I will bless you, and make your name great, so that you will be a blessing" (Gen. 12:2).

Everyone Gets Their Fair Share (1 Corinthians 9:7–10)

In chapter 9, Paul explains why he initially chose not to accept direct financial support from the Corinthian church even though he had a right to it. He begins by asserting the right of workers, including apostles, to receive wages for their work. We serve the Lord in our work, and the Lord intends that we draw sustenance from it in return. Paul gives three examples from daily life that illustrate this point. Soldiers, vintners, and shepherds all derive economic benefit for their labors. Paul, however, rarely appeals to convention alone to make his case, so he quotes Deuteronomy 25:4 ("You shall not muzzle an ox while it is treading out the grain") in support of his argument. If even animals deserve a share of the fruits of their labor, then surely any person who participates in bringing about some benefit should share in that benefit.

---

[10] Fee, 336.

This text has clear implications for the workplace, especially for employers. Workers deserve a fair wage. In fact, the Bible threatens employers with dire consequences if they deny their employees just compensation (Lev. 19:13; Deut. 24:14; James 5:7). Paul knows that a variety of factors affect the determination of a fair wage, and he does not try to prescribe a figure or formula. Likewise, the complexities of supply and demand, regulation and unionization, wages and benefits, and power and flexibility in today's labor markets are beyond the scope of this chapter. But the principle is not. Those who employ human labor cannot neglect the needs of those whose work they employ.

Nonetheless, Paul chooses not to make use of his right to receive wages for his work as an apostle. Why? Because in his case, given the sensitivities in the church in Corinth, to do so might "put an obstacle in the way of the gospel of Christ." As it happens, God has made it possible for him to earn a living there by introducing him to fellow tentmakers (or leatherworkers), Priscilla and Aquila, who live in Corinth (Acts 18:1–3; Rom. 16:3). Paul doesn't expect that God will arrange things so that all church workers can afford to work for free. But in this case, God did, and Paul accepts God's provision with thanks. The point is that only the worker has the right to offer to work without fair remuneration. The employer has no right to demand it.

God's Glory Is the Ultimate Goal (1 Corinthians 10)

In the course of an extended argument beginning in chapter 8 on an issue of critical importance to believers in Corinth—the propriety of eating meat that had previously been offered to idols—Paul articulates a broad principle concerning the use of the earth's resources. He says, quoting Psalm 24:1, "The earth and its fullness are the Lord's" (1 Cor. 10:26). That is, because everything comes from God, any food may be eaten irrespective of its previous use for pagan cultic purposes. (In a Roman city, much of the meat sold in the market would have been offered to idols in the course of its preparation.[11]) There are two aspects of this principle that apply to work.

---

[11] Hans Conzelman, *1 Corinthians,* trans. James W. Leitch (Philadelphia: Fortress Press, 1975), 176, incl. nn. 11–13.

First, we may extend Paul's logic to conclude that believers may use all that the earth produces, including food, clothing, manufactured goods, and energy. However, Paul sets a sharp limit to this use. If our use harms another person, then we should refrain. If the context of a dinner party at which meat offered to idols is the issue, then another person's conscience may be the reason we need to refrain from eating it. If the context is worker safety, resource scarcity, or environmental degradation, then the well-being of today's workers, the access to resources by today's poor, and the living conditions of tomorrow's population may be the reasons we refrain from consuming certain items. Since God is the owner of the earth and its fullness, the use we make of the earth must be in line with his purposes.

Second, we are expected to engage in commerce with nonbelievers, as we have already seen from 1 Corinthians 5:9–10. If Christians were buying meat only from Christian butchers, or even from Jews, then of course there would have been no reason to worry whether it had been offered to idols. But Paul asserts that believers are to engage in commerce with society at large. (The concerns in chapter 8 also assume that Christians will engage in social relationships with nonbelievers, although that is not our topic here.) Christians are not called to withdraw from society but to engage society, including society's places of work. As noted earlier, Paul discusses the limits to this engagement in 2 Corinthians 6:14–18 (see "Working with Nonbelievers" in 2 Corinthians).

"Therefore, whatever you eat or drink, or whatever you do, do everything for the glory of God," says Paul (1 Cor. 10:31). This verse by no means legitimates every conceivable activity. It should not be construed to mean that absolutely anything could be done in a way that brings glory to God. Paul's point is that we have to discern whether our actions—including work—are consistent with God's purposes in the world. The criterion is not whether we associate with nonbelievers, whether we use materials that could be used for ill by others, whether we deal with people who are not friends with God, but whether the work we do contributes to God's purposes. If so, then whatever we do will indeed be done for the glory of God.

The upshot is that all vocations that add genuine value to God's created world in a way that benefits humanity are true callings that bring

God glory. The farmer and grocery clerk, the manufacturer and the emissions regulator, the parent and the teacher, the voter and the governor can enjoy the satisfaction of serving in God's plan for his creation.

Gifted Communities (1 Corinthians 12:1–14:40)

The use of what have come to be called "spiritual gifts" (12:1) seems to have caused much contention in the church of Corinth. It seems that the gift of tongues (i.e., Spirit-led ecstatic utterances) in particular was being used to accentuate status differences in the church, with those who practiced this gift claiming to be more spiritual than those who didn't (see 12:1–3, 13:1, 14:1–25).[12] In countering, Paul articulates a broad understanding of the gifts of God's Spirit that has major applications to work.

The first thing to observe is that the term "spiritual gifts" is too narrow to describe what Paul is talking about. They are "spiritual" in the broad sense of originating from God's Spirit, not in the narrow sense of being disembodied or paranormal. And "gift" is only one of a number of terms Paul uses for the phenomenon he has in mind. In chapter 12 alone, he calls the various gifts "services" (12:5), "activities" (12:6), "manifestations" (12:7), "deeds," "forms," and "kinds" (12:28). The exclusive use of the term "spiritual gift" to refer to what Paul also calls "manifestation of God's spirit for the common good" or "kind of service" tends to skew our thinking.[13] It suggests that God's Spirit supersedes or ignores the "natural" skills and abilities God has given us. It implies that the recipient of the "gift" is its intended beneficiary. It makes us think that worship, rather than service, is the primary purpose of the Spirit's working. All of these are false assumptions, according to 1 Corinthians. The Holy Spirit does not dispense with our bodily abilities, but honors and employs them (12:14–26). The community or organization, not merely the individual, benefits (12:7). The purpose is to build up the community (14:3–5) and

---

[12] See Dale B. Martin, *The Corinthian Body* (New Haven: Yale University Press, 1995), 87–92.

[13] For a scholarly discussion of the problems involving the term "spiritual gifts," see Kenneth Berding, "Confusing Word and Concept in 'Spiritual Gifts': Have We Forgotten James Barr's Exhortations?" *Journal of the Evangelical Theological Society* 43 (2000): 37–51.

serve outsiders (14:23–25), not merely to improve the quality of worship. "Giftings" might be a better term to use, since it carries these important connotations better.

Second, Paul seems to be providing a number of examples rather than an exhaustive list. Paul also lists gifts of God in Romans 12:6–8, Ephesians 4:11, and 1 Peter 4:10–11, and the differences among the lists suggest they are illustrative rather than exhaustive. Among them there is no standard list or even a standard way of referring to the various ways the gifts are given. Contrary to much popular literature on the subject, then, it is impossible to compile a definitive list of *the* spiritual gifts. They exhibit a striking variety. Some are what we would call supernatural (speaking in unknown languages), while others seem to be natural abilities (leadership) or even personality traits (mercy). As we have seen, Paul tells us to "do everything for the glory of God" (1 Cor. 10:31), and here he lists a few of the amazing things God will give us the ability to do.

Paul has the church in mind here (14:4, 12), and some Christians suppose this passage to mean that the Spirit gives gifts *only* for use inside the church. However, Paul gives no reason to suppose that these gifts are limited to the confines of the church. God's kingdom encompasses the whole world, not just the institutions of the church. Believers can and should exercise their giftings in every setting, including the workplace. Many of the giftings named here—such as leadership, service, and discernment—will be of immediate benefit in the workplace. Others will no doubt be given to us as needed to serve God's purposes in whatever work we do. We should by all means develop the giftings we have been given and use them for the common good in every sphere of life.

In fact, the most important question is not who, where, what, or how we exercise the giftings of God's Spirit. The most important question is why we employ the gifts. And the answer is, "For love." Gifts, talents, and abilities—coming as they do from God—are sources of excellence in our work. But as he begins to discuss the importance of love, Paul says, "I will show you a still more excellent way" (12:31), "for the greatest of these is love" (13:13). If I exercise every wondrous gifting of God's Spirit "but do not have love," says Paul, "I am nothing" (13:2). Chapter 13 is often read at weddings, but it is actually a perfect manifesto for the workplace.

Love is patient; love is kind; love is not envious or boastful or arrogant
or rude. It does not insist on its own way; it is not irritable or resentful;
it does not rejoice in wrongdoing, but rejoices in the truth. It bears all
things, believes all things, hopes all things, endures all things. (13:4–7)

If Christians would exhibit these kinds of love in our places of work,
how much more productive and enriching would work be for everyone?
How much glory would it bring our Lord? How much closer would we
come to God's fulfillment of our prayer, "Thy kingdom come on earth"?

Our Work Is Not in Vain (1 Corinthians 15:58)

In chapter 15, Paul conducts a lengthy discussion of the resurrection,
and he applies his conclusions directly to work. "[Excel] in the work in
the Lord because you know that in the Lord your labor is not in vain"
(1 Cor. 15:58). How does a correct understanding of the resurrection—
that believers will be raised bodily—ground the conclusion that our labor
for the Lord is of lasting significance ("not in vain")?

First of all, we must recognize that if life in the fallen world around
us were all there were to life, our labor would be in vain (1 Cor. 15:14–19).
Paul's use of the word *vain* brings to mind Ecclesiastes' extended medi-
tation on the vanity of work under the conditions of the Fall. (See Ecclesiastes and Work at www.theologyofwork.org.) Even if there is life
beyond the fallen state of the present world, our work would be in vain
if the new world were completely disconnected from the present one. At
most, it would launch us (and perhaps others) into the new world. But
we have already seen that work done according to God's ways survives
into eternity (1 Cor. 3:10–15). In the second half of chapter 15, Paul develops this matter further by stressing a fundamental continuity between
pre- and post-resurrection bodily existence, in spite of vast differences
in their respective substances. "This perishable body must put on imper-
ishability, and this mortal body must put on immortality" (1 Cor. 15:53).
Our soul does not change out of the old body into a new body—as if
donning a new suit of clothes—but our present body "puts on immortality." The old continues into the new, though radically transformed. It is

precisely this continuity that lends meaning to our present existence and guarantees that our labor for God is of lasting value.[14]

We Share Our Resources with Those in Hardship (1 Corinthians 16:1–3)

One ongoing project that Paul pursued throughout his missionary journeys was that of collecting money for congregations in Judea suffering economic hardship.[15] He mentions this collection not only here but also in Galatians 2:10, and he explains the theological rationale for it more thoroughly in Romans 15:25–31 and 2 Corinthians 8–9. For our purposes, it is important to note that, according to Paul, part of what a believer earns should be given for the benefit of those who cannot provide adequately for themselves. For Paul, one of the essential functions of the church is to take care of its worldwide members' needs. The Old Testament prescribed both fixed tithes and free-will offerings,[16] which together supported the operations of the temple, the maintenance of the state, and the relief of the poor. But this system had ceased with the demise of the Jewish kingdoms. Paul's collection for the poor in Judea essentially assumes for the church the relief aspect once provided by the Old Testament tithes and offerings.

The New Testament nowhere affirms certain fixed percentages, but Paul encourages generosity (see 2 Cor. 8–9), which would hardly mean less than Old Testament levels. Over the next several centuries, as the church grew, its role as a social service provider became an essential element of society, outlasting even the Roman Empire.[17] Whatever the amount given, believers are expected to determine it ahead of time as

---

[14] N. T. Wright, *The Resurrection of the Son of God*, vol. 3 of Christian Origins and the Question of God (Minneapolis: Fortress Press 2003), 359–60.

[15] For an overview, see Scot McKnight, "Collection for the Saints" in *Dictionary of Paul and His Letters*, ed. Gerald F. Hawthorne et al. (Downers Grove, IL: InterVarsity Press, 1993), 143–47.

[16] See E. P. Sanders, *Judaism: Practice and Belief, 63 BCE-66 CE (London: SCM Press,* 1992).

[17] Jeannine E. Olson, *Calvin and Social Welfare* (Selinsgrove, PA: Susquehanna University Press, 1989), 18.

a part of their budget and bring their offerings regularly to the weekly gatherings of the congregation. In other words, it takes a sustained lifestyle change to reach this level of generosity. We are not talking about pocket change.

These principles demand renewed consideration in our time. Governments have displaced the church as the prime providers of social welfare, but are there some forms of service that God equips Christians to do uniquely well? Could Christians' work, investment, and other economic activity be a means of serving those facing economic hardship? In Paul's day, there was limited scope for Christians to start businesses, engage in trade, or provide training and education, but today those could be means of creating jobs or providing for economically disadvantaged people. Is the purpose of giving merely to bind the church more closely together around the world (certainly one of Paul's objectives), or also to care for our neighbors? Could it be that today God calls believers to give money *and* to conduct business, government, education, and every other form of work as a means of taking care of people in hardship? (These questions are explored in depth in "Provision and Wealth" at www.theologyofwork.org.)

Conclusion to 1 Corinthians

First Corinthians has much to contribute to a biblical understanding of work. Above all, it establishes a healthy sense of calling to every legitimate kind of work. In his opening words, Paul stresses that God has called both him and the Corinthian believers to follow Christ. God provides every believer with spiritual resources and concrete giftings for the service of others. Our effectiveness does not depend on our own merits, but on God's power. Depending on his power, we can and must seek to do good work. God leads us to a common vision and purpose in our work, which requires a diverse array of people working in a wide variety of jobs. Leaders are needed to bring this diversity and variety into effective focus.

Leaders in God's kingdom are servants of those they lead, responsible for accomplishing their groups' tasks while at the same time meeting their needs. Whatever our position, it is more important to work each day according to God's purposes than to spend all our time and energy looking for the perfect job. Because we know Christ will return to fulfill God's restoration of the world to his original intent, we have the confidence to work diligently toward Christ's coming kingdom. When we work according to our abilities, God rewards our work with a fair share of the fruits of our labor. Christians are called to standards of fair wages and fair work.

Our ultimate goal is God's kingdom and his glory. This gives us freedom to use the resources of the world, but we must steward them for the benefit of all people, including future generations. In fact, we should not even think in terms of balancing the needs of one individual versus another, but in terms of building up communities of mutual support and service. Love is the mainspring of God's kingdom, and when we work out of love for the people for whom Christ worked and died, our work is not in vain. It has eternal significance and survives along with us into the new world of God's kingdom fulfilled. In the meantime, we take extra care to use the resources at our disposal to care for those in need.

2 CORINTHIANS AND WORK

Introduction to 2 Corinthians

If 1 Corinthians gives us unparalleled insight into the everyday life of a New Testament church, 2 Corinthians offers us a unique glimpse into the heart and soul of the apostle whose work founded and built that church. We see Paul at work, teaching and exemplifying transparency, joy, good relationships, sincerity, reputation, service, humility, leadership, performance and accountability, reconciliation, working with nonbelievers, encouragement, generosity, timely fulfillment of obligations, and the proper use of wealth.

These workplace topics arose because of the daily struggles and opportunities Paul encountered in his own work as an apostle. During the period leading up to the composition of 2 Corinthians, Paul faced any number of "disputes without and fears within," as he describes them (2 Cor. 7:5). These clearly left their mark on him, and the result is a letter like no other in the New Testament—intensely personal, exhibiting a full range of emotions from anguish and agitation to exuberance and confidence. As a result of this adversity, Paul became a more effective leader and worker. All those who want to learn how to be more effective in their work—and who are willing to trust God for the ability to do so—will find a practical model in Paul and his teachings in 2 Corinthians.

Paul's Interactions with the Church in Corinth (2 Corinthians)

In the introduction to 1 Corinthians we noted that Paul established the church of Corinth during his first sojourn there (winter 49/50 through summer 51). Later he wrote one letter to the Corinthian church that no longer exists (it is mentioned in 1 Cor. 5:9) and one letter that does—our 1 Corinthians. He also visited the church three times (2 Cor. 12:14; 13:1). We know from Romans 16:1 that Paul wrote his epistle to the Romans during one of his stays in Corinth.

Nonetheless, Paul's relationship with the church in Corinth was strained. At one point he wrote them what has come to be known as the "severe letter"[1]—that apparently was quite harsh (see 2 Cor. 2:4). He sent it off to the Corinthians with Titus in the hope it would bring about a change of heart among his antagonists in Corinth. The unresolved conflict with the church in Corinth made Paul restless as he waited to hear back from them (2 Cor. 1:12–13). When Titus finally arrived in the autumn of 55 he brought good news from Corinth. Paul's severe letter had, in fact, proven to be remarkably beneficial. The believers in Corinth who had been the cause of so much sorrow were truly grieved about the rupture in their relationship with Paul, and their sorrow had led to repentance (2 Cor. 7:8–16).

In response to that news, Paul wrote 2 Corinthians, or more precisely the first seven chapters, to express his joy and gratitude both to God and to the Corinthians for the restored relationship between them. In these chapters he models the kind of transparency, joy, attention to relationships, integrity, reputation, service, dependence on God, ethical conduct, character, and encouragement that God calls all Christians to embody. Following this, in chapters 8 and 9, he turns to the topics of generosity and timely fulfillment of obligations as he exhorts the Corinthians to contribute to the relief of Christians in Jerusalem, which they had promised to do. In this section Paul highlights how our needs are met by God's generosity, not only so we lack nothing we need but also so we have plenty to share with others. In chapters 10 through 13 he describes the marks of godly leadership, apparently in response to disturbing news he received about so-called "super-apostles" who were leading some of the Corinthian church astray. Although we are not concerned here with church leadership per se, Paul's words in this section are directly applicable to all workplaces.

Thank God for Relationships (2 Corinthians 1:1–11)

Second Corinthians begins with Paul's sincere thanks for the deep relationship he has with the Corinthians. They are so closely knit together

---

[1] See Charles H. Talbert, *Reading Corinthians: A Literary and Theological Commentary on 1 and 2 Corinthians* (New York: Crossroad, 1987), xviii–xxi.

that whatever happens to one, it is as if it happens to all. He writes, "If we are being afflicted, it is for your consolation and salvation" (2 Cor. 1:6). "As you share in our sufferings, so you also share in our consolation" (2 Cor. 1:7). Paul's description of the relationship sounds almost like a marriage. Given the strained relationship between Paul and the church that comes into view during the letter, this intimacy may be surprising. How could people with huge disagreements, disappointments, and even anger at each other say things such as, "Our hope for you is unshaken" (2 Cor. 1:7)?

The answer is that good relationships do not arise from mutual agreement but mutual respect in the pursuit of a common goal. This is a crucial point for our lives at work. We generally do not choose our co-workers, just as the Corinthians did not choose Paul to be their apostle and Paul did not choose those God would lead to faith. Our relationships at work are not based on mutual attraction but on the need to work together to accomplish our common tasks. This is true whether our work is to plant churches, manufacture auto parts, process insurance or government forms, teach at a university, or any other vocation. The more difficult things are, the more important good relationships become.

How do we build good relationships at work? In a sense, the rest of 2 Corinthians is an exploration of various means of building good working relationships—transparency, integrity, accountability, generosity, and so on. We will discuss all of them in this context. But Paul makes it clear that we cannot achieve good relationships through skills and methods alone. What we need above all is God's help. For this reason, praying for each other is the cornerstone of good relationships. "Join in helping us by prayers," Paul asks and then speaks of "the blessing granted to us through the prayers of many" (2 Cor. 1:11).

How deeply do we invest in relationships with the people we work among? The answer might be measured by the extent to which we pray for them. Do we care enough about them to pray for them? Do we pray for their specific needs and concerns? Do we bother to learn enough about their lives so that we *can* pray for them in concrete ways? Do we open our own lives enough so that others can pray for us? Do we ever ask the people in our workplaces whether we can pray for them or them for us? They may not share our faith, but people almost always appreciate an authentic offer to pray for them or a request to pray (or hope) for us.

Transparency (2 Corinthians 1:12–23)

As Paul moves into the body of his second letter to the Corinthians, he addresses the complaint that he had not been open and honest with them. Although he promised to visit Corinth again, Paul had backed out twice. Was Paul being insincere or speaking out of both sides of his mouth? Was he maneuvering behind the scenes to get his way behind others' backs? Paul addresses these questions in 2 Corinthians 1:12–14. He is proud that his behavior among the Corinthians has been transparent at all times. His actions were not the machinations of what he calls "fleshly wisdom" (2 Cor. 1:12). He cancelled his visits, not to gain an advantage for himself or save face, but because he did not want to shame or rebuke the Corinthians again. Therefore, he delayed coming back to Corinth in the hope that, when he did come, he could bring joy rather than recrimination and reproof (2 Cor. 1:23–24).

Though Paul's integrity had been questioned, he knew that because of his history of transparency with them, they would continue to trust him. "We have behaved in the world with frankness and godly sincerity," he reminds them (2 Cor. 1:12). Because they have seen him in action, they know he says what he means without vacillating (2 Cor. 1:17–20). This makes him sure they "will understand until the end" (2 Cor. 1:1–13), once they know all the factors he has had to consider. His proof of their trust is that even without knowing everything, Paul tells them, "You have already understood us in part" (2 Cor. 1:13).

In our work today, are we transparent enough so that people have a reason to trust us? On a daily basis, every person, company, and organization faces temptations to hide the truth. Are we obscuring our motivations in order to falsely gain trust from a customer or a rival? Are we making decisions in secret as a way of avoiding accountability or hiding factors others would object to? Are we pretending to support co-workers in their presence, but speaking derisively behind their backs? Paul's example shows us that these actions are wrong. Moreover, whatever brief advantage we might gain from them is more than lost in the long term because our co-workers learn not to trust us. And if our co-workers cannot trust us, can God?

This doesn't mean, of course, that we always reveal all the information we have. There are confidences, personal and organizational, that cannot be broken. Not everyone needs to be privy to all information. At times the honest answer may be, "I can't answer that question because I have a duty of privacy to someone else." But we shouldn't use confidentiality as an excuse to prevaricate, to gain an edge on others, or to portray ourselves in a falsely positive light. If and when questions surface about our motives, a solid track record of openness and reliability will be the best antidote for misplaced doubts.

Transparency is so important to Paul's work with the Corinthians that he returns to the theme throughout the letter. "We refuse to practice cunning or to falsify Gods word; but by the open statement of the truth we commend ourselves" (2 Cor. 4:2). "We have spoken frankly to you Corinthians; our heart is wide open to you" (2 Cor. 6:11).

Working for the Joy of Others (2 Corinthians 1:24)

Joy is the next means of building relationships that Paul discusses. "I do not mean to imply that we lord it over your faith; rather we are workers with you for your joy, because you stand firm in the faith" (2 Cor. 1:24). Even though he was an apostle with God-given authority, Paul brought joy to others by the way he led them—not lording it over them but working alongside them. This explains why he was such an effective leader and why the people associated with him became strong and reliable co-workers. Paul's words echo what Jesus said to his disciples when they were arguing about who among them was the greatest:

> The kings of the Gentiles lord it over them; and those in authority over them are called benefactors. But not so with you; rather the greatest among you must become like the youngest, and the leader like one who serves. (Luke 22:25–26)

The essence of Christian work, Paul maintains, is nothing less than working alongside others to help them attain greater joy.

What would our workplaces look like if we tried to bring others joy through the way we treat them?[2] This does not mean trying to make

---

[2] Dennis W. Bakke, *Joy at Work: A Revolutionary Approach to Fun on the Job* (Seattle: PVG, 2005), and Raymond Bakke, William Hendricks, and Brad

everyone happy all the time, but treating co-workers as people of value and dignity, as Paul did. When we pay attention to others' needs at work, including the need to be respected and the need to be entrusted with meaningful work, we follow Paul's own example.

The Priority of Relationships (2 Corinthians 2:12–16)

Another means to healthy interactions at work is simply taking the time and effort to develop and invest in relationships. Having left Ephesus, Paul went to Troas, a port city in the northwest corner of Asia Minor, where he expected Titus to arrive from his visit to Corinth (see the introduction above for details). While Paul was there he went about his missionary work with his usual vigor, and God blessed his efforts. But in spite of a promising beginning in a city of great strategic importance,[3] Paul cut short his work in Troas because, as he puts it, "my mind could not rest because I did not find my brother Titus there" (2 Cor. 2:13). He simply could not attend to his work, his very passion, because of the anguish he felt over his strained relationship with the Corinthian believers. So he left for Macedonia in the hope of finding Titus there.

Two things are striking about this passage. First, Paul places significant value on his relationships with other believers. He cannot remain aloof and unburdened when these relationships are in disrepair. We cannot say with absolute certainty that he was familiar with Jesus' teaching about leaving one's gift at the altar and being reconciled to one's brother (Matt. 5:23–24), but he clearly understood the principle. Paul is eager to see things patched up, and he invests a great deal of energy and prayer in pursuing that end. Second, Paul places a high priority on bringing about reconciliation, even if it causes significant delay in his work schedule. He does not try to convince himself that he has a great opportunity for ministry that will not come around again, and that therefore he can't be

---

Smith, *Joy at Work Bible Study Companion* (Lake Mary, FL: Charisma House, 2005) explore this question in detail.

[3] See Jerome Murphy-O'Connor, *Paul: A Critical Life* (Oxford: Clarendon, 1996), 300.

bothered with the Corinthians and their momentary needs. Repairing the rupture in his relationship with them takes precedence.

The lesson for us is obvious. Relationships matter. Clearly, we cannot always drop what we're doing at a moment's notice and attend to strained relationships. But no matter what our task, relationships *are* our business. Tasks are important. Relationships are important. So, in the spirit of Matthew 5:23–24, when we learn—or even suspect—that a relationship has been strained or broken in the course of our work, we do well to ask ourselves which is more pressing at the moment, the completion of the task or the restoration of a relationship. The answer may vary, depending on circumstances. If the task is big enough, or the strain in relationship serious enough, we do well not only to ask which is more pressing but also to seek counsel from a respected brother or sister.

Sincerity (2 Corinthians 2:17)

As in 2 Corinthians 1:12, Paul again addresses lingering questions about his delay in visiting Corinth. The Corinthians seem offended because he did not initially accept financial support from the church in Corinth. His response is that supporting himself was a matter of sincerity. Could people trust that he really believed what he was preaching, or was he doing it just to make money like the "peddlers of God's word" (2 Cor. 2:17) who could be found in any Roman city? It appears he did not want to be lumped together with the philosophers and rhetoricians of his day who charged hefty fees for their speeches.[4] Instead he and his co-workers were "persons of sincerity." They were quite clearly not going from place to place preaching the gospel in order to get rich, but they understood themselves as individuals who were sent by God and answered to God.

This reminds us that motivation is not just a private matter, especially when it comes to money. The way we handle money shines like a laser pointer on the question of our sincerity as Christians. People want to see whether we handle money in accordance with our high principles or ditch our principles when there's money to be made. Are we lax with

---

[4] See Murray J. Harris, *The Second Epistle to the Corinthians: A Commentary on the Greek Text* (Grand Rapids: Eerdmans, 2005), 253–54.

our expense accounts? Do we hide income under the table? Do we engage in dubious tax shelters? Do we push for raises, commissions, and bonuses at the expense of others? Do we take financial advantage of people in difficult circumstances? Do we twist contracts to gain a disproportionate financial gain? The question is not only whether we can justify ourselves, but also whether those around us can recognize that our actions are consistent with Christian beliefs. If not, we bring dishonor to ourselves and to the name of Christ.

A Genuine Reputation (2 Corinthians 3)

Paul begins this section of 2 Corinthians with two rhetorical questions, both of which expect a negative answer.[5] "Are we beginning to commend ourselves again? Surely we do not need, as some do, letters of recommendation to you or from you, do we?" (2 Cor. 3:1). Paul—their old friend—wryly asks whether he needs the letters of introduction or commendation that others who had presented themselves to the church apparently possessed. Such letters were common in the ancient world, and generally it was necessary to take them with a grain of salt. The Roman statesman Cicero wrote scores of them, for instance, making lavish use of the stereotypical language of praise the genre demanded. Recipients became so jaded, however, that sometimes he felt it necessary to write a second letter so that the recipients would know whether to take the first letter seriously.[6] Letters of commendation, in other words, were often not worth the papyrus they were written on.

Paul had no need of them in any case. The Corinthian believers knew him intimately. The only letter of recommendation he required was already written on their hearts (2 Cor. 3:3). Their very existence as a church, as well as their individual conversions in response to Paul's preaching, was all the commendation Paul needed or wanted concern-

---

[5] Harris, 258.

[6] See Cicero, *Epistulae ad Familiares (The Letters to His Friends)*, 13.6a. For a thorough discussion see Peter Marshall, *Enmity in Corinth: Social Conventions in Paul's Relations with the Corinthians*, Wissenschaftliche Untersuchungen zum Neuen Testament 2.23 (Tübingen: Mohr Siebeck, 1987), 91–129, esp. 93–95.

ing his apostleship. They could see the fruit of Paul's labor, which left no doubt that he was an apostle sent by God. Further, Paul insists, he is not claiming competence in his own strength. "Our competence is from God" (2 Cor. 3:5), he writes. The question is not whether Paul has piled up credentials and recommendations, but whether his work is a contribution to the kingdom of God.

How do we build our reputations today? In the United States, many young people choose their activities based not on how they can best contribute to their communities, or even on what they actually enjoy, but upon how the activities will look on a university or graduate school application. This can continue during our working lives, with every job assignment, professional affiliation, dinner party, and social event calculated to associate us with prestigious people and institutions. Paul chose his activities based on how he could best serve the people he loved. Following his lead, we should work so as to leave solid evidence of jobs well done, of lasting results, and of people whose lives have been impacted for the better.

Leading and Serving (2 Corinthians 4)

Second Corinthians 4 brings together themes that are closely related in Paul's work—transparency, humility, weakness, leadership, and service. Because we are seeing Paul at work in a real-life situation, the themes are entangled as Paul tells the story. But we will try to discuss the themes one at a time in order to explore each one as clearly as possible.

Transparency and Humility (2 Corinthians 4)

In chapter 4 Paul returns to the theme of transparency, as we noted in our discussion of 2 Corinthians 1:12–23. This time he emphasizes the importance of humility for maintaining transparency. If we are going to let everyone see the reality of our life and work, we had better be prepared to be humbled.

Naturally, it would be much easier to be transparent with people if we had nothing to hide. Paul himself says, "We have renounced the shameful things that one hides" (2 Cor. 4:2). But transparency requires that we remain open, even if we have engaged in conduct that is not commendable.

For the truth is, we are all susceptible to errors of intention and execution. "We have this treasure in clay jars," Paul reminds us (2 Cor. 4:7), alluding to the typical household vessels of his day that were made of common clay and easily breakable. Anyone who visits the remains of the Ancient Near East can testify to the shards of these vessels lying scattered everywhere. Paul reinforces this idea later by recounting that God gave him a "thorn in the flesh" in order to restrain his pride (2 Cor. 12:7).

Maintaining transparency when we know our own weaknesses requires humility and especially the willingness to offer a genuine apology. Many apologies by public figures sound more like thinly veiled justifications than actual apologies. This may be because, if we depend on ourselves as the source of our confidence, to apologize would be to risk our ability to carry on. Yet Paul's confidence is not in his own rightness or ability, but in his dependence on the power of God. "We have this treasure in clay jars, so that it may be made clear that this extraordinary power belongs to God and does not come from us" (2 Cor. 4:7). If we too acknowledged that the good things we accomplish are not a reflection on us but on our Lord, then maybe we could have the courage to admit our mistakes and look to God to put us back on track again. At the very least, we could stop feeling that we have to maintain our image at all costs, including the cost of deceiving others.

Weakness as the Source of Strength (2 Corinthians 4)

Our weakness, however, is not just a challenge to our transparency. It is actually the source of our true abilities. Enduring suffering is not an unfortunate side effect experienced in some circumstances; it is the actual means of bringing about genuine accomplishment. Just as the power of Jesus' resurrection came about *because* of his crucifixion,[7] so the apostles' fortitude in the midst of adversity testifies to the fact that the same power is at work in them.

In our culture, no less than in Corinth, we project strength and invincibility because we feel they are necessary to climb the ladder of success. We try to convince people that we are stronger, smarter, and more competent than we really are. Therefore, Paul's message of vulnerability

---

[7] Harris, 349.

may sound challenging to us. Is it apparent in the way you go about your work that the strength and vitality you project is not your own, but rather God's strength on display in your weakness? When you receive a compliment, do you allow it to add to your aura of brilliance? Or do you recount the ways God—perhaps working through other people—made it possible for you to exceed your native potential? We usually want people to perceive us as ultra-competent. But aren't the people we admire most the ones who help *other* people bring their gifts to bear?

If we hold up under difficult circumstances without trying to conceal them, it will become apparent that we have a source of power outside of ourselves, the very power that effected Jesus' resurrection from the dead.

Serving Others by Leading (2 Corinthians 4)

Humility and weakness would be unbearable if our purpose in life were to make something great of ourselves. But service, not greatness, is the Christian's purpose. "We do not proclaim ourselves; we proclaim Jesus Christ as Lord and ourselves as your slaves for Jesus' sake" (2 Cor. 4:5). This verse is one of the classic biblical statements of the concept that has come to be known as "servant leadership." Paul, the foremost leader of the Christian movement beyond the confines of Palestine, calls himself "your slave for Jesus' sake" (2 Cor. 4:5).

Again, Paul seems to be reflecting on Jesus' own teaching here (see 2 Cor. 1:24 above). As leaders, Jesus and his followers served others. This fundamentally Christian insight should inform our attitude in any leadership position. This does not mean that we refrain from exercising legitimate authority or that we lead timidly. Rather, it implies that we use our position and our power to further others' well-being and not only our own. In fact, Paul's words "your slaves for Jesus' sake" are stricter than they may at first appear. Leaders are called to seek other people's well-being *ahead* of their own, as slaves are compelled to do. A slave, as Jesus pointed out, works all day in the fields, then comes in and serves dinner to the household, and only afterwards may eat and drink (Luke 17:7–10).

Leading others by serving will inevitably lead to suffering. The world is too broken for us to imagine there is a chance we may escape suffering while serving. Paul suffered affliction, perplexity, and persecution nearly to the point of death (2 Cor. 4:8–12). As Christians, we should not accept leadership positions unless we intend to sacrifice the privilege of taking care of ourselves before taking care of others.

Performance and Accountability
(2 Corinthians 5:1–15)

In 2 Corinthians 5 Paul, who constantly faced situations that could result in his death, reminds the Corinthians that at the final judgment each person will be "recompensed according to what he has done in the body, whether good or evil" (2 Cor. 5:10) These are unusual words for Paul (though not as unusual as one might expect; see Rom. 2:6–10), whom we normally associate with the doctrine of grace, meaning that our salvation is entirely unmerited and not the result of our own works (Eph. 2:8–9). It is, however, important that we allow our picture of Paul to be formed by what he actually says, rather than by some caricature. When we analyze Paul's teaching in its entirety, we find it is in harmony with that of Jesus, James, and even the Old Testament. For all of them, faith that does not express itself in good works is no faith at all. Indeed, faith and obedience are so closely intertwined that even Paul can, as he does here, refer to the latter rather than the former when he actually has both in mind. What we do in the body cannot help but reflect what God's grace has done for us. What pleases the Lord can be described either as faith or, as here, as works of righteousness made possible by God's grace.

In any case, Paul's message is clear enough: How we live our lives matters to God. In workplace terms, our performance matters. Moreover, we will have to give an account to the Lord Jesus for all that we have done and left undone. In workplace terms, this is accountability. Performance and accountability are profoundly important to the Christian life, and we cannot dismiss them as secular concerns of no importance to God. God cares whether we are slacking off, neglecting our duties, not showing up for work, or going through the motions without genuine attention to our work.

This does not mean that God always agrees with what our workplaces expect from us. God's idea of good performance may be different from that of our manager or supervisor. In particular, if meeting our employer's performance expectations requires unethical activities or harming others, then God's review of our performance will be different from our employer's. If your boss expects you to mislead customers or denigrate co-workers, for God's sake aim for a poor performance review from your boss and a good review from God.

God holds us to a high standard of conduct. One day we will answer for the way we have treated our co-workers, bosses, employees, and customers, not to mention our family and friends. This does not negate the doctrine of grace, but instead shows us how God intends his grace to transform our lives.

Reconciling the Whole World (2 Corinthians 5:16–21)

If it sounds as if Paul is calling us to grit our teeth and try harder to be good, then we are missing the point of 2 Corinthians. Paul intends for us to see the world in a completely new way, so that our actions stem from this new understanding, not from trying harder.

> If anyone is in Christ, there is a new creation: everything old has passed away; see, everything has become new! All this is from God, who reconciled us to himself through Christ, and has given us the ministry of reconciliation; that is, in Christ God was reconciling the world to himself, not counting their trespasses against them, and entrusting the message of reconciliation to us. (2 Cor. 5:17–19)

Paul wants us to become so thoroughly transformed that we become members of a "new creation." The mention of "creation" immediately takes us back to Genesis 1–2, the story of God's creation of the world. From the beginning God intended that men and women work together (Gen. 1:27; 2:18), in concert with God (Gen. 2:19), to "till the ground" (Gen. 2:15), "give names" to the creatures of the earth, and exercise "dominion" (Gen. 1:26) over the earth as God's stewards. God's intent for creation, in other words, includes work as a central reality of existence. When humans disobeyed God and marred the creation, work became cursed (Gen. 3:17–18), and humans no longer worked alongside God.

Thus when Paul says, "Everything has become new," *everything* includes the world of work as a core element.

God brings the new creation into existence by sending his Son into the old creation to transform or "reconcile" it. "In Christ, God was reconciling *the world* to himself." Not just one aspect of the world, but the whole world. And those who follow Christ, who are reconciled to God by Christ, are appointed to carry on Christ's work of reconciliation (2 Cor. 5:18). We are agents to bring reconciliation to all spheres of the world. Every day as we go out to do our work we are to be ministers of this reconciliation. This includes reconciliation between people and God (evangelism and discipleship), between people and people (conflict resolution), and between people and their work (goods and services that meet genuine needs and improve the quality of life and care for God's creation).

There are three essential elements of the work of reconciliation. First, we must understand accurately what has gone wrong among people, God, and the creation. If we do not truly understand the ills of the world, then we cannot bring genuine reconciliation any more than an ambassador can effectively represent one country to another without knowing what's going on in both. Second, we must love other people and work to benefit them rather than to judge them. "We regard no one from a human point of view," Paul tells us (2 Cor. 5:16)—that is, as an object to be exploited, eliminated, or adulated, but as a person for whom "Christ died and was raised" (2 Cor. 5:15). If we condemn the people in our workplaces or withdraw from the daily places of life and work, we are regarding people and work from a human point of view. If we love the people we work among and try to improve our workplaces, products, and services, then we become agents of Christ's reconciliation. Finally, being seeds of God's creation, of course, requires that we remain in constant fellowship with Christ. If we do these things, we will be in a position to bring Christ's power to reconcile the people, organizations, places, and things of the world so that they too can become members of God's new creation.

Transparency Revisited (2 Corinthians 6:11)

As we noted earlier (in 2 Cor. 1:12–23), transparency is a recurring theme in this letter. It crops up again here when Paul writes, "We have spoken frankly to you Corinthians; our heart is wide open to you" (2 Cor. 6:11). We might say that his life was an open book before them. Though he adds nothing new to what he has said previously, it becomes more and more apparent how important the topic of transparency is for him. When questions arise about his ministry, he can appeal to his earlier dealings with the Corinthians with absolute certainty that he has always been honest with them about himself. Can we say the same of ourselves?

Working with Nonbelievers (2 Corinthians 6:14–18)

In 2 Corinthians 6:14–18 Paul takes up the question of close relationships with non-Christians. Up to this point, Paul has vividly portrayed the importance of good relationships with the people with whom we work. Paul says in 1 Corinthians 5:9–10 that we should work with non-Christians, and he discusses how to do so in 1 Corinthians 10:25–33 (see 1 Corinthians 10).

But perhaps there are limits to the intimacy of Christians' working relationships with non-Christians. Paul tells the Corinthians, "Do not be mismatched with unbelievers," as the NRSV puts it, or to translate the Greek term (*heterozygountes*) more literally, "Do not be unequally yoked with unbelievers." His words are reminiscent of Leviticus 19:19, which prohibits mating different kinds of animals together, and Deuteronomy 22:10, which prohibits yoking an ox and donkey together while plowing. These two Old Testament precedents refer to mating and to work, respectively. We are concerned here with work.

What, then, are the limits in working with nonbelievers? Perhaps the key is the term "yoked." When two animals are yoked together, they must move in lockstep. If one turns left, the other also turns left, whether or not it consents. This is different from, say, animals grazing in a herd, which cooperate but still have the freedom to move separately and even to depart from the herd if they choose. If two animals—or, metaphorically, two people—are yoked, each is bound by whatever the other chooses to do. Two people are yoked if one person's choices compel the other person to follow the same choices, even without their consent. A yoking is when either person is bound by the unilateral decisions and actions of the other.

Paul does not want us to be *un*equally yoked. So what would it mean to be *equally* yoked? Jesus has already given us the answer to that question. "Take my yoke upon you," he calls to those who follow him (Matt. 11:29a). Paul tells us not to be unequally yoked with nonbelievers because we are already yoked to Jesus. One part of his yoke is around us, and the other is on Jesus' shoulders. Jesus, like the lead ox in a team, determines the bearing, the pace, and the path of the team, and we submit to his leadership. Through his yoke, we feel his pull, his guidance, his direction. By his yoke, he trains us to work effectively in his team. His yoke is what leads us, sensitizes us, and binds us to Jesus. Being yoked to Jesus makes us partners with him in restoring God's creation in every sphere of life, as we explored in 2 Corinthians 5:16–21. No other yoke that would pull us away from the yoke of Jesus could ever be equal to that! "My yoke is easy, and my burden is light," Jesus tells us (Matt. 11:29b), yet the work we are doing with him is no less than the transformation of the entire cosmos.

When Paul tells us not to be unequally yoked in working relationships, he is warning us not to get entangled in work situations that prevent us from doing the work Jesus wants us to do or that prevent us from working in Jesus' ways. This has a strong ethical element. "What partnership is there between righteousness and lawlessness?" Paul asks (2 Cor. 6:14). If the dictates of a work situation lead us to harm customers, deceive constituents, mislead employees, abuse co-workers, pollute the environment, or such, then we would be yoked into a violation of our duties as stewards of God's kingdom. Yet ethics is not the only element. Besides *preventing* us from doing anything unethical, being yoked with Jesus also *leads* us to work to reconcile or restore the world to God's vision for it. At the very least, this suggests that we pay careful attention to the motivations, values, integrity, working methods, and similar factors when deciding where and with whom we work.

To be unequally yoked with unbelievers, then, is to be in a situation or relationship that binds you to the decisions and actions of people who have values and purposes incompatible with Jesus' values and purposes.

A few examples may help. A business partnership—joint, unlimited ownership of a business—would generally seem to be a form of yoking.

If one partner signs a contract, spends money, buys or sells property—or even violates the law—the other partner is bound by that action or decision. To form a business partnership in this sense would very likely be a form of unequal yoking. Even if the believer trusts that the nonbelieving partner(s) would not do anything unethical, is it possible that the non-believing partner(s) would want to run the business for the purposes of transforming the world to be more as God intends it to be? Even if the partnership does not force the believer to do evil, would it hinder him or her from doing all the good Christ desires? Joining an army, making a pledge of office, raising money for a nonprofit organization, or buying property jointly might have similar consequences.

In contrast, a single commercial transaction—buying or selling an item between two parties—would generally not seem to be a form of yoking. The parties agree in advance on a single item of business and then perform what they agreed to. (The Christian, of course, should only agree to do the transaction if it is in accordance with God's values and purposes.) Neither party is bound by anything the other party might do after the transaction. Teaching a class, writing or being interviewed for a newspaper article, volunteering in a civic event, and babysitting a child are other examples similarly limited in scope and duration.

Buying stock is probably somewhere in between. As part owners in the corporation, stock owners are morally—though probably not legally—bound by the decisions of the directors, executives, and other employees, but only for as long as they own the stock. Likewise, getting a job, joining a faculty, raising money for a nonprofit organization or political campaign, and signing a contract all commit us to living with the consequences of others' choices, but not forever.

As these examples show, there is no hard-and-fast rule for what it means to be unequally yoked. In practice, it may be difficult to say whether a particular working relationship is a form of yoking. Getting a job in a secular organization is probably not a form of yoking. But going so far into debt that you can't afford to quit your job probably turns any employee relationship into a de facto yoking. You have lost the freedom to resign if the organization engages in ungodly activities. One rising lawyer was offered a partnership in a prestigious law firm, but declined when he observed how many of those who became partners got divorced soon after.[8] It seemed to him that accepting a partnership would yoke him to values and practices incompatible with the commitment he made to put his wife first among the people in his life.

Finally, we must be careful to not turn Paul's words into an us-versus-them mentality against nonbelievers. Paul knew as well as any-one that believers fall far short of the values and purposes of God. We should be careful not to be unequally yoked, even with Christians whose conduct would pull us away from the yoke of Christ. Even more, we need to receive Christ's grace every day so that being yoked with us doesn't cause someone else to be pulled away from working according to Christ's ways and purposes. Nor can we judge or condemn nonbelievers as inherently unethical, since Paul himself refused to do so. "For what have I to do with judging those outside? Is it not those who are inside that you are to judge? God will judge those outside" (1 Cor. 5:12–13). We are called not to judge but to discern whether our working relation-ships are leading us to work for the purposes and according to the ways of Christ.

Perhaps the best guidance is to ask ourselves the question Paul asks, "What does a believer share with an unbeliever?" (2 Cor. 6:15). If the answer is that we share similar values and goals with respect to the work we may undertake together, then it may serve God's will to work closely with nonbelievers. You can assess the opportunities and risks by explor-ing in advance all the commitments entailed in any work relationship. Consider how your individual capabilities and limitations might reduce or exacerbate the risk of being pulled away from working as God intends. This means that the decision whether to participate may be different for each person. Considering our differing strengths and weaknesses, a free association for one person could be a binding yoke for another. A recent graduate, for example, might find it relatively easy to quit a job, compared to a CEO with a large investment and reputation at stake. In other words, the larger our role in a working relationship, the more im-portant it is to make sure we're not yoking ourselves into a situation we won't be able to handle in a godly way. In any case, all Christians would

---

[8] An incident reported confidentially to a member of the Theology of Work Project Steering Committee. Recorded August 24, 2011 at the Theology of Work Project 2011 summer conference in Los Angeles.

do well to consider carefully the entanglements that can arise in every workplace relationship, job, partnership, and transaction.

The Encouragement of Praise (2 Corinthians 7)

Immediately after admonishing the Corinthians, Paul praises them. "I often boast about you; I have great pride in you" (2 Cor. 7:4) It may come as a surprise for some to find Paul boasting so unapologetically about the church in Corinth. Many of us have been brought up to believe that pride is a sin (which is, of course, quite true) and even that pride in someone else's accomplishments is questionable. Further, we might wonder whether Paul's pride in the Corinthians is misplaced. This was a congregation beset with many difficulties, and there are some stinging rebukes in his letters to them. He wears no rose-colored glasses when it comes to the Corinthians. But Paul is entirely unabashed by such concerns. He does not shy away from giving praise where praise is due, and it seems that he is genuinely proud of the progress the believers in Corinth have made in spite of his tense relations with them. He notes his pride in them is well deserved, not a cheap trick of flattery (2 Cor. 7:11–13). He repeats in 2 Corinthians 7:14 the point that praise must be genuine when he says, "Everything we said to you was true, so our boasting to Titus has proved true as well."

This reminds us of the importance of specific, accurate, and timely praise for co-workers, employees, and others with whom we interact at work. Inflated or generalized praise is hollow and may seem insincere or manipulative. And unrelenting criticism destroys rather than builds up. But words of genuine appreciation and gratitude for work well done are always appropriate. They are evidence of mutual respect, the foundation of true community, and they motivate everyone to continue their good work. We all look forward to hearing the Lord say, "Well done, good and faithful servant" (Matt. 25:21, NIV), and we do well to give similar praise whenever it's warranted.

Generosity Is Not Optional (2 Corinthians 8:1–9)

As we noted in the introduction, 2 Corinthians 8 and 9 form a separate section of Paul's letter in which he addresses the topic of the collection for the churches in Judea. This project was a passion of the apostle's, and he promoted it vigorously in his churches (1 Cor. 16:1–3). Paul begins this section by pointing to the exemplary generosity of the churches in Macedonia and implying that he expects no less from the Corinthians. Just as the believers in Corinth have displayed an abundance of faith, ability to proclaim the truth,[9] knowledge, enthusiasm, and love, so they should also strive to abound in the "gift" (Gk. *charis*) of generosity. The term "gift" has a double meaning here. It has the sense of "spiritual gift," referring to God's gift to them of the virtue of generosity, and it has the sense of "donation," referring to their gifts of money to the collection. This makes the point doubly clear that generosity is not an option for Christians, but part of the Spirit's work in our lives.

In the workplace, a generous spirit is the oil that makes things run smoothly on a number of levels. Employees who sense that their employers are generous will be more willing to make sacrifices for their organizations when they become necessary. Workers who are generous with their co-workers will create a ready source of help for themselves and a more joyful and satisfying experience for everyone.

Generosity is not always a matter of money. To name only a few examples, employers can be generous by taking time to mentor workers, providing a workplace of beauty, offering opportunities for training and development, genuinely listening to someone with a problem or complaint, or visiting an employee's family member in the hospital. Co-workers can offer generosity by helping others do their work better, making sure no one is left out socially, standing up for those who suffer misuse, offering true friendship, sharing praise, apologizing for offenses, and simply learning the names of workers who might otherwise be invisible to us. Steve Harrison tells of two surgical residents at the University of Washington who competed to see who could learn the names of more nurse's aides, custodians, transport, and dietary staff and then greet them by name whenever they saw them.[10]

---

[9] Literally, "in speech." See Harris, 574.

[10] Steve Harrison, *The Manager's Book of Decencies* (New York: McGraw-Hill, 2007), 67.

Timely Fulfillment of Obligations (2 Corinthians 8:10–12)

Paul reminds the believers in Corinth that they had already signaled their intentions to participate in the collection for the churches in Judea during the previous year. They seem, however, to have become sidetracked. Perhaps lingering doubts about Paul's ministry and the tensions that surfaced during his previous visit play a role here. In any case, their effort is flagging, and at the time of Paul's writing they have not yet gathered all the contributions from individual members, as he had previously instructed them to do (1 Cor. 16:1–3).

Paul's advice is straightforward. "Finish doing it, so that your eagerness may be matched by completing it according to your means" (2 Cor. 8:11). Paul's advice is as relevant now as it was then, especially in our work. What we start we should finish. Obviously, there are many situations in which circumstances change or other priorities take precedence so that we have to adjust our commitments. This is why Paul adds, "according to your means." But often, as in the Corinthians' situation, the problem is merely one of dragging our feet. Paul reminds us of the need to carry through on our commitments. Other people are counting on us.

This advice may seem too simple to need mentioning in the word of God. Yet Christians underestimate how important this is as a matter of witness, in addition to productivity. If we do not fulfill ordinary commitments at work, how can our words or actions possibly convince people that our Lord will fulfill his promise of eternal life? Better to deliver a report, a part, or a raise on time than to deliver a lunchtime argument for the divinity of Christ.

Sharing the Wealth (2 Corinthians 8:13–15)

Paul reminds the Corinthians of the underlying principle behind the collection. "It is a question of a fair balance between your present abundance and their need" (2 Cor. 8:14). It is not that the Judean churches should experience relief to the detriment of the Gentile churches, but rather that there should be an appropriate balance between them. The

Judean believers were in need, and the Corinthian church was experiencing a measure of prosperity. The time might come when the tables would be turned, and then aid would flow in the other direction, "so that their abundance may be for your need" (2 Cor. 8:14).

Paul invokes two images to explain what he means. The first one, balance, is abstract, but in the ancient world, as now, it appeals to our sense that in the natural world and in society equilibrium leads to stability and health.[11] The recipient benefits because the gift alleviates an abnormal lack. The giver benefits because the gift prevents acclimation to an unsustainable abundance. The second image is concrete and historical. Paul reminds the Corinthians of the ancient days when God gave the people of Israel manna to sustain themselves (Exod. 16:11–18). Though some gathered much and others comparatively little, when the daily ration was distributed, no one had either too little or too much.

The principle that the richer should give their wealth to the poorer to the degree that everyone's resources are in "balance" is challenging to modern notions of individual self-reliance. Apparently, when Paul calls Christians "slaves for Jesus' sake" (2 Cor. 5:4), he means that 100 percent of our wages and our wealth belong directly to God, and that God might want us to distribute them to others to the point that the income we keep for our personal use is in equal balance with theirs.

We must be careful, however, not to make simplistic applications to the structures of today's world. A full discussion of this principle among Christians has become difficult because it gets caught up in the political debates about socialism and capitalism. The question in those debates is whether the state has the right—or duty—to compel the balance of wealth by taking from the richer and distributing to the poorer. This is a different matter from Paul's situation, in which a group of churches asked their members to voluntarily give money for distribution by another church for the benefit of its poor members. In fact, Paul does not say anything at all about the state in this regard. As for himself, Paul says he has no plans to compel anyone. "I do not say this as a command" (2 Cor. 8:8), he tells us, nor is collection to be made "reluctantly or under compulsion" (2 Cor. 9:7).

---

[11] Harris, 590.

Paul's purpose is not to create a particular social system but to ask those who have money whether they are truly ready to put it at God's service on behalf of the poor. "Show them the proof of your love and of our reason for boasting about you," he implores (2 Cor. 8:24). Christians should engage in plenty of discussion about the best ways to alleviate poverty. Is it through giving alone, or investment, or something else, or some mix? What role do the structures of the church, business, government, and nonprofit organizations have? Which aspects of legal systems, infrastructure, education, culture, personal responsibility, stewardship, hard work, and other factors must be reformed or developed? Christians need to be on the forefront of developing not only generous but effective means of bringing poverty to an end.[12]

But there can be no question about the pressing urgency of poverty and no reluctance to balance our use of money with the needs of others around the world. Paul's forceful words show that those who enjoy superabundance cannot be complacent when so many people in the world suffer extreme poverty.

You Can't Out-Give God (2 Corinthians 9)

In urging the Corinthian believers to give generously, Paul is aware that he must address a very human concern in a world of limited resources. Some of his hearers must have been thinking, "If I give as altruistically as Paul is urging me to give, there may not be enough to meet my own needs." Making use of an extended agricultural metaphor, Paul assures them that in God's economy things work differently. He has already alluded to a principle from the book of Proverbs, noting that the "one who sows sparingly will also reap sparingly, and the one who sows bountifully will also reap bountifully" (compare 2 Cor. 9:6 with Prov. 11:24–25). He followed this up by quoting an aphorism from the Greek version of Proverbs 22:8, that "God loves a cheerful giver" (2 Cor. 9:7).

---

[12] John Stott, *The Grace of Giving: 10 Principles of Christian Giving*, Lausanne Didasko Files (Peabody, MA: Hendrickson Publishers, 2012), discusses giving in depth, based on his reading of 2 Corinthians 8–9.

From this he infers a promise that for the one who gives generously, God can and will cause all sorts of blessings[13] to abound.

Paul, therefore, assures the Corinthians that their generosity does not come at the risk of future poverty. On the contrary, generosity is the route to *prevent* future deprivation. "God is able to provide you with every blessing in abundance, *so that* by always having enough of everything, you may share abundantly in every good work" (2 Cor. 9:8). In the next two verses he assures those who sow (or "scatter") generously to the poor that God will provide them with enough seed for that sowing *and* for bread for their own needs. He underscores this when he says, "You will be enriched in every way for your great generosity, which will produce thanksgiving to God through us" (2 Cor. 9:11), a promise that encompasses and goes beyond material blessings.

Although Paul is clearly speaking of material generosity and blessing, we must be careful not to turn an assurance of God's provision into an expectation of getting rich. God is no pyramid scheme! The "abundance" Paul speaks of means "having *enough* of everything," not getting rich. The so-called "prosperity gospel" profoundly misunderstands passages like this. Following Christ is not a money-making scheme, as Paul has been at pains to say throughout the letter.

This has obvious applications in giving away the fruits of our labor, that is, in donating money and other resources. But it applies equally well in giving of ourselves *during* our labor. We need not fear that by helping others succeed at work we will compromise our own well-being. God has promised to give us all that we need. We can help others look good at work without fearing it will make us look lackluster by comparison. We can compete fairly in the marketplace without worrying that it takes a few dirty tricks to make a living in a competitive business. We can pray for, encourage, support, and even assist our rivals because we know that God, not our competitive advantage, is the source of our provision. We must be careful not to distort this promise into the false

---

[13] The term for "every" or "all" (*pan*) here has the connotation of "every kind of" rather than "every possible" blessing. Cf. Gerhard Kittel, Gerhard Friedrich, and Geoffrey William Bromiley, eds., *Theological Dictionary of the New Testament* (Grand Rapids: Eerdmans, 1985), 631c.

gospel of health and wealth, as many have done. God does not promise true believers a big house and an expensive car. But he does assure us that if we look to the needs of others, he will make sure that our needs will be met in the process.

Assessing Performance (2 Corinthians 10–13)

As we noted in the introduction, 2 Corinthians 10 through 13 constitute the third section of the letter. The most relevant parts for work come in chapters 10 and 11, which expand the discussion of on-the-job performance that began in chapter 5. Here Paul is defending himself in the face of attacks by a few people he facetiously calls "super-apostles" (2 Cor. 11:5). In doing so, he offers specific insights directly applicable to performance assessment.

The false super-apostles had been criticizing Paul for not measuring up to them in terms of eloquence, personal charisma, and evidence of signs and wonders. Naturally, the "standards" they chose were nothing more than self-descriptions of themselves and their ministries. Paul points out what an absurd game they were playing. People who judge by comparing others to themselves will always be self-satisfied. Paul refuses to go along with such a self-serving scheme. As far as he is concerned, as he had already explained in 1 Corinthians 4:1–5, the only judgment—and therefore the only commendation—that is worth its salt is the judgment of the Lord Jesus.

Paul's perspective has direct relevance to our workplaces. Our performance on the job will likely be assessed in quarterly or annual reviews, and there is certainly nothing wrong with that. Problems arise when the standards by which we measure ourselves or others are biased and self-serving. In some organizations—typically those only loosely accountable to their owners and customers—a small circle of intimates may gain the ability to judge the performance of others primarily based on whether it falls in line with the insiders' self-interests. Those outside the inner circle are then evaluated primarily in terms being "with us" or "against us." This is a difficult spot to find ourselves in, yet because Christians measure success by God's assessment rather than promotion, pay, or even continued employment, we may be the very people who can bring redemption to such corrupt organizations. If we should find ourselves as beneficiaries of corrupt, self-dealing systems, what better witness to Christ could we find than to stand up for the benefit of others who have been harmed or marginalized, even at the expense of our own comfort and security?

Conclusion to 2 Corinthians

The unique circumstances that led Paul to write 2 Corinthians resulted in a letter with many important lessons for work, workers, and workplaces. Paul repeatedly stresses the importance of transparency and integrity. He urges his readers to invest in good and joyful relationships at work and to pursue reconciliation when relationships are broken. He measures godly work in terms of service, leadership, humility, generosity, and the reputations we earn through our actions. He argues that performance, accountability, and the timely fulfillment of obligations are essential duties of Christians at work. He gives standards for unbiased performance evaluation. He explores the opportunities and challenges of working with nonbelievers. He implores us to use the wealth we gain from work for the good of the community, even to the point of making equal use of it to benefit others as we do to benefit ourselves. He assures us that in doing so we increase, rather than decrease, our own financial security because we come to depend on God's power rather than our own weakness.

Paul's words are extremely challenging because he says that serving others, even to the point of suffering, is the way to be effective in God's economy, just as Jesus himself effected our salvation by his suffering on the cross. Paul, while falling far short of Jesus' divine perfection, is willing to live his life as an open book, an example of how God's strength overcomes human frailty. Because of his openness, Paul is credible when he claims that working according to God's ways, purposes, and values is truly the way to a fuller life. He passes on to us the words of the Lord Jesus himself, "My grace is sufficient for you, for power is made perfect in weakness" (2 Cor. 12:9). This admonition is just as important to our work today as it was to the Corinthians when Paul wrote this fascinating letter.

GALATIANS, EPHESIANS, PHILIPPIANS, AND WORK

Galatians, Ephesians and Philippians are three short but rich books among the letters of Paul in the New Testament. Because of their brevity, their contribution to the theology of work is combined here into a single chapter. However, the three letters have their own distinctive themes, and we will explore each letter on its own.

Galatians and Work

> For you were called to freedom, brothers and sisters; only do not use your freedom as an opportunity for self-indulgence, but through love become slaves to one another. (Gal. 5:13)

Introduction to Galatians

How do we live as believers in Jesus Christ? If the Christian life begins when we put our faith in Christ as Savior and Lord, how do we express this faith in our daily lives, including our work?

For many of us, the answer to these questions lies in ordering our behavior according to certain basic rules. Thus, for example, when it comes to the workplace, we might adopt the following to-do list: (1) Show respect to colleagues; (2) don't use inappropriate language; (3) don't gossip; (4) be guided by biblical values when making decisions; and (5) speak of faith in Christ if possible. Although this list could easily be much longer, it contains valuable guidance that reflects biblical priorities.

But there is a danger for Christians in such a list, whether in the workplace or elsewhere. It's the danger of legalism, of turning the Christian life into a set of rules rather than our free response to God's grace in Christ and a network of relationships centered in Christ. Moreover, those who approach the Christian life legalistically often tend to put on their to-do list items that are inessential or perhaps even incorrect.

Paul and the Galatians

This is exactly what happened with the believers in Galatia in the mid-first century. In response to the preaching of the Apostle Paul, they had put their faith in Christ and began living as Christians. But, before long, they started shaping their lives according to a list of do's and don'ts. In this effort, the Galatians were influenced by outsiders who claimed to be Christians and who insisted that the Christian life required keeping the Law of Moses as understood by certain contemporary schools of thought. In particular, these "Judaizers" were persuading the Galatians to live like Jews in matters of circumcision (Gal. 5:2–12) and the ceremonial law (Gal. 4:10).

Paul wrote the letter we call "Galatians" in order to get the Christians in Galatia back on the right track. Though he did not address workplace issues directly, his basic instructions on the nature of the Christian life speak incisively to our interests in faith and work. Moreover, Galatians contains work-related imagery, especially drawn from the first-century practice of slavery. Christians, according to Paul, are to live in freedom, not in slavery to the Law of Moses and other earthly powers (Gal. 4:1–11). Yet, ironically, those who exercise their freedom in Christ should choose to "become slaves to one another" through love (Gal. 5:13).

Biblical scholars almost unanimously agree that Galatians was written by the Apostle Paul to a group of churches in the Roman province of Galatia, in what is now central Turkey, sometime between AD 49 and 58.[1] Paul was writing to churches he had founded through the preaching of the good news of Jesus Christ. These churches existed in a culturally and religiously diverse environment and had recently been influenced by Judaizers (Jewish Christians who argued that all Christians must keep the whole law if they want to experience the full Christian life).

---

[1] See Richard N. Longenecker, *Galatians*, vol. 41 of the *Word Biblical Commentary* (Waco, TX: Word, 1990), lxxiii–lxxxvii.

Paul underscores the freedom we have in Christ in his response to the Galatians and the Judaizers who were corrupting them. Applied to the workplace, Galatians helps us understand and engage in our work with a freedom that is essential to the gospel of Jesus Christ.

After introducing himself, Paul greets the Galatians, referring to Christ as one "who gave himself for our sins to set us free from the present evil age" (Gal. 1:3). Thus he introduces the theme of freedom, which is central to the letter to the Galatians and to living as a believer in Jesus.

Understanding Life in Christ (Galatians 1:6–4:31)

Paul begins by identifying the problem among the Galatians. They "are turning to a different gospel" (Gal. 1:6). This "gospel" requires Gentiles "to live like Jews" (Gal. 2:14). In order to show that this "gospel" is really not a gospel—that is, good news—at all, Paul presents a variety of arguments, including his autobiography (Gal. 1:10–2:21), the receiving of the Spirit through faith (Gal. 3:1–5), the offspring of Abraham through faith (Gal. 3:6–29), the analogy of slaves and children (Gal. 4:1–11), a personal, emotional appeal (Gal. 4:12–20), and the allegory of the slave woman and the free woman (Gal. 4:21–31).

At several points in chapters 1–4 in his explication of the Christian life, Paul uses the language and imagery of slavery to fortify his understanding of life in Christ. Slavery, which in Galatians signifies primarily the absence of freedom, is that from which the Galatians had been delivered by their faith in Christ. "You are no longer a slave but a child" (Gal. 4:7). Their desire to follow the Law of Moses rather than to rely on their faith is, in effect, a senseless return to the bondage of slavery (Gal. 4:8–10). Even the Law of Moses, when understood properly, commends freedom rather than slavery to the law itself (Gal. 4:21–31).

So we see that Paul uses workplace imagery (slavery) to illustrate a spiritual point about religious legalism. Yet the point does apply directly to the workplace itself. A legalistic workplace—in which bosses try to control every motion, every word, every thought that employees have—is contrary to freedom in Christ. Workers of all types owe obedience to their legitimate superiors. And organizations of all types owe freedom to their workers to the full extent compatible with the true needs of the work.

Living in Christ (Gal. 5–6)

Galatians 5:1 completes the crescendo of the first four chapters with a roaring call to freedom. "For freedom Christ has set us free. Stand firm, therefore, and do not submit again to a yoke of slavery." Yet this does not mean that Christians should do whatever they please, gratifying their own sinful desires and neglecting those around them. On the contrary, Paul explains, "For you were called to freedom, brothers and sisters; only do not use your freedom as an opportunity for self-indulgence, but through love become slaves to one another" (Gal. 5:13). Christians are free in Christ from slavery to this world and its power, including the Law of Moses. Yet in this freedom, they should choose out of love to serve one another with humility. Such "slavery" is not bondage, but an ironic exercise of true freedom in Christ.

Living in the Spirit (Galatians 5:13–23)

The Spirit of God, given to Christians when they believe the good news of Christ (Gal. 3:2–5), helps us to live out our faith each day (Gal. 5:16). Those who "live by the Spirit" will reject and be safe from the "works of the flesh," which include "fornication, impurity, licentiousness, idolatry, sorcery, enmities, strife, jealousy, anger, quarrels, dissensions, factions, envy, drunkenness, carousing, and things like these" (Gal. 5:19–21). Parts of this list sound all too similar to life in many workplaces—strife, jealousy, anger, quarrels, dissensions, factions and envy. Even seemingly religious practices such as idolatry and sorcery have real manifestations in the workplace. If we are called to live in the Spirit at all, then we are called to live in the Spirit at work.

Paul specifically warns us against "self-indulgence" in the name of freedom (Gal. 5:13). Instead, we should choose to "become slaves [or servants] to one another." At work, this means we are to assist our co-workers even when we are in competition or at odds with them. We are to confront fairly and resolve our jealousies, angers, quarrels, dissensions, factions, and envy (see Matt. 18:15–17), rather than nurture resentment. We are to create products and services that exceed our customers' legitimate expectations, because a true servant seeks what is best for the person served, not merely what is adequate.

The Spirit of God is not, however, simply a divine naysayer who keeps us out of trouble. Rather, the Spirit at work in believers produces new attitudes and actions. In agriculture, fruit is a delicious result of long-term growth and cultivation. The metaphor "fruit of the Spirit" signals that God cares about the kind of people we are becoming, rather than only what we are doing today. We are to cultivate "love, joy, peace, patience, kindness, generosity, faithfulness, gentleness, and self-control" (Gal. 5:22–23) over the course of a lifetime. We have no reason to believe that this fruit is meant only for relationships among Christians in our churches and families. On the contrary, just as we are to be guided by the Spirit in every facet of life, so we are to demonstrate the fruit of the Spirit wherever we are, including the places in which we work. Patience in the workplace, for example, does not refer to indecisiveness or failure to act urgently in business matters. Instead, it means a freedom from the anxiety that would tempt us to act before the time is ripe, such as firing a subordinate in a fit of anger, berating a colleague before hearing an explanation, demanding a response before a student has time to consider, or cutting a customer's hair before being completely sure what kind of style the customer wants. If the fruit of the Spirit seems to have little to do with work, perhaps we have narrowed our imagination of what spiritual fruit really is.

Working for the Good of Others (Galatians 6:1–10)

The first part of Galatians 6 employs a variety of work-related words to instruct Christians in how to care for others in tangible ways. Christians are to be generous to others as we "bear one another's burdens" (Gal. 6:2). Yet, lest we be overtaken by pride and imagine that our work on behalf of others excuses poor work of our own, believers must "test their own work" and "carry their own loads" (Gal. 6:4–5).

The analogy of sowing and reaping allows Paul to encourage the Galatians to focus on the life of the Spirit rather than the flesh (Gal. 6:7–8). Sowing in the Spirit involves purposeful effort: "Let us *work* for the good of all, and especially for those of the family of faith" (Gal. 6:10). Christians are to labor for the common good, in addition to caring for their fellow believers. Surely, if we are to *work* for the good of others, one place we should do it is in the workplace.

The Center of the Gospel (Galatians 6:11–18)

In his closing remarks, Paul reminds the Galatians of the center of the gospel, which is the cross of Christ: "May I never boast of anything except the cross of our Lord Jesus Christ, by which the world has been crucified to me, and I to the world" (Gal. 6:14).

Conclusion to Galatians

In his concluding use of crucifixion language (Gal. 6:14), Paul echoes what he had said earlier in the letter: "I have been crucified with Christ; and it is no longer I who live, but it is Christ who lives in me. And the life I now live in the flesh I live by faith in the Son of God, who loved me and gave himself for me" (Gal. 2:19b-20). Faith in Christ is not only believing certain facts about his life, death, and resurrection, but also dying with Christ so that he might live in us. This "Christ in us" reality does not disappear when we enter our offices, warehouses, shops, and boardrooms. Rather, it urges and empowers us to live for Christ, in the power of the Spirit, every moment, in every place.

The Christian life is based upon faith. But faith is not passive assent to the truth of the gospel. Rather, in the daily experience of the Christian, faith becomes alive and active. According to Paul, faith can even be said to be "*working* through love" (Gal. 5:6). Thus faith at work in our lives energizes loving actions, even as the Spirit of God helps us to be more loving both in heart and in action (Gal. 5:22). We reject the slavery of trying to justify ourselves by our work. However, when we embrace our freedom in Christ through faith, our work leads to love, joy, peace, patience, kindness, generosity, faithfulness, gentleness, and self-control. We see our work as a primary context in which to exercise our freedom in Christ so as to love others and "work for the good of all" (Gal. 6:10). If we do not see the fruit of faith in our places of work, then we are cutting off a major part of our life from Christ's mastery.

Ephesians and Work

I therefore, the prisoner in the Lord, beg you to lead a life worthy of the calling to which you have been called. (Eph. 4:1)

Introduction to Ephesians

What is the place of our work in the grand scheme of things? Is work just an activity we need to get by in life? Or is it also a place where we find meaning, healing, and personal integration?[2] Does our work have a place in the cosmos of God's creation? Does it mean anything alongside Christ's work of redeeming the world?

The letter to the Ephesians tells the story of God's cosmic work, beginning before the creation of the world, continuing in Christ's work of redemption, and leading up to the present moment and beyond. It draws us into this work both as awestruck observers of the drama and as active participants in God's work.

Thus Ephesians gives a new perspective, not only about God but also about ourselves. Our lives, our actions, and indeed our work take on fresh meaning. We live differently, we worship differently, and we work differently because of what God has done and is doing in Christ. We do what we do with our lives, including our professional lives, in response to God's saving activity and in fulfillment of the assignment he has given us to cooperate with him. Each one of us has been called by God to participate in God's work in the world (Eph. 4:1).

The letter we know as "Ephesians" is both similar to and different from other New Testament letters attributed to the Apostle Paul. It is similar most of all to Colossians, with which it shares common themes, structures, and even sentences (Eph. 6:21–22; Col. 4:7–8).[3] Ephesians is different from the other Pauline letters in its exalted style, distinctive vocabulary, and in some of its theological perspectives. Moreover, it is much

---

[2] See, for example, Dan P. McAdams, *The Redemptive Self: Stories Americans Live By* (New York: Oxford University Press, 2005); Donald E. Polkinghorne, *Narrative Knowing and the Human Sciences* (Albany: State University of New York, 1988).

[3] See "Colossians & Philemon and Work."

less oriented to a particular situation in the life of a particular church than Paul's other letters.[4] In this commentary, authorship by Paul is assumed.

Rather than focusing on the needs of one particular congregation, the letter to the Ephesians presents an expansive theological perspective on the work of God in the universe and the central role of the church of Jesus Christ within that work. Each individual believer contributes to this ecclesial effort as one who has been "created in Jesus Christ for good works" (Eph. 2:10) and who is essential to the growth and ministry of the church (Eph. 4:15–16).

God's Grand Plan: A Theological Vision (Ephesians 1:1–3:21)

The first half of Ephesians unfolds the grand narrative of God's salvation of the whole cosmos. Even before the "foundation of the world," God graciously chose us in Christ for relationship with him and to live out his purpose in the world (Eph. 1:4–6). At the core of this purpose, God will "gather up all things in Christ, things in heaven and things on earth" (Eph. 1:10). To put it differently, God will restore the whole cosmos, once broken by sin, under the authority of Christ. The fact that God will renovate his creation reminds us that this world—including farms, schools, and corporations—matters to God and has not been abandoned by him.

God's restoring work, centered in Christ, involves human beings, both as recipients of God's grace and as participants in his ongoing work of gracious restoration. We are saved by grace because of faith, not because of our works (Eph. 2:8–9). But our works are vital to God, "for we are what he has made us, created in Christ Jesus for good works, which God prepared beforehand to be our way of life" (Eph. 2:10). Thus we are not saved by works but for works. These works, which include all that we do, are a part of God's renewal of creation. Therefore, our activity in the workplace is one crucial element of that which God has prepared for us to do in fulfillment of his purpose for us.

---

[4] For discussion of these issues and their implications, see Andrew T. Lincoln, *Ephesians*, vol. 42 of the *Word Biblical Commentary* (Nashville: Thomas Nelson, 1990), xlvii–lxxiv; "Ephesians, Letter to the" in *Dictionary of Paul and His Letters*, eds. Gerald F. Hawthorne, Ralph P. Martin, and Daniel G. Reid (Downers Grove, IL: InterVarsity Press, 1993).

The church features prominently in God's plan for putting the world back together in Christ. His death on the cross not only made possible our personal salvation (Eph. 2:4–7), but also mended the breach between Jews and Gentiles (Eph. 2:13–18). This unity between former enemies epitomizes the unifying work of God. Thus the church serves as a demonstration to the whole universe of the nature and ultimate success of God's cosmic plan (Eph. 3:9–10). But the church is not merely a unit of people who gather once a week to do religious activities together. Rather, the church is the community of all believers, doing everything they do in all the places of life, whether working together or separately. In every sphere of life, we have "the power at work within us [which] is able to accomplish abundantly far more than all we can ask or imagine" (Eph. 3:20). Notice that Paul uses the civic term "citizens" (Eph. 2:19) to describe Christians, rather than the religious term "worshippers." In fact, Ephesians gives virtually no instructions about what the church should do when it gathers, but several instructions about how its members should work, as we will see momentarily.

God's Grand Plan: A Practical Guide (Ephesians 4:1–6:24)

The second half of Ephesians begins with an exhortation to live out the vision of the first half of the letter. "I therefore, the prisoner in the Lord, beg you to lead a life worthy of the calling to which you have been called" (Eph. 4:1). Every Christian shares in this calling. Thus our truest and deepest *vocation* (from the Latin word for "calling") is to do our part to advance the multifaceted mission of God in the world. This calling shapes everything else we do in life, including our work—or what we sometimes refer to as our "vocation." Of course, God may call us to specific jobs for expressing our fundamental calling to live for the praise of God's glory (Eph. 1:12). Thus as doctors and lawyers, clerks and waiters, actors and musicians, and parents and grandparents, we lead a life worthy of our calling to Christ and his activity in the world.

Working Hard for Good and for Giving (Ephesians 4:28)

Among the practical exhortations in Ephesians 4–6, two passages deal specifically with work-related concerns. The first has to do with the purpose of work. "Thieves must give up stealing; rather let them labor and work honestly with their own hands, so as to have something to share with the needy" (Eph. 4:28). Though pointed immediately at those who steal, Paul's advice is relevant to all Christians. The Greek translated in the NRSV as "honestly" (*to agathon*) literally means "to the good." God is always leading Christians to the good. The workplace is a crucial setting for us to do many of the good works that God has prepared for us (Eph. 2:10).

Through our work, we also earn sufficient resources to share with the needy, whether directly through the church or by other means. Although a theology of work is not quite the same as a theology of charity, this verse explicitly links the two. The overall message is that the purpose of work is to do good both by what our work accomplishes directly and by what our work enables us to give to others outside of work.

Mutuality in Working for the Lord (Ephesians 5:21–6:9)

The second practical consideration is relationships. Our calling as Christians impacts our basic relationships, especially those in the family and the workplace. (Prior to the industrial age, households were equally places of family life and places of work.) Ephesians 5:21–6:9 underscores this point by including specific instructions for relationships within the household (wives/husbands, children/fathers, slaves/masters). Lists of this sort were common in the moral discourse of the Greco-Roman world and are represented in the New Testament (see, for example, Col. 3:18–4:1 and 1 Pet. 2:13–3:12).[5]

We are particularly interested in Ephesians 6:5–9, a passage that addresses the relationship between slaves and masters. Paul addresses Christians who are masters, Christians who are slaves under Christian masters, and Christians who are slaves under nonbelieving masters. This text is similar to a parallel passage in Colossians (Col. 3:22–4:1). (See "Colossians" in "Colossians & Philemon and Work" for the historical background on slavery in the first-century Roman Empire, which is helpful for understanding this section of Ephesians.) To summarize briefly,

---

[5] See David Noel Freedman, "Haustafeln" and "Household Codes" in *The Anchor Bible Dictionary* (New York: Doubleday, 1992).

Roman slavery has both similarities to and differences from paid work in the twenty-first century. The chief similarity is that both ancient slaves and contemporary workers serve under the authority of masters or supervisors. With regard to the work itself, both groups have a duty to meet the expectations of those in authority over their work. The chief difference is that ancient slaves (and those in modern times as well) owe not only their work but also their lives to their masters. Slaves cannot quit, they have limited legal rights and remedies for mistreatment, they do not receive pay or compensation for their work, and they do not negotiate working conditions. In short, the scope for abuse of power by masters over slaves is far greater than that for supervisors over workers.

We will begin by exploring this section of Ephesians as it applies to actual slaves. Then we will consider applications to the form of paid labor that dominates developed economies today.

Christian Slaves (Ephesians 6:6–8)

The letter to the Ephesians encourages slaves to see themselves as "slaves of Christ" who "render service with enthusiasm" for the Lord rather than their human masters (Eph. 6:6–7). The fact that their work is for Christ will encourage them to work hard and well. Paul's words are therefore a comfort when masters order slaves to do good work. In that case, God will reward the slave (Eph. 6:8) even if the master doesn't, as is typically the case with slaves (Luke 17:8).

But why would slaving away for an earthly master necessarily be "doing the will of God" (Eph. 6:6)? Surely a master could order a slave to do work that is far from the will of God—abusing another slave, cheating a customer, or encroaching on someone else's fields. Paul clarifies, "Slaves, obey your earthly masters with fear and trembling, in singleness of heart, *as you obey Christ*" (Eph. 6:5). Slaves can only do for their masters what could be done *for Christ*. If a master orders slaves to do evil work, then Paul's words are dreadfully challenging, for the slave would have to refuse the master's orders. This could lead to unpleasant consequences, to say the least. Nonetheless, Paul's command is inescapable. "Render service . . . as to the Lord, and not to men and women" (Eph. 6:7). The Lord's commands supersede the commands of any master. Indeed, what else could "singleness of heart" mean, if not to set aside every order that conflicts with duty to Christ? "No one can serve two masters," said Jesus (Matt. 6:24). The punishment for disobeying an earthly master may be fearsome, but it may be necessary to suffer it in order to work "as to the Lord."

Christian Masters (Ephesians 6:5–11)

It is cruel for a master to force a slave to choose between obedience to the master and obedience to Christ. Therefore, Paul tells masters to "stop threatening" their slaves (Eph. 6:9). If masters order slaves to do good work, then threats should not be necessary. If masters order slaves to do evil work, then their threats are like threats against Christ. As in the letter to the Colossians, Ephesians agrees that masters should remember that they have a Master in heaven. But Ephesians underscores the fact that both slaves and masters "have the *same* Master" (Eph. 6:9). For this reason, Ephesians says that masters are to "do the same for your slaves" (Eph. 6:9)—that is, to give orders to slaves as though they were giving the orders to (or for) Christ. With this in mind, no Christian master could order a slave to do evil work, or even excessive work. Though the earthly distinction of master and slave remains intact, their relationship has been altered with an unprecedented call to mutuality. Both parties are subject to Christ alone "in singleness of heart" (Eph. 6:5). Neither can lord it over the other, since only Christ is Lord (Eph. 6:7). Neither can shirk the duty of love to the other. This passage accepts the economic and cultural reality of slavery, but it contains fertile seeds of abolitionism. In Christ's kingdom, "there is no longer slave or free" (Gal. 3:28).

Slavery continues to flourish in our world today, much to our shame, though it's often called human trafficking or forced labor. The inner logic of Ephesians 6:5–9, as well as the broader story of Ephesians, motivates us to work for the end of slavery. Most of us, however, will not experience slavery in a personal way, either as slaves or as masters. Yet we do find ourselves in workplace relationships where someone has authority over another person. By analogy, Ephesians 6:5–9 teaches both employers and employees to order, perform, and reward only work that could be done by or for Christ. When we are ordered to do good work, the issue is simple, though not always easy. We do it to the best of our ability, regardless of the compensation or appreciation we receive from our bosses, customers, regulators, or anyone else in authority over us.

When we are ordered to do evil work, the situation is more complicated. On the one hand, Paul tells us to "obey your earthly masters . . . as you obey Christ." We cannot lightly disobey those in earthly authority over us, any more than we can lightly disobey Christ. This has even caused some to question whether whistleblowing, work stoppages, and complaints to regulatory authorities are legitimate for Christian employees. At the very least, a difference of opinion or judgment is not by itself good enough cause to disobey a valid order at work. It is important not to confuse "I don't want to do this work, and I don't think it's fair for my boss to tell me to do it" with "It is against God's will for me to do this work." Paul's instruction to "obey your earthly masters with fear and trembling" suggests that we obey the orders of those in authority over us unless we have strong reason to believe doing so would be wrong.

Yet Paul adds that we obey earthly masters as a way of "doing the will of God from the heart." Surely, if we are ordered to do something clearly against God's will—for example, a violation of biblical commands or values—then our duty to our higher master (Christ) is to resist the ungodly order from a human boss. The crucial distinction often requires finding out whose interests would be served by disobeying the order. If disobeying would protect the interests of another person or the larger community then there is a strong case for disobeying the order. If disobeying the order would protect only our personal interests, the case is weaker. In some cases, protecting others could even jeopardize our careers or cost us our livelihoods. No wonder Paul says, "Be strong in the Lord" and "Put on the whole armor of God" (Eph. 6:10, 11).

Yet surely we express compassion for those—including maybe ourselves at times—who face the choice of obeying a genuinely ungodly order or suffering personal loss such as getting fired. This is especially true in the case of workers near the bottom of the economic ladder, who may have few alternatives and no financial cushion. Workers are routinely ordered to perform a variety of petty evils, such as lying ("Tell her I'm not in the office"), cheating ("Put an extra bottle of wine on table 16's tab—they're too drunk to even notice"), and idolatry ("I expect you to act like this job is the most important thing in the world to you"). Do we have to resign over every one of them? Other times, workers may be ordered to do serious evils. "Threaten to drag her name through the mud if she won't agree to our terms." "Find an excuse to fire him before he uncovers any more falsified quality control records." "Dump it in the river tonight when no one is around." Yet the alternative of losing a job and seeing our family slide into poverty may be—or seem—even worse than following the ungodly order. Often it's not clear which alternatives are more in accord with biblical values and which are less. We must acknowledge that the decisions can be complex. When we are pressured to do something wrong, we need to depend on God's power to stand firmer against evil than we ever believed we could. Yet we also need to bear Christ's word of compassion and forgiveness when we find that Christians cannot overcome all the evils of the world's workplaces.

When we are the ones in authority, then, we should order only work that Christ would order. We do not order subordinates to harm themselves or others in order to benefit ourselves. We do not order others to do what in good conscience we will not do. We do not threaten those who refuse our orders out of conscience or justice. Though we are bosses, we have bosses of our own, and Christians in authority still have a heightened duty to serve God by the way we command others. We are Christ's slaves, and we have no authority to order or obey anyone else in opposition to Christ. For each of us, no matter our position in the workplace, our work is a way of serving—or failing to serve—God.

Conclusion to Ephesians

Only a few verses of Ephesians deal precisely with the workplace and even these are directed at thieves, slaves, and masters. But when we glimpse how God is restoring all of creation through Christ, and when we discover that our work plays an essential role in that plan, then our workplace becomes a primary context for us to do the good works that God has prepared for us. Ephesians does not tell us specifically what good works God has prepared for each of us in our work. We must look to other sources to discern that. But it does tell us that God calls us to do all of our work for the good. Relationships and attitudes in the workplace are transformed as we see ourselves and our co-workers mainly in terms of our relationship with Jesus Christ, the one true Lord.

Ephesians encourages us to take a new perspective on our lives, one in which our work is an outgrowth of God's own work of creating the world and redeeming it from sin. We work in response to God's call to follow Jesus in every aspect of our lives (Eph. 4:1). At work, we discover the opportunity to do many of the good works that God intends for us to do. Thus in our offices, factories, schools, households, stores, and every other place of work, we have the opportunity to "render service with enthusiasm" to the Lord (Eph. 6:7).

Philippians and Work

> Work out your own salvation with fear and trembling; for it is God who is at work in you, enabling you both to will and to work for his good pleasure. (Phil. 2:11b-12)

Introduction to Philippians

Work requires effort. Whether we do business or drive trucks, raise children or write articles, sell shoes or care for the disabled and aged, our work requires personal effort. If we don't get up in the morning and get going, our work won't get done. What motivates us to get out of bed each morning? What keeps us going throughout the day? What energizes us so that we can do our work with faithfulness and even excellence?

There are a wide variety of answers to these questions. Some might point to economic necessity. "I get up and go to work because I need the money." Other answers might refer to our interest in our work. "I work because I love my job." Still other answers might be less inspiring. "What gets me up and keeps me going all day? Caffeine!"

Paul's letter to the Christians in Philippi provides a different sort of answer to the question of where we find strength to do our work. Paul says that our work is not the result of *our own* effort, but that *God's* work in us is what gives us our energy. What we do in life, including on the job, is an expression of God's saving work in Christ. Moreover, we find the strength for this effort by the power of God within us. Christ's work is to serve people (Mark 10:35), and God empowers us to serve alongside him.

Almost all scholars agree that the Apostle Paul wrote the letter we know as Philippians sometime between AD 54 and 62.[6] There is no unanimity about the place from which Paul wrote, though we know it was written during one of his several imprisonments (Phil. 1:7).[7] It is clear that Paul wrote this personal letter to the church in Philippi, a community he planted during an earlier visit there (Phil. 1:5; Acts 16:11–40). He wrote in order to strengthen his relationship with the Philippian church, to update them on his personal situation, to thank them for their support of his ministry, to equip them to confront threats to their faith, to help them get along better, and, in general, to assist them in living out their faith.

Philippians uses the word *work* (*ergon* and cognates) several times (Phil. 1:6; 2:12–13, 30; 4:3). Paul uses it to describe God's work of salvation and the human tasks that flow from God's saving work. He doesn't directly address issues in the secular workplace, but what he says about work has important applications there.

God's Work in Us (Philippians 1:1–26)

In the context of his opening prayer for the Philippians (Phil. 1:3–11), Paul shares his conviction of God's work in and among the Philippian believers. "I am confident of this, that the one who began a good work among you will bring it to completion by the day of Jesus Christ" (Phil. 1:6). The "work" Paul refers to is the work of new birth in Christ, which leads to salvation. Paul himself had a hand in that work by preaching the gospel to them. He continues that work as their teacher and apostle, and he says it is "fruitful *labor* for me" (Phil. 1:22). Yet the underlying worker is not Paul but God, for God is "the one who began a good work among you" (Phil. 1:6). "This is God's doing" (Phil. 1:28).

---

[6] Gerald F. Hawthorne, *Philippians*, rev. and exp. by Ralph P. Martin, in vol. 43 of the *Word Biblical Commentary* (Nashville: Thomas Nelson, 2004), xxvii–xxix, xxxix–l.

[7] See Gerald F. Hawthorne, Ralph P. Martin, and Daniel G. Ried, eds., "4.3. Place and Date" of "Philippians, Letter to the," in *Dictionary of Paul and His Letters* (Downers Grove, IL: InterVarsity Press, 1993).

The NRSV speaks of God's work "among you," while most English translations speak of God's work "in you." Both are apropos, and the Greek phrase *en humin* can be rendered either way. God's good work begins *in* individual lives. Yet it is to be lived out *among* believers in their fellowship together. The main point of verse 6 is not to restrict God's work either to individuals or the community as a whole, but rather to underscore the fact that all of their work is God's work. Moreover, this work isn't completed when individuals "get saved" or when churches are planted. God continues working in and among us until his work is complete, which happens "by the day of Jesus Christ." Only when Christ returns will God's work be finished.

Paul's job is evangelist and apostle, and there are marks of success and ambition in his profession, as in any other. How many converts you win, how much funding you raise, how many people praise you as their spiritual mentor, how your numbers compare to other evangelists—these can be points of pride and ambition. Paul admits that these motivations exist in his profession, but he insists that the only proper motivation is love (Phil. 1:15–16). The implication is that this is true in every other profession as well. We are all tempted to work for the marks of success—including recognition, security, and money—which can lead to "selfish ambition" (*eritieias*, perhaps more precisely translated as "unfair self-promotion").[8] They are not entirely bad, for they often come as we accomplish the legitimate purposes of our jobs (Phil. 1:18). Getting the work done is important, even if our motivation is not perfect. Yet in the long run (Phil. 3:7–14), motivation is even more important and the only Christ-like motivation is love.

Do Your Work in a Worthy Manner (Philippians 1:27–2:11)

Since our work is actually God's work in us, our work should be worthy, as God's work is. But apparently we have the ability to hinder God's work in us, for Paul exhorts, "Live your life in a manner worthy of the gospel of Christ" (Phil. 1:27). His topic is life in general, and there

---

[8] James Strong, *Enhanced Strong's Lexicon* (Ontario: Woodside Bible Fellowship, 1995), G2052.

is no reason to believe he means to exclude work from this exhortation. He gives three particular commands:

1. "Be of the same mind" (Phil. 2:2).

2. "Do nothing from selfish ambition or conceit, but in humility regard others as better than yourselves" (Phil. 2:3).

3. "Look not to your own interests, but the interests of others" (Phil. 2:4).

Again, we can work according to these commands only because our work is actually God's work in us, but this time he says it in a beautiful passage often called the "Hymn of Christ" (Phil. 2:6–11). Jesus, he says, "did not regard equality with God as something to be exploited, but emptied himself taking the form of a slave, and being born in human likeness. And being found in human form, he humbled himself and became obedient to the point of death—even death on a cross" (Phil. 2:8–9). Therefore God's work in us—specifically Christ's work in us—is always done humbly with others, for the benefit of others, even if it requires sacrifice.

"Be of the Same Mind" (Philippians 2:2)

The first of the three commands, "Be of the same mind," is given to Christians as a body. We shouldn't expect it to apply in the secular workplace. In fact, we don't always want to have the same mind as everyone around us at work (Rom. 12:2). But in many workplaces, there is more than one Christian. We should strive to have the same mind as other Christians where we work. Sadly, this can be very difficult. In church, we segregate ourselves into communities in which we generally agree about biblical, theological, moral, spiritual, and even cultural matters. At work we don't have that luxury. We may share the workplace with other Christians with whom we disagree about such matters. It may even be hard to recognize others who claim to be Christians as Christians, according to our judgments.

This is a scandalous impediment to both our witness as Christians and our effectiveness as co-workers. What do our non-Christian colleagues think of our Lord—and us—if we get along worse with each other than with nonbelievers? At the very least, we ought to try to identify other Christians in our workplaces and learn about their beliefs and practices. We may not agree, even about matters of great importance, yet it is a far better witness to show mutual respect than to treat others who call themselves Christians with contempt or bickering. If nothing else, we should set aside our differences enough to do excellent work together, if we really believe that our work truly matters to God.

Having the same mind as Christ means "having the same love" as Christ (Phil. 2:2). Christ loved us to the point of death (Phil. 2:8), and we are to have the same love he had (Phil. 2:5). This gives us something in common not only with other believers but also with nonbelievers in our workplaces: we love them! Everyone at work can agree with us that we should do work that benefits them. If a Christian says, "My job is to serve you," who would disagree with that?

"Do Nothing from Selfish Ambition or Conceit" (Philippians 2:3)

Regarding others as better than ourselves is the mind-set of those who have the mind of Christ (Phil. 2:3). Our humility is meant to be offered to all the people around us, and not just to Christians. For Jesus' death on the cross—the ultimate act of humility—was for sinners and not for the righteous (Luke 5:32; Rom. 5:8; 1 Tim. 1:15).

Workplaces offer unlimited opportunities for humble service. You can be generous in giving credit to others for success and stingy in passing out blame for failure. You can listen to what someone else is saying instead of thinking ahead to your reply. You can try another person's idea instead of insisting on your own way. You can give up your envy at another person's success or promotion or higher salary, or, failing that, you can take your envy to God in prayer instead of to your buddies at lunch.

Conversely, workplaces offer unlimited opportunities for selfish ambition. As we have seen, ambition—even competition—is not necessarily bad (Rom. 15:20; 1 Cor. 9:24; 1 Tim. 2:5), but unfairly advancing your own agenda is. It forces you to adopt an inaccurate, inflated assessment of yourself ("conceit"), which puts you into an ever more remote fantasyland where you can be effective neither in work nor in faith. There are two antidotes. First, make sure your success depends on and contributes to others' success. This generally means operating in genuine teamwork with others in your workplace. Second, continually seek accurate feedback about yourself and your performance. You may find that your performance is actually excellent, but if you learn that from accurate sources, it is not conceit. The simple act of accepting feedback from others is a form of humility, since you subordinate your self-image to their image of you. Needless to say, this is helpful only if you find accurate sources of feedback. Submitting your self-image to people who would abuse or delude you is not true humility. Even as he submitted his body to abuse on the cross, Jesus maintained an accurate assessment of himself (Luke 23:43).

"Look Not to Your Own Interests, But to the Interests of Others" (Philippians 2:4)

Of the three commands, this may be the hardest to reconcile with our roles in the workplace. We go to work—at least in part—in order to meet our needs. How then can it make sense to avoid looking to our own interests? Paul does not say. But we should remember that he is speaking to a community of people, to whom he says, "Let each of you look not to your own interests, but to the interests of others" (Phil. 2:4). Perhaps he expects that if everyone looks not to their individual needs, but to the needs of the whole community, then everyone's needs will be met. This is consistent with the body analogy Paul uses in 1 Corinthians 12 and elsewhere. The eye does not meet its need for transportation but relies on the foot for that. So each organ acts for the good of the body, yet finds its own needs met.

Under ideal circumstances, this might work for a close-knit group, perhaps a church of equally highly committed members. But is it meant to apply to the nonchurch workplace? Does Paul mean to tell us to look to the interests of our co-workers, customers, bosses, subordinates, suppliers, and myriad others around us, instead of our own interests? Again, we must turn to Philippians 2:8, where Paul depicts Jesus on the cross as our model, looking to the interests of sinners instead of his own. He lived out this principle in the world at large, not the church, and so must we. And Paul is clear that the consequences for us include suffering and loss, maybe even death. "Whatever gains I had, these I have come to regard as loss because of Christ." There is no natural reading of Philippians 2 that lets us off the hook of looking to the interests of others at work instead to our own.

Following Christ as Ordinary Christians (Philippians 2:19–3:21)

In fact, Philippians gives us three examples—Paul, Epaphroditus, and Timothy—to show us how all Christians are meant to follow Christ's model. "Join in imitating me, and observe those who live according to the example you have in us," Paul tells us (Phil. 3:17). He depicts each of these examples in a framework based on the "Hymn of Jesus" in chapter 2.

Person	Sent to a difficult place	In obedience/ slavery	Taking grave risks	For the benefit of others
Jesus	Found in human form (2:7)	Taking the form of a slave (2:7)	Obedient to the point of death (2:8)	Emptied himself (2:7)
Paul	Live in the flesh (1:22)	Servant of Jesus Christ (1:1)	Imprisonment (1:7) Becoming like Christ in death (3:10)	For your progress and joy (1:25)
Timothy	Send Timothy to you soon (2:19)	Like a son with a father (2:22)	(Not specified in Philippians, but see Rom. 6:21)	Will be genuinely concerned for your welfare (2:20)
Epaphroditus	Send you Epaphroditus (2:25)	Your messenger (2:25)	Came close to death (2:30)	To minister to my need (2:25)

The message is clear. We are called to do as Jesus did. We cannot hide behind the excuse that Jesus is the only Son of God, who serves others so we won't have to. Nor are Paul, Epaphroditus, and Timothy supermen whose exploits we can't hope to duplicate. Instead, as we go to work we are to put ourselves into the same framework of sending, obedience, risk, and service to others:

Person	Sent to a difficult place	In obedience/ slavery	Taking grave risks	For the benefit of others
Workplace Christians	Go to non-Christian workplaces	Work under the authority of others	Risk career limitation for our motivation to love as Christ loves	Are called by God to put others' interests ahead of our own

Are we allowed to temper the command to serve others *instead of* ourselves with a little common sense? Could we, say, look first to the interests of others whom we can trust? Could we look to the interests of others *in addition* to our own interests? Is it okay to work for the common good in situations where we can expect to benefit proportionally, but look out for ourselves when the system is stacked against us? Paul doesn't say.

What should we do if we find ourselves unable or unwilling to live quite so daringly? Paul says only this, "Do not worry about anything, but in everything by prayer and supplication with thanksgiving let your requests be made known to God" (Phil. 4:6). Only by constant prayer, supplication, and thanksgiving to God can we get through the difficult decisions and demanding actions required to look to the interests of others instead of our own. This is not meant as abstract theology but as practical advice for daily life and work.

Everyday Applications (Philippians 4:1–23)

Paul describes three everyday situations that have direct relevance for the workplace.

Resolving Conflict (Philippians 4:2–9)

Paul asks the Philippians to help two women among them, Euodia and Syntyche, come to peace with each other (Phil. 4:2–9). Although our instinctive reflex is to suppress and deny conflict, Paul lovingly brings it into the open where it can be resolved. The women's conflict is not specified, but they are both believers who Paul says "have struggled beside me in the work of the gospel" (Phil. 4:3). Conflict occurs even between the most faithful Christians, as we all know. Stop nurturing resentment, he tells them, and think about what is honorable, just, pure, pleasing, commendable, excellent, and praiseworthy in the other person (Phil. 4:8). "The peace of God, which surpasses all understanding" (Phil. 4:7) seems to begin with appreciating the good points of those around us, even (or especially) when we are in conflict with them. After all, they are people for whom Christ died. We should also look carefully at ourselves and find God's reserves of gentleness, prayer, supplication, thanksgiving, and letting go of worry (Phil. 4:6) inside ourselves.

The application to today's workplace is clear, though seldom easy. When our urge is to ignore and hide conflict with others at work, we must instead acknowledge and talk (not gossip) about it. When we would rather keep it to ourselves, we should ask people of wisdom for help—in humility, not in hopes of gaining an upper hand. When we would rather build a case *against* our rivals, we should instead build a case *for* them, at least doing them the justice of acknowledging whatever their good points are. And when we think we don't have the energy to engage the other person, but would rather just write off the relationship, we must let God's power and patience substitute for our own. In this we seek to imitate our Lord, who "emptied himself" (Phil. 2:7) of personal agendas and so received the power of God (Phil. 2:9) to live out God's will in the world. If we do these things, then our conflict can be resolved in terms of what the true issues are, rather than our projections, fears, and resentments. Usually this leads to a restored working relationship and a kind of mutual respect, if not friendship. Even in the unusual cases where no reconciliation is possible, we can expect a surprising "peace of God, which surpasses all understanding" (Phil. 4:7). It is God's sign that even a broken relationship is not beyond the hope of God's goodness.

Supporting Each Other in Work (Philippians 4:10–11, 15–16)

Paul thanks the Philippians for their support for him, both personal (Phil. 1:30) and financial (Phil. 4:10–11, 15–16). Throughout the New Testament, we see Paul always striving to work in partnership with other Christians, including Barnabas (Acts 13:2), Silas (Acts 15:40), Lydia (Acts

16:14–15), and Priscilla and Aquila (Rom. 16:3). His letters typically end with greetings to people with whom he has worked closely, and are often from Paul and a co-worker, as Philippians is from Paul and Timothy (Phil. 1:1). In this he is following his own advice of imitating Jesus, who did almost everything in partnership with his disciples and others.

As we noted in Philippians 2, Christians in the secular workplace don't always have the luxury of working alongside believers. But that doesn't mean we can't support one another. We could gather with others in our professions or institutions to share mutual support in the specific challenges and opportunities we face in our jobs. The "Mom-to-Mom" program[9] is a practical example of mutual support in the workplace. Mothers gather weekly to learn, share ideas, and support each other in the job of parenting young children. Ideally, all Christians would have that kind of support for their work. In the absence of a formal program, we could talk about our work in our usual Christian communities, including worship and sermons, Bible studies, small groups, church retreats, classes, and the rest. But how often do we? Paul went to great lengths to build community with the others in his calling, even employing messengers to make long sea voyages (Phil. 2:19, 25) to share ideas, news, fellowship, and resources.

Handling Poverty and Plenty (Philippians 4:12–13, 18)

Finally, Paul discusses how to handle both poverty and plenty. This has direct workplace relevance because work makes the difference between poverty and plenty for us, or at least for those of us who are paid for our work. Again, Paul's advice is simple, yet hard to follow. Don't idolize your work in expectation that it will always provide plenty for you. Instead, do your work because of the benefit it brings to others, and learn to be content with however much or little it provides for you. Tough advice indeed. Some professions—teachers, health workers, customer service people, and parents, to name a few—may be used to working overtime without extra pay to help people in need. Others expect to be amply rewarded for the service they perform. Imagine a senior executive or investment banker working without a contract or bonus target say-

---

[9] See www.momtomom.org.

ing, "I take care of the customers, employees, and shareholders, and am happy to receive whatever they choose to give me at the end of the year." It's not common, but a few people do it. Paul says simply this:

> I know what it is to have little, and I know what it is to have plenty. In any and all circumstances I have learned the secret of being well-fed and of going hungry, or having plenty and of being in need. I can do all things through him who strengthens me. . . . I have been paid in full and have more than enough; I am fully satisfied. (Phil. 4:12–13, 18)

The point is not how much or how little we are paid—within reason—but whether we are motivated by the benefit our work does for others or only for our self-interest. Yet that motivation itself should move us to resist institutions, practices, and systems that result in extremes of either too much plenty or too much poverty.

Conclusion to Philippians

Though Paul does not address the workplace distinctly in Philippians, his vision of God's work in us lays a foundation for our considerations of faith and work. Our jobs provide a major context in which we are to live out the good work God has begun in us. We are to seek the same mind as other Christians in our places of life and work. We are to act as though others are better than ourselves. We are to look to the interests of others instead of our own. Without directly addressing work, Paul seems to demand the impossible from us in the workplace! But what we do in the workplace is not just our effort—it is God's work in and through us. Because God's power is unlimited, Paul can say boldly, "I can do all things through him who strengthens me" (Phil. 4:13).

COLOSSIANS & PHILEMON AND WORK

Introduction to Colossians and Philemon

Whatever you do, in word or deed, do everything in the name of the Lord Jesus, giving thanks to God the Father through him. Whatever your task, put yourselves into it, as done for the Lord and not for your masters, since you know that from the Lord you will receive the inheritance as your reward; you serve the Lord Christ. (Col. 3:17, 23–24)

Why would the Apostle Paul[1] insist that the Christians at Colossae live their daily lives under such a comprehensive mandate of controlling every word and deed? In these two brief but rich letters Paul explores in detail both the theological rationale behind these two overlapping commands and the implications of this lifestyle in all of the primary relationships of life—with our spouses and families, and with our colleagues, employees, or bosses in the workplace.

Background on Colossae and the Colossians

The City of Colossae

Cities grow as they develop commercial centers that provide jobs for their residents. The ancient city of Colossae was built on a major trade route through the Lycus River Valley in the Roman province of Asia

---

[1] The authorship of the letter to the Colossians has been questioned by a number of scholars, but because it is not the purpose of this commentary to address authorship, the letter's self-attribution to Paul will be accepted here. This debate has a negligible effect on understanding the letter's application to the workplace.

Minor (in the southwest corner of modern-day Turkey). There the Colossians manufactured a beautiful dark red wool cloth (*colossinum*) for which the city became famous. But Colossae's importance as a business center diminished significantly around 100 BC, when the neighboring city of Laodicea was founded as an active and commercially aggressive competitor. The two towns, along with neighboring Hierapolis, were destroyed by earthquakes in AD 17 (in the reign of Tiberius) and again in 60 (in the reign of Nero). Rebuilt after each earthquake, Colossae never regained its early prominence, and by 400 the city no longer existed.

The Colossian Church

The Apostle Paul had spent two years planting a church in Ephesus, and in Acts 19:10 we learn that, radiating from that center, "all the residents of Asia, both Jews and Greeks, heard the word of the Lord." Whether Paul himself fanned out in missionary activity throughout the province or whether some of his converts did so, a church was planted in Colossae. It is likely that Epaphras founded the Colossian church (Col. 1:7), and from 1:21 we assume that the church was composed mainly of Gentiles.

Philemon was a citizen of Colossae and an upright leader in that church. He also was a slaveholder whose slave Onesimus had escaped, had later encountered the Apostle Paul, and had responded to the gospel message about Jesus. In the letter to the Colossians, Paul addresses how our relationship to God through Jesus Christ affects us in the workplace. Specifically, he writes about how slaves are to do their work for their masters and how masters are to treat their slaves. The short personal letter to Philemon extends our understanding of Paul's command in Colossians 4:1.

The Purpose of the Letter

The letters to the Colossians and to Philemon are believed to have been written by Paul from prison sometime circa 60 to 62. At that time, Nero was the cruel and insane emperor of the Roman Empire who could ignore the claims of Paul's Roman citizenship.

From prison, Paul had heard that the Colossian Christians, who had at one time been strong in their faith, were now vulnerable to deception about the faith (2:4, 8, 16, 18, 21–23). He wrote to refute each of the theological errors the Colossians were tempted to embrace. The letters, however, take readers far beyond these issues of deception. Paul cared deeply that all of his readers (today as well as the Colossians two thousand years ago) understood the context of their lives within God's story, and what that looks like in their relationships on the job.

God at Work, Jesus at Work (Colossians 1:15–20)

The first half of Paul's letter to the Colossians can be summarized in nine words:

Jesus made it all.
Then Jesus paid it all.

Jesus Made It All

The Colossian letter assumes that the reader is familiar with the opening lines of the first book of the Bible, "In the beginning when God created the heavens and the earth" (Gen. 1:1). The second chapter of Genesis then states that "on the seventh day God finished the work that he had done, and he rested on the seventh day from all the work that he had done" (Gen. 2:2). The creation of all that exists was *work*, even for God. Paul tells us that Christ was present at the creation and that God's work in creation is Christ's work:

He is the image of the invisible God, the firstborn of all creation; for in him all things in heaven and on earth were created, things visible and invisible, whether thrones or dominions or rulers or powers—all things have been created through him and for him. He himself is before all things, and in him all things hold together. (Col. 1:15–17)

In other words, Paul attributes all of creation to Jesus, a theme also developed in the Gospel of John (1:1–4).

Jesus Paid It All

Paul then goes on to make clear to his readers that Jesus was not only the agent who created all that exists, but he is also the agent of our salvation:

> For in him all the fullness of God was pleased to dwell, and through him God was pleased to reconcile to himself all things, whether on earth or in heaven, by making peace through the blood of his cross. (Col. 1:19–20)

Paul puts Christ's work in creation side by side with his work in redemption, with themes of creation dominating the first part of the passage (Col. 1:15–17) and themes of redemption dominating the second half (Col. 1:18–20). The parallelism is especially striking between 1:16, "in him all things in heaven and on earth were created," and 1:20, "to reconcile to himself all things." The pattern is easy to see: God created all things through Christ, and he is reconciling those same things to himself through Christ. James Dunn writes,

> What is being claimed is quite simply and profoundly that the divine purpose in the act of reconciliation and peacemaking was to restore the harmony of the original creation . . . resolving the disharmonies of nature and the inhumanities of humankind, that the character of God's creation and God's concern for the universe in its fullest expression could be so caught and encapsulated for them in the cross of Christ.[2]

In sum, Jesus made it all and then Jesus paid it all so that we can have a relationship with the living God.

God Worked in Creation, Making Humans Workers in His Image (Colossians 1:1–14)

In Colossians 1:6, by allusion Paul takes us back to Genesis 1:26–28.

Then God said, "Let us make humankind in our image, according to our likeness; and let them have dominion over the fish of the sea, and over the

---

[2] James D. G. Dunn, *The Epistles to the Colossians and to Philemon: A Commentary on the Greek Text*, The New International Greek Testament Commentary (Grand Rapids: Eerdmans, 1996), 104.

birds of the air, and over the cattle, and over all the wild animals of the earth, and over every creeping thing that creeps upon the earth." So God created humankind in his image, in the image of God he created them; male and female he created them. God blessed them, and God said to them, "Be fruitful and multiply, and fill the earth and subdue it; and have dominion over the fish of the sea and over the birds of the air and over every living thing that moves upon the earth."

Here is God the creator at work, and the apex of his activity is the creation of humanity in the divine image and likeness. To the newly minted man and woman, he gives two tasks (the tasks are given to both the male and the female): they are to be fruitful and multiply, filling the earth they are then to subdue or govern. Paul picks up the language of Genesis 1 in Colossians 1:6, giving thanks to God that the gospel is progressing in their midst, "bearing fruit and growing" as it goes out into the entire world. He then repeats this in 1:10—the Colossians are to bear fruit and grow in their understanding of God and in their work on his behalf. Whether the tasks are the work of parenting, the multifaceted work of subduing the earth and governing it, or the work of ministry, in our work they and we are image-bearers of God who works. We were created as workers in the beginning, and Christ redeems us as workers.

Jesus, the Image of the Invisible God (Colossians 1:15–29)

What difference does it make that we are bearers of the divine image in our work? One implication of this is that in our work we will reflect God's work patterns and values. But how do we know God so that we know what those patterns and values are? In Colossians 1:15, Paul reminds us that Jesus Christ is "the image of the invisible God." Again, "For in him the whole fullness of deity dwells bodily" (Col. 2:9). It is "in the face of Jesus Christ" that we can know God (2 Cor. 4:6). During Jesus' earthly ministry, Philip asked him, "Lord, show us the Father, and we will be satisfied." Jesus responded, "Have I been with you all this time, Philip, and you still do not know me? Whoever has seen me has seen the Father. How can you say, 'Show us the Father'?" (John 14:8–9).

Jesus reveals God to us. He shows us how we as God's image-bearers are to carry out our work. If we need help in grasping this, Paul spells it out: first, he describes Jesus' infinite power in creation (Col. 1:15–17), and then he immediately ties that to Jesus' willingness to set that power aside, to incarnate God on earth in word and deed, and then to die for our sins. (Paul says this directly in Philippians 2:5–9.) We look at Jesus. We listen to Jesus to understand how we are called to image God in our work.

How, then, can God's patterns and values apply in our work? We start by looking specifically at Jesus' work as our example.

Forgiveness

First, we see that God "has rescued us from the power of darkness and transferred us into the kingdom of his beloved Son" (Col. 1:13). Because Jesus has done that, Paul can appeal to us to "bear with one another and, if anyone has a complaint against another, forgive each other; just as the Lord has forgiven you, so you also must forgive" (Col. 3:13). It was on this basis that Paul could ask Philemon, the slave master, to forgive and receive Onesimus as a brother, no longer as a slave. We are doing our work in the name of the Lord Jesus when we bring that attitude to our relationships in the workplace: we make allowances for others' faults and we forgive those who offend us.

Self-sacrifice for the Benefit of Others

Second, we see Jesus with infinite power creating all that is, "things visible and invisible, whether thrones or dominions or rulers or powers" (Col. 1:16). Yet we also see him setting aside that power for our sake, "making peace through the blood of his cross" (Col. 1:20), so that we might have a relationship with God. There are times when we may be called on to set aside the authority or power we have in the workplace to benefit someone who may be undeserving. If Philemon is willing to set aside his slave-owner authority over Onesimus (who does not deserve his mercy) and take him back in a new relationship, then in this way Philemon images the invisible God in his workplace.

Freedom from Cultural Accommodation

Third, we see Jesus living a new reality that he offers to us: "If you have been raised with Christ, seek the things that are above, where Christ is, seated at the right hand of God. Set your minds on things that are above, not on things that are on earth, for you have died, and your life is hidden with Christ in God" (Col. 3:1–3). We are no longer bound by cultural mores that stand in contrast to the life of God within us. We are in the world, but we are not of the world. We can march to a different drumbeat. The culture of the workplace can work against our life in Christ, but Jesus calls us to set our hearts and our minds on what God desires for us and in us. This calls for a major reorientation of our attitudes and values.

Paul called Philemon to this reorientation. First-century Roman culture gave slaveholders complete power over the bodies and lives of their slaves. Everything in the culture gave Philemon full permission to treat Onesimus harshly, even to have him killed. But Paul was clear: As a follower of Jesus Christ, Philemon had died and his new life was now in Christ (Col. 3:3). That meant rethinking his responsibility not only to Onesimus but also to Paul, to the Colossian church, and to God his judge.

"I'm Doing Alright by Myself" (Colossians 2:1–23)

Paul warns the Colossians against falling back into the old orientation toward self-help. "See to it that no one takes you captive through philosophy and empty deceit, according to human tradition, according to the elemental spirits of the universe, and not according to Christ" (Col. 2:8). In "A Good Man is Hard to Find," Flannery O'Connor ironically put those words—"I'm doing alright by myself"—in the mouth of a serial killer proclaiming that he doesn't need Jesus.[3] This is an apt summary of the ethos of the false teachers plaguing the saints at Colossae. In their "self-imposed piety" (Col. 2:23), spiritual progress could be attained by

---

[3] Flannery O'Connor, "A Good Man Is Hard to Find," in *Collected Works* (New York: Library of America, 1988).

rough treatment of the body, mystical visions (Col. 2:18), and observing special days and food laws (Col. 2:16, likely derived from the Old Testament). These teachers believed that by marshaling the resources at their disposal, they could overcome sin on their own.

This important point forms the foundation for Paul's exhortations to workers later in the letter. Genuine progress in the faith—including progress in the way we glorify God in our workplace—can spring only out of our trust in God's work in us through Christ.

Heavenly Living for Earthly Good: The Shape of our Reorientation (Colossians 3:1–16)

This call to reorientation means that we reshape our lives to think and do according to Jesus' ethics in situations he never encountered. We cannot relive Jesus' life. We must live our own lives for Jesus. We have to respond to questions in life for which Jesus does not give specific answers. For example, when Paul writes, "Set your minds on things above, not on the things that are on earth" (Col. 3:2), does this mean that prayer is preferable to painting a house? Does Christian progress consist of thinking less and less about our work and more and more about harps and angels and clouds?

Paul does not abandon us to raw speculation about these things. In Colossians 3:1–17, he makes it clear that "to set your minds on things that are above" (Col. 3:2) means expressing the priorities of God's kingdom *precisely in the midst of everyday earthly activities.* In contrast, to set your mind on earthly things is to live by the values of the world system that sets itself up in opposition to God and his ways.

What does this putting to death "whatever belongs to your earthly nature" (Col. 3:5) look like in concrete daily life? It does not mean wearing a hair shirt or taking ice-cold baths for spiritual discipline. Paul has just said that "severe treatment of the body" does no good in stopping sin (Col. 2:23).

First, it does mean putting to death "fornication, impurity, passion, evil desire, and greed (which is idolatry)" (Col. 3:5). We are called to turn aside from sexual immorality (as if degraded sex could bring you an upgraded life) and greed (as if more stuff could bring more life). The assumption, of course, is that there is in fact a proper place for gratification of sexual desire (marriage between a man and a woman) and a proper degree for the gratification of material desire (that which results from trust in God, diligent labor, generosity toward neighbors, and thankfulness for God's provision).

Second, Paul states, "You must get rid of all such things—anger, wrath, malice, slander, and abusive language from your mouth. Do not lie to one another, seeing that you have stripped off the old self with its practices and have clothed yourselves with the new self, which is being renewed in knowledge according to the image of its creator" (Col. 3:8–10). The words "to one another" indicate that Paul is speaking to the church, that is, to those who are believers in Christ. Does this mean it is permissible to continue to lie to others outside the church? No, for Paul is not talking about a change in behavior alone but a change in heart and mind. It is difficult to imagine that having taken on a "new self," you could somehow put back on the old self when dealing with nonbelievers. Once you "get rid of all such things," they are not meant to be brought back.

Of these vices, three are particularly relevant to the workplace: greed, anger, and lying. These three vices can appear within what would otherwise be legitimate business pursuits.

- *Greed* is the unbridled pursuit of wealth. It is proper and necessary for a business to make a profit or for a nonprofit organization to create added value. But if the desire for profit becomes boundless, compulsive, excessive, and narrowed to the quest for personal gain, then sin has taken hold.

- *Anger* can appear in conflict. It is necessary for conflict to be expressed, explored, and resolved in any workplace. But if conflict is not dealt with openly and fairly, it degenerates into unresolved anger, rage, and malicious intent, and sin has taken hold.

- *Lying* can result from promoting the company's prospects or the product's benefits inaccurately. It is proper for every enterprise to have a vision for its products, services, and its organization that goes beyond what is presently in place. A sales brochure ought to describe the product in its highest, best use, along with warnings about the product's limitations. A stock prospectus ought to describe what the company hopes to accomplish if it is successful, and also the risks the company may encounter along the way. If the desire to portray a product, service, company, or person in a visionary light crosses the line into deception (an unbalanced portrayal of risks vs. rewards, misdirection, or plain fabrication and lies), then sin once again reigns.

Paul does not attempt to give universal criteria to diagnose when the proper virtues have degenerated into vices, but he makes it clear that Christians must learn to do so in their particular situations.

When Christians "put to death" (Col. 3:5) the person they used to be, they are then to put on the person God wants them to be, the person God is recreating in the image of Christ (Col. 3:10). This does not consist in hiding one's self away for constant prayer and worship (though we are all called to pray and worship, and some may be called to do that as a full-time vocation). Rather, it means reflecting God's own virtues of "compassion, kindness, humility, meekness and patience" (Col. 3:12) in whatever we do.

An encouraging word comes from Paul's exhortation to "put up with one another" (Col. 3:13, as it may be translated). Most translations read "bear with one another," but this does not fully capture Paul's point. He seems to be saying that there are all kinds of people in the church (and we can readily apply this to the workplace as well) with whom we won't naturally get along. Our interests and personalities are so different there can be no instinctive bonding. But we put up with them anyway. We seek their good, we forgive their sins, and we endure their irritating idiosyncrasies. Many of the character traits Paul extols in his letters can be summarized in the phrase "He/she works well with others." Paul himself mentions co-workers Tychicus, Onesimus, Aristarchus, Mark, Justus, Epaphras, Luke, Demas, Nympha, and Archippus (Col. 4: 7–17). Being a "team player" is not simply a résumé-enhancing cliché. It is a foundational Christian virtue. Both putting to death the old and putting on the new are immensely relevant to daily work. Christians are meant to show the new life of Christ in the midst of a dying world, and the workplace is perhaps the main forum where that type of display can take place.

- Christians may be tempted, for example, to fit in at work by participating in the gossip and the complaining that permeates many workplaces. It is likely that every workplace has people whose on- and off-hours actions make for juicy stories. It is not lying, is it, to repeat the stories?

- It is likely that every workplace has unfair policies, bad bosses, nonfunctional processes, and poor channels of communication. It is not slander, is it, to complain about those grievances?

Paul's exhortation is to live differently even in fallen workplaces. Putting to death the earthly nature and putting on Christ means directly confronting people who have wronged us, instead of gossiping about them behind their backs (Matt. 18:15–17). It means working to correct inequities in the workplace and forgiving those that do occur.

Someone may ask, "Don't Christians run the risk of being rejected as cheerless, 'holier-than-thou' types if they don't speak the way others do?" This could be the case if such Christians disengage from others in an effort to show that they are better than other people. Co-workers will sniff that out in a second. But if, instead, Christians are genuinely clothing themselves with Christ, the vast majority of people will be happy to have them around. Some may even secretly or openly appreciate the fact that someone they know is at least trying to live a life of "compassion, kindness, humility and patience" (Col. 3:12). In the same way, Christian workers who refuse to employ deception (whether by rejecting misleading advertising copy or balking at glorified Ponzi schemes) may find themselves making some enemies as the price of their honesty. But it also is possible that some co-workers will develop a new openness to Jesus' way when the Securities and Exchange Commission knocks on the office door.

Doing Our Work as for the Lord (Colossians 3:17, 23)

So what does it mean to do our work "in the name of the Lord Jesus" (Col. 3:17)? How do we do our work wholeheartedly, "as done for the Lord and not for your masters" (Col. 3:23)? To do our work in the name of the Lord Jesus carries at least two ideas:

- We recognize that we represent Jesus in the workplace. If we are Christ-followers, how we treat others and how diligently and faithfully we do our work reflects on our Lord. How well do our actions fit with who he is?

- Working in "Jesus' name" also implies that we live recognizing that he is our master, our boss, the one to whom we are ultimately accountable. This leads into Paul's reminder that we work for the Lord and not for human masters. Yes, we most likely have horizontal accountability on the job, but the diligence we bring to our work comes from our recognition that, in the end, God is our judge.

When Paul writes, "Whatever you do, in word or deed, do everything in the name of the Lord Jesus, giving thanks to God the Father through him" (Col. 3:17), we can understand this verse in two ways: a shallow way and a deeper way. The shallow way is to incorporate some Christian signs and gestures into our workplace, like a Bible verse posted on our cubicle or a Christian bumper sticker on our truck. Gestures like this can be meaningful, but in and of themselves they do not constitute a Christ-centered work-life. A deeper way to understand Paul's challenge is to pray specifically for the work we are in the midst of doing: "God, please show me how to respect both the plaintiff and the defendant in the language I use in this brief."

An even deeper way would be to begin the day by imagining what our daily goals would be if God were the owner of our workplace. With this understanding of Paul's injunction, we would do all the day's work in pursuit of goals that honor God. The apostle's point is that in God's kingdom, our work and prayer are integrated activities. We tend to see them as two separate activities that need to be balanced. But they are two aspects of the same activity—namely, working to accomplish what God wants accomplished in fellowship with other people and with God.

Of Slaves and Masters, Ancient and Contemporary (Colossians 3:18–4:1)

At this point, Colossians moves on to what is called a "household code," a set of specific instructions to wives and husbands, children and parents, slaves and masters. These codes were common in the ancient world. In the New Testament, they occur in one form or another six times—in Galatians 3:28; Ephesians 5:15–6:9; Colossians 3:15–4:1; 1 Timothy 5:1–22; 6:1–2; Titus 2:1–15; and 1 Peter 2:11–3:9. For our purposes here, we will explore only the section in Colossians having to do with the workplace (slaves and masters in 3:18–4:1).

If we are to appreciate fully the value of Paul's words here for con- temporary workers, we need to understand a bit about slavery in the ancient world. Western readers often equate slavery in the ancient world with the chattel system of the pre-Civil War South in the United States, a system notorious for its brutality and degradation. At the risk of over- simplification, we might say that the slave system of the ancient world was both similar to and different from the former U.S. system. On the one hand, in ancient times, foreign captives of war laboring in mines were arguably far worse off than slaves in the American South. At the other extreme, however, some slaves were well-educated, valued mem- bers of the household, serving as physicians, teachers, and estate manag- ers. But all were considered to be their master's property, so that even a household slave could be subject to horrific treatment with no necessary legal recourse.[4]

What relevance does Colossians 3:18–4:1 have for workers today? Much as working for wages or a salary is the dominant form of labor in developed countries today, slavery was the dominant form of labor

---

[4] For a fuller description of first-century slavery, see S. Scott Bartchy, *MAL- LON CHRESAI: First Century Slavery and the Interpretation of 1 Corinthians 7:21*, Society of Biblical Literature Dissertation Series No. 11 (Missoula: Scholars Press, University of Montana, 1973; reprinted by Wipf & Stock, 2003).

in the Roman Empire. Many slaves worked in jobs we would recognize today as occupations, receiving food, shelter, and often a modicum of comforts in return. Slaveholders' power over their slaves was similar in some respects to, but much more extreme than, the power that employers or managers have over workers today The general principles Paul puts forward concerning slaves and masters in this letter can be applied to modern managers and employers, provided we adjust for the significant differences between our situation now and theirs then.

What are these general principles? First, and perhaps most important, Paul reminds slaves that their work is to be done in integrity in the presence of God, who is their real master. More than anything else, Paul wants to recalibrate the scales of both slaves and masters so that they weigh things with the recognition of God's presence in their lives. Slaves are to work "fearing the Lord" (Col. 3:22) because "you serve the Lord Christ" (Col. 3:24). In sum, "Whatever your task, put yourselves into it [literally, "work from the soul"] as done for the Lord and not for your masters" (Col. 3:23). In the same way, masters [literally, "lords"] are to recognize that their authority is not absolute—they "have a Master in heaven" (Col. 4:1). Christ's authority is not bounded by church walls. He is Lord of the workplace for both workers and bosses.

This has several practical consequences. Because God is watching workers, there is no point in being a mere "people pleaser" who gives "eye service" (literal translations of the Greek terms in Col. 3:22). In today's world, many people try to curry favor with their bosses when they are around, and then slack off the moment they are out the door. Apparently it was no different in the ancient world. Paul reminds us that the Ultimate Boss is always watching and that reality leads us to work in "sincerity of heart," not putting on a show for management, but genuinely working at the tasks set before us. (Some earthly bosses tend to figure out over time who is playacting, though in a fallen world slackers can sometimes get away with their act.)

The danger of being caught for dishonesty or poor work is reinforced in Colossians 3:25. "For the wrongdoer will be paid back for whatever wrong has been done, and there is no partiality." Because the previous verse refers to a reward from God for faithful service, we may presume that God is also in view as the punisher of the wicked. However, it is noteworthy here that the fear of punishment is not the prime motivation. We do not do our jobs well simply to avoid a bad performance review. Paul wants good work to spring out of a good heart. He wants people to work well because it is the right thing to do. Implicit here is an affirmation of the value of labor in God's sight. Because God created us to exercise dominion over his creation, he is pleased when we fulfill that by pursuing excellence in our jobs. In this sense, the words "Whatever your task, put yourselves into it!" (Col. 3:23) are as much a promise as a command. By the spiritual renewal offered us in Christ by God's grace, we can do our jobs with zest.

Colossians 3:22–4:1 makes it clear that God takes all labor seriously, even if it is done under imperfect or degrading conditions. The cataracts removed by a well-paid ocular surgeon matter to God. So, too, does the cotton picked by a sharecropper or even by a plantation slave. This does not mean that exploitation of workers is ever acceptable before God. It does mean that even an abusive system cannot rob workers of the dignity of their work, because that dignity is conferred by God himself.

One of the noteworthy things about the New Testament household codes is the persistence of the theme of *mutuality*. Rather than simply telling subordinates to obey those over them, Paul teaches that we live in a web of interdependent relationships. Wives and husbands, children and parents, slaves and masters all have obligations to one another in Christ's body. Thus hard on the heels of the commands to slaves comes a directive to masters: "Masters, treat your slaves justly and fairly, for you know that you also have a Master in heaven" (Col. 4:1). Whatever leeway the Roman legal system might have given to slaveholders, they must ultimately answer in God's courtroom where justice for all is upheld. Of course, justice and fairness must be interpreted afresh in each new situation. Consider the concept of the "just wage," for example. A just wage on a Chinese farm may have a different cash value from a just wage in a Chicago bank. But there is mutual obligation under God for employers and employees to treat each other justly and fairly.

Philemon

A workplace application of the theme of mutuality is alluded to in Colossians and discussed in Paul's letter to Philemon, the shortest book of the Bible. In Colossians, Paul mentions "the faithful and beloved brother," Onesimus (Col. 4:9). The letter to Philemon tells us that Onesimus was the slave of a Christian named Philemon (Philem. 16). Onesimus apparently escaped, became a Christian himself, and then became an assistant to Paul (Philem. 10–11, 15). Under Roman law, Philemon had the right to punish Onesimus severely. On the other hand, Paul—as an apostle of the Lord—had the right to command Philemon to release Onesimus (Philem. 17–20). But instead of resorting to a hierarchy of rights, Paul applies the principle of mutuality. He requests that Philemon forgive Onesimus and forego any punishment, while at the same time requesting that Onesimus return voluntarily to Philemon. He asks both men to treat each other as brothers, rather than as slave and master (Philem. 12–16). We see a three-way application of the principle of mutuality among Paul, Philemon, and Onesimus. Each of them owes something to the others. Each of them has a claim over the others. Paul seeks to have all the debts and claims relinquished in favor of a mutual respect and service. Here we see how Paul applies the virtues of compassion, kindness, humility, gentleness, patience, and putting up with each other's faults (Col. 3:12–13) in a real workplace situation.

Paul's use of persuasion, rather than command (Philem. 14), is a further application of the mutuality principle. Rather than dictating a solution to Philemon, Paul approaches him with respect, lays out a persuasive argument, and leaves the decision in Philemon's hands. Philemon could not have failed to notice Paul's clear desire and his statement that he would be following up with him (Philem. 21). But Paul manages the communication in an artful way that provides a model for resolving issues in the workplace.

Conclusion to Colossians and Philemon

Colossians gives us a picture of God's standard for work. As employees, we serve our employers with integrity, giving a full measure of work for the wages we are paid (Col. 3:23). As supervisors, we treat those under us as God treats us—with compassion, kindness, humility, gentleness, and patience (Col. 3:12). God intends that our work be done in reciprocal relationships, in which each party contributes to, and benefits from, the overall work. But even if the other parties fail in their reciprocal duty, Christians fulfill their obligations (Col. 3:22–4:1). Following Jesus' example, we offer forgiveness in the face of conflict (Col. 1:13) and we lay aside our power when necessary for the good of others (Col. 1:20). This does not mean we lack rigorous standards or accountability, or that Christians in business and other workplaces cannot compete vigorously and successfully. It does mean that we offer forgiveness. It does mean that Christians cannot always go along with what their workplace culture deems acceptable (Col. 3:1–3), particularly if it would lead to unfair or unjust treatment of a co-worker or employee (Col. 4:1). We see this illustrated in the case of Onesimus and Philemon. Whatever our work, we strive for excellence, for we do it in the name of the Lord Jesus, not merely for human masters, knowing that we will receive an inheritance from the Lord as a reward (Col. 3:23–24).

1 & 2 THESSALONIANS AND WORK

Introduction to 1 & 2 Thessalonians

"We work hard, so you don't have to." That's the advertising line for a modern bathroom cleaner,[1] but—with a little adjustment—it might have fit well as a slogan for some Christians in the ancient city of Thessalonica. "Jesus worked hard so I don't have to." Many believed the new way of living offered by Jesus was cause to abandon the old way of living that involved hard work, and so they became idle. As we will see, it is difficult to know exactly why some Thessalonians were not working. Perhaps they mistakenly thought that the promise of eternal life meant that this life no longer mattered. But these idlers were living off the largesse of the more responsible members of the church. They were consuming the resources intended to meet the needs of those genuinely unable to support themselves. And they were becoming troublesome and argumentative.

In his letters to the Thessalonians, Paul would have none of this. He made it clear that Christians need to keep at their labors, for the way of Christ is not idleness but service and excellence in work.

Thessalonica and Its Church

The capital of the Roman province of Macedonia and a major Mediterranean seaport, Thessalonica had a population of over 100,000.[2] Not only did it have a natural harbor, it was also located on key north-south trade routes and on the busy east-west Ignatian Way, the road that linked

---

[1] From a U.S. television commercial for a bathroom cleaning product with "Scrubbing Bubbles."

[2] Rainer Riesner, *Die Frühzeit des Apostels Paulus: Studien zur Chronologie, Missionsstrategie, und Theologie,* in Wissenschaftliche Untersuchungen zum Neuen Testament (Tübingen: Mohr, 1994), 301.

Italy to the eastern provinces. People were drawn from nearby villages to this great city, which was a bustling center of trade and philosophy. Thessalonica's natural resources included timber, grain, continental fruits, and gold and silver (although it is questionable if the gold and silver mines were operational in the first century AD). Thessalonica was also notably pro-Roman and self-governing, and it enjoyed the status of a free city. As its citizens were Roman citizens, it was exempt from paying tribute to Rome.[3]

The church at Thessalonica was founded by Paul and his co-workers Timothy and Silas during the so-called Second Missionary Journey in AD 50. God worked mightily through the missionaries and many became Christians. While some Jews believed (Acts 17:4), the majority of the church was Gentile (1 Thess. 1:9–10). Although it did have some relatively wealthy members—such as Jason, Aristarchus, and a number of "the leading women" (Acts 17:4, 6–7; 20:4)—it seems to have consisted largely of manual laborers (1 Thess. 4:11) and presumably some slaves. In 2 Corinthians, Paul states that the "churches of Macedonia" were marked by "extreme poverty" (2 Cor. 8:2), and the Thessalonian church would have been included in their ranks.

The precise situations that prompted Paul to write these two letters[4] have been much debated. For our purposes, it is sufficient to say that Paul wanted to encourage believers who were trying to live faithful Christian lives in a hostile pagan environment. In addition to the typical struggles against things such as idolatry and sexual immorality, they were also confused about the end times, the role of everyday work, and the life of faith.

---

[3] For further information on Thessalonica, see Gene L. Green, *The Letters to the Thessalonians* (Grand Rapids: Eerdmans, 2002), 1–47.

[4] Paul's authorship of 2 Thessalonians is taken at face value here (2 Thess. 1:1; 3:17), although the question of authorship has been debated at length, as is discussed in the general-purpose commentaries. (By comparison, Paul's authorship of 1 Thessalonians is not significantly disputed.) In any case, the question of authorship has little or no bearing on the contribution of either letter to understanding work in the Christian perspective.

Working Faith, Finishing Up, and Keeping the Faith (1 Thessalonians 1:1–4:8; 4:13–5:28; 2 Thessalonians 1:1–2:17)

Working Faith (1 Thessalonians 1:1–4:8)

In light of the problems with work that will emerge later in the epistles, it is interesting that Paul begins by remembering the Thessalonians' "work of faith, and labor of love, and perseverance of hope in our Lord Jesus Christ" (1 Thess. 1:3). Paul writes his letters carefully and, if nothing else, this opening serves to introduce the vocabulary of labor into his discussion. The verse reminds us that faith is not simply mental assent to the propositions of the gospel. It takes work. It is the total life response to the commands and promises of the God who renews us and empowers us through his Spirit. The Thessalonians are apparently responding well in their daily lives of faith, though they need encouragement to keep living lives of moral purity (1 Thess. 4:1–8).

The question of work emerges directly again in chapter 2, when Paul reminds the Thessalonians that he and his friends worked night and day so that they would not be a burden to them (1 Thess. 2:9). Paul says this so that the Thessalonians will be certain how much Paul cares for them, despite his physical absence from them. But it may also serve as a rebuke to members of the congregation who might have been sponging off of the generosity of fellow believers. If anyone had a right to receive from the Thessalonians, it was Paul, whose hard work had mediated the new life of Christ to them in the first place. But Paul took no money from the Thessalonians in compensation. Instead, he labored hard as a tradesman as an expression of his concern for them.

Finishing Up (1 Thessalonians 4:13–5:28)

Paul goes on to console the Thessalonians about those in their community who have died. They are not dead but only sleeping, because Jesus will awaken them on the last day (1 Thess. 4:13–18). They don't need to worry about when that day will come, because that is in the Lord's hands. Their only concern should be to keep walking in the light, remaining faithful and hopeful in the midst of a dark world (1 Thess. 5:11). Among other things, this means that they are to respect those who work (1 Thess. 5:12–13; the reference may be to the "work" of instructing people in the faith, but it could equally be workers in general, in distinction from the idlers) and to rebuke the slackers among them (1 Thess. 5:14). The promise of eternal life is more reason—not less—for working hard in this life. This is so because the good we do lasts forever, because "we belong to the day" of Christ's redemption, rather than to the night of oblivion (1 Thess. 5:4–8). Each day gives us an opportunity to "do good to one another and to all" (1 Thess. 5:15).

Keeping the Faith (2 Thessalonians 1:1–2:17)

As 2 Thessalonians opens, we learn that Paul is still happy that the Thessalonians are maintaining their faith in a difficult environment, and he encourages them that Jesus will return to set all things right (2 Thess. 1:1–12). But some of them are worried that the Day of the Lord has already come and that they have missed it. Paul lets them know that the day has not come, and in fact it will not come until Satan makes one last grand attempt to deceive the world through "the lawless one" (presumably the figure we commonly call "the Antichrist"; 2 Thess. 2:8). They should take heart: God will judge Satan and his minions, but bring eternal blessing to his beloved children (2 Thess. 2:9–17).

Faithful Work (1 Thessalonians 4:9–12 and 2 Thessalonians 3:6–16)

First Thessalonians 4:9–12 and 2 Thessalonians 3:6–16 address work directly.[5] Scholars continue to debate precisely what led to the

---

[5] On the relationship between the instructions about sexual purity in 1 Thessalonians 4:3–7 and the instructions in 4:9–12, see Traugott Holtz, *Der erste Brief an die Thessalonicher* in Evangelisch-katholischer Kommentar zum Neuen Testament (Zürich: Benziger, 1986), 161–62; Karl P. Donfried, "The Cults of Thessalonica and the Thessalonian Correspondence," *New Testament Studies* 31, no. 3 (1985): 341–42; and Earl J. Richard, *First and Second Thessalonians, Sacra Pagina* (Collegeville: Michael Glazier, 1995), 194, 202.

problem of idleness at Thessalonica. While we are most concerned to hear how Paul wants the problem solved, it will be helpful to make some suggestions as to how the problem might have arisen in the first place.

- Many believe that some of the Thessalonians had stopped working because the end times were at hand.[6] They might have felt that they were already living in God's kingdom, and there was no need to work; or they might have felt that Jesus was coming at any minute, and thus there was no point to work. The Thessalonian letters do speak quite a bit about misunderstandings about the end times, and it is interesting that the passages about idleness in 1 Thessalonians 4:9–12 and 2 Thessalonians 3:6–16 both come in the context of teaching on the end times. On the other hand, Paul does not make an explicit connection between idleness and eschatology.

- Others have suggested a "nobler" reason for the idleness: people had given up their day jobs in order to preach the gospel. (One could see how such a move would be eased if they had the sort of eschatological fervor noted in the first view.)[7] Such would-be evangelists stand in sharp contrast to Paul, the foremost evangelist, who nonetheless works with his own hands lest he become a burden to the church. The churches in Macedonia were known

---

[6] See, e.g., G. Agrell, *Work, Toil and Sustenance: An Examination of the View of Work in the New Testament, Taking into Consideration Views Found in Old Testament, Intertestamental and Early Rabbinic Writings*, trans. S. Westerholm and G. Agrell (Lund: Ohlssons, 1976), 122–23; John A. Bailey, "Who Wrote II Thessalonians?" *New Testament Studies* 25, no. 02 (1979): 137; Peter Müller, *Anfänge der Paulusschule: Dargestellt am zweiten Thessalonicherbrief und am Kolosserbrief, in Abhandlungen zur Theologie des Alten und Neuen Testaments* (Zürich: Theologischer, 1988), 162–67; K. Romanuik, "Les Thessaloniciens étaient-ils des parassuex?" *Ephemerides Theologicae Lovanienses* 69 (1993): 142–45; and A. M. Okorie, "The Pauline Work Ethic in 1 and 2 Thessalonians," *Deltio Biblikon Meleton* 14 (1995): 63–64.

[7] See, e.g., John Barclay, "Conflict in Thessalonica," *Catholic Biblical Quarterly* 55 (1993), 512–30; Trevor J. Burke, *Family Matters: A Socio-Historical Study of Kinship Metaphors in 1 Thessalonians* (London: T&T Clark, 2003), 213ff.

for their evangelistic zeal, yet it remains unclear whether the idle in Thessalonica were necessarily using their free time for evangelistic labors.

- A third view sees the problem as more sociological than theological.[8] Some manual laborers were unemployed (whether through laziness, persecution, or general economic malaise) and had become dependent on the charity of others in the church. They discovered that life as the client of a rich patron was significantly easier than life as a laborer slogging out a day's work. The injunction for Christians to care for one another formed a ready pretext for them to continue in this parasitic lifestyle.

It is difficult to choose between these different reconstructions. They all have something in the letters to support them, and it is not hard to see modern analogies in the modern church. Many people today undervalue everyday work because "Jesus is coming soon, and everything is going to burn up anyway." Plenty of Christian workers justify substandard performance because their "real" purpose in the workplace is to evangelize their co-workers. And questions of unhelpful dependence on the charity of others arise both in the local context (e.g., pastors who are asked to give money to a man whose mother died . . . for the third time this year) and the global context (e.g., the question of whether some foreign aid does more harm than good).

We can, however, move forward even in the absence of complete certainty about what was going on to cause the problem of idleness in Thessalonica. First, we may note that the views above share a common, but false, supposition—namely, *Christ's coming into the world has radically diminished the value of everyday labor.* People were using

---

[8] See, with various points of emphasis, D. E. Aune, "Trouble in Thessalonica: An Exegetical Study of 1 Thess. 4:9–12, 5:12–14 and II Thess. 6:6–15 in Light of First-Century Social Conditions," ThM thesis (Regent College, 1989); Colin R. Nicholl, *From Hope to Despair: Situating 1 & 2 Thessalonians*, Society for New Testament Studies Monograph Series (Cambridge: Cambridge University Press, 2004), 157ff; Ben Witherington, *1 and 2 Thessalonians: A Socio-Rhetorical Commentary* (Grand Rapids, Eerdmans, 2006), 43–44.

some aspect of Christ's teaching—whether it was his second coming, or his commission to evangelize the world, or his command for radical sharing in the community—to justify their idleness. Paul will have none of it. Responsible Christian living embraces work, even the hard work of a first-century manual laborer. It is equally clear that Paul is disturbed when people take advantage of the generosity of others in the church. If people can work, they should work. Finally, the idleness of Christians appears to have given the church a bad name in the pagan community.

Christians Are Expected to Work
(1 Thessalonians 4:9–12; 5:14)

Christians are Expected to Work, to the Degree They are Able

Paul highlights that God expects every Christian who can work to do so (1 Thess. 4:11–12). He exhorts the Thessalonians "to work with [their] hands" (1 Thess. 4:11) and to "have need of no one" (1 Thess. 4:12). Rather than evading work, the Thessalonian Christians are to be industrious, laboring so as to earn their own living and thereby avoid putting undue burdens on others. Being a manual laborer in a Greco-Roman city was a hard life by modern and ancient standards, and the thought that it might not be necessary must have been appealing. However, abandoning work in favor of living off the work of others is unacceptable. It is striking that Paul's treatment of the issue in 1 Thessalonians is framed in terms of "brotherly love" (1 Thess. 4:9). The idea is plainly that love and respect are essential in Christian relationships, and that living off the charity of others unnecessarily is unloving and disrespectful to the charitable brother(s) or sister(s) concerned.

It is important to remember that work does not always mean paid work. Many forms of work—cooking, cleaning, repairing, beautifying, raising children, coaching youth, and thousands of others—meet the needs of family or community but do not receive remuneration. Others—the arts come to mind—may be offered free of charge or at prices too low to support those who do them. Nonetheless, they are all work.

Christians are not necessarily expected to earn money, but to work to support themselves, their families, and the church and community.

The Creation Mandate Remains in Effect

The mandate in Genesis 2:15 ("The Lord God took the man and put him in the Garden of Eden to work it and keep it") is still in effect. The work of Christ has not eliminated or supplanted humanity's original work, but it has made it more fruitful and ultimately valuable. Paul may have the Genesis 2:15 text in view when he refers to the idlers with the Greek adjective, adverb, and verb derived from the root *atakt-* ("disorder") in 1 Thessalonians 5:14, 2 Thessalonians 3:6 and 11, and 1 Thessalonians 5:7, respectively. These words all portray the idlers' behavior as disorderly, betraying an "irresponsible attitude to the obligation to work."[9] The order being violated may well be the work mandate in Genesis 2.

Paul's insistence on the ongoing validity of work is not a concession to a bourgeois agenda, but rather reflects a balanced perspective on the already/not yet of God's kingdom. Already, God's kingdom has come to earth in the person of Jesus, but it has not yet been brought to completion (1 Thess. 4:9–10). When Christians work with diligence and excellence, they demonstrate that God's kingdom is not an escapist fantasy, but a fulfillment of the world's deepest reality.

Christians are to Work with Excellence

Given the importance of work, Christians are to be the best workers they can be. Failure to work with excellence may bring the church into disrepute. Many Cynics in the Greco-Roman world abandoned their jobs, and this behavior was widely regarded as disgraceful.[10] Paul is aware that

---

[9] Gerhard Kittel, Gerhard Friedrich, and Geoffrey William Bromiley, eds., *Theological Dictionary of the New Testament* (Grand Rapids: Eerdmans, 1985), 8:48. For a helpful study, see Ceslas Spicq, "Les Thessalonicien 'inquiets' etaient-ils des parrassuex?" *Studia theologica* 10 (1956): 1–13.

[10] See Abraham J. Malherbe, *The Letters to the Thessalonians*, Anchor Bible (New York: Doubleday, 2000), 258–29; idem, *Paul and the Thessalonians: The Philosophic Tradition of Pastoral Care* (Philadelphia: Fortress, 1987), 99–107.

when Christians evade their responsibility to work, the standing of the church as a whole is undermined. In 1 Thessalonians 4:11–12, Paul is evidently concerned that society is getting a wrong view of the church. In the context of the Greco-Roman world his concern makes a lot of sense, for what was happening in the Thessalonian church not only fell below society's standards for decency, but it also made the charitable Christians look gullible and foolish. Paul does not want Christians to fall below society's standards in regard to work, but rather to exceed them. Moreover, by failing to fulfill their proper role within society, these Christians are in danger of stirring up more anti-Christian rumors and resentment. Paul is eager that those who persecute the church should have no legitimate grounds for their hostility. With respect to work, Christians should be model citizens. By placing the idlers under discipline, the church would effectively be distancing itself from their defective behavior.

Mature Christians are to set an example for young Christians by modeling a good work ethos. Although Paul knew it was the right of the minister of the gospel to be financially supported (1 Tim. 5:17–18), he himself refused to take advantage of this (1 Thess. 2:9; 2 Thess. 3:8). He saw the need to set new converts an example of what the Christian life looked like, and that meant joining them in manual labor. Itinerant philosophers in the Greco-Roman world were often quick to burden their converts financially, but Paul did not care about having an easy life or projecting an image of superiority over his spiritual charges. Christian leadership is servant leadership, even in the arena of work.

Manual Labor and Hard Work Are Honorable

The positive view of hard work that Paul was promoting was countercultural. The Greco-Roman world had a very negative view of manual labor.[11] To some extent, this is understandable in view of how unpleasant urban workhouses were. If the idle in Thessalonica were in fact

---

[11] So, e.g., Gustav Wohlenberg, *Der erste und zweite Thessalonicherbrief,* Kommentar zum Neuen Testament (Leipzig: Deichert, 1903), 93; I. Howard Marshall, *1 and 2 Thessalonians,* New Century Bible Commentary (London: Marshall, Morgan, and Scott, 1983), 223; Ernest Best, *The First and Second Epistles to the Thessalonians,* 2nd ed., British New Testament Conference (London: A & C Black, 1986), 338.

unemployed manual laborers, it is not difficult to appreciate how easy it would have been to rationalize this exploitation of the charity of their brothers and sisters over against returning to their workhouses. After all, weren't all Christians equal in Christ? However, Paul has no time for any rationalizations. He approaches the matter from an understanding strongly rooted in the Old Testament, where God is portrayed as creating Adam to work, and Adam's manual labor is not divorced from worship, but rather is to be a form of worship. In Paul's assessment, manual labor is not beneath Christians, and Paul himself had done what he demands that these idle brothers do. The apostle plainly regards work as one way believers may honor God, show love to their fellow-Christians, and display the transforming power of the gospel to outsiders. He wants the idle brothers to embrace his perspective and to set an impressive, not disgraceful, example for their unbelieving contemporaries.

Those Truly Unable to Work Should Receive Assistance (1 Thessalonians 4:9–10)

Paul is an advocate of social welfare and charitable giving, but only for those who are genuinely in need. Paul clearly regards the early manifestations of generous provision for the unemployed Thessalonian Christians as appropriate expressions of Christian love (1 Thess. 4:9–10). Moreover, even after the expression of love on the part of some was selfishly exploited by others, he still calls for the church to continue to do good by giving to those in genuine need (2 Thess. 3:13). It would have been easy for the benefactors to become disillusioned with charitable giving in general and to shy away from it in the future.

The key factor in determining whether someone unemployed was worthy of charity or welfare was a willingness to work (2 Thess. 3:10). Some who are perfectly capable of working do not, simply because they do not want to—they do not merit financial or material assistance. On the other hand, some cannot work due to some incapacity or mitigating circumstance—they are clearly deserving of financial and material assistance. Verse 13 assumes that there are legitimate charitable cases in the Thessalonian church.

In practice, of course, it is difficult to determine who is slacking versus who is willing yet genuinely unable to work or find a job. If the close-knit members of the Thessalonian church had a hard time discerning who among them was worthy to receive financial support, imagine how much more difficult it is for a far-flung modern city, province, or nation. This reality has led to deep divisions among Christians with respect to social policy, as practiced by both the church and the state. Some prefer to err on the side of mercy, providing relatively easy access and generous, sometimes long-term, benefits to people in apparent financial hardship. Others prefer to err on the side of industriousness, requiring relatively stringent proof that the hardship is due to factors beyond the recipient's control, and providing benefits limited in amount and duration. A particularly thorny question has been support of single mothers with small children and of all persons unemployed for long periods during economic recessions. Does such support provide care to the most vulnerable members of society, particularly children in vulnerable families? Or does it subsidize a culture of removal from working society, to the detriment of both the individual and the community? These are difficult, challenging issues. Biblical passages such as those in the Thessalonian letters should figure deeply in Christians' social and political understanding. Our conclusions may put us in opposition with other Christians, but this is not necessarily a cause to withdraw from political and social participation. Yet we should engage politics and social discourse with respect, kindness, a healthy humility that our views are not infallible, and an awareness that the same passages may lead other believers to contrary conclusions. The Thessalonian letters reveal God's values and insights applied to the ancient Thessalonian context. But they do not constitute an indisputable social or party program as applied in today's very different contexts.

It is clear that Paul has in mind both that all the Thessalonian Christians should work to the degree they are able and that the church should take care of those in genuine need. He wants the finances of the benefactors in the church to be used strategically rather than frittered away idly. Indeed, if the idle get back to work, they too will be in a position to be givers rather than recipients, and the church's capacity to spread the gospel and minister to the poor and needy within and without the church will be increased. The biblical insistence that Christians should work so as to be self-supporting wherever possible ultimately has in view the extension of the kingdom of God on the earth.

Idleness (2 Thessalonians 3:6–15)

Idleness Is a Matter for the Christian Community, Not Just the Individual

The words of 2 Thessalonians 3:10 are critical. "If anyone is not willing to work, neither should he eat." God regards shirking work as a grave offense, so grave that the church is called to correct its idle members. Paul exhorts the church to "warn" those dodging their obligation to work (1 Thess. 5:14) and issues a "command in the name of our Lord Jesus Christ" in 2 Thessalonians 3:6–15 that the church impose disciplinary measures on the offending brothers. The discipline is relatively harsh, which underscores that idleness was no minor foible in Paul's assessment. The church is called upon to "disassociate from" those who shirk their responsibility to work, presumably meaning that they are to avoid including them when they gather together in Christian fellowship. The intention was, of course, to induce a short, sharp shock in the offending brothers by alienating them, and thereby bring them back into line.

Idleness Leads to Mischief

The negative consequences of shirking work go beyond the burden placed on others. Those who evade work often end up spending their time on unwholesome pursuits. Paul's exhortation of the Thessalonian manual laborers "to aspire to lead a quiet life" and "to attend to [their] own business" (1 Thess. 4:11) hints at what 2 Thessalonians 3:11 states explicitly, "We hear that some among you are living in a disorderly manner, not doing their own work but being busybodies." The Greek word *periergazomai* ("busybodies") refers to meddling in other people's affairs.[12] A similar

---

[12] Johannes P. Louw and Eugene A. Nida, *Greek-English Lexicon of the New Testament Based on Semantic Domains,* 2 vols. (New York: UBS, 1988),

thought is expressed by Paul in 1 Timothy 5:13, where Paul says of younger widows being supported by the church that "they are not only lazy, but also gossips and busybodies, talking about things they should not." It seems that the Thessalonian idlers were interfering in other people's business and being argumentative. Idleness breeds trouble.

Conclusion to 1 & 2 Thessalonians

Workplace themes are woven into the fabric of the Thessalonian letters. They are most visible in several explicit passages, and especially in 2 Thessalonians. Underlying both letters is the principle that Christians are called to work to the degree they are able. Work is required to put food on the table, so eaters should be workers. Moreover work is honorable, reflecting God's intent for humanity in creation. Not everyone has equal capacity to work, so the measure of work is not the quantity of achievement, but the attitude of service and commitment to excellence. Therefore, those who work as hard and as well as they are able have a full share in the community's bounty. In contrast, those who shirk their duty to work should be confronted by the church. If they continue to be idle, they should not be supported by others' means. As a last resort, they should even be removed from the community, for idleness leads to not only consuming the fruit of others' labor, but also to active disruption of the community by meddling, gossip, and obstruction.

---

§88.243; Horst Balz and Gerhard Schneider, *Exegetical Dictionary of the New Testament,* 3 vols., trans. J. W. Medendorp and Douglas W. Scott (Grand Rapids: Eerdmans, 1990–93), 3:73.

THE PASTORAL EPISTLES AND WORK

Introduction to the Pastoral Epistles

The Pastoral Epistles were written to leaders in the early church. Yet much of what they say applies to Christians in other workplaces as well. In applying them to nonchurch work, the critical task will be to reflect on the similarities and differences between churches and other workplace organizations. Both types are voluntary organizations (generally) with structures and goals. Both are ultimately governed by the same Lord. Both are composed of human beings made in God's image. Both face major challenges at times, yet are designed to endure and adapt in future generations. These similarities suggest that many of the same biblical principles will apply to each, as will be discussed in depth.

From ancient times, the letters 1 Timothy, 2 Timothy, and Titus have been grouped together as the "Pastoral Epistles." These letters outline the qualification, development, and promotion of leaders; organizational structures for the care, compensation, and discipline of members; and the setting and execution of individual and organizational goals. They are concerned with the good governance, effectiveness, and growth of an organization—in particular, the church. In 1 Timothy 3:14–15 Paul expresses the major theme of all three letters: "I am writing these instructions to you so that, if I am delayed, you may know how one ought to behave in the household of God, which is the church of the living God, the pillar and bulwark of the truth."

But there are differences as well. The church has as its mission the calling and equipping of people to commit their lives to Christ, to serve his kingdom, and to worship God. It was instituted by God as the body of Christ, and he has promised it will remain a going concern until Christ's return. Other organizations have different missions, such as creating economic value (businesses), protecting members (labor unions), educating children and adults (schools and universities), and administering defense, justice, and other civic needs (governments). They are instituted as bodies (corporations or states) by charters and constitutions, and may come in and out of existence. These differences do not mean that other organizations are inferior to the church, but rather that each kind must be respected for its particular mission. Nonetheless, the Pastoral Epistles provide fertile material for reflecting on how relationships within nonchurch workplaces ought to be created and maintained, while highlighting the special role of the church community. Although the Pastoral Epistles are concerned primarily with organizations, they do not necessarily exclude those who work in families, sole proprietorships, and other such workplaces. For brevity, from here forward, the term "workplace" will be used to mean the nonchurch workplace only.

1 Timothy: Working for Order in God's Household

Each of the three Pastoral Epistles takes the form of a letter from the Apostle Paul giving counsel to one of his co-workers.[1] In 1 Timothy, Paul gives instructions his younger colleague Timothy about how to minister within the church and how to deal with false teachers. Yet the last words of the letter—"Grace be with you [plural]" (1 Tim. 6:21)—indicate that the letter is meant to be overheard by the whole church in Ephesus so that all may benefit from Paul's counsel to Timothy.

Because the letters share some common themes, we will combine our discussion of related passages among the letters. The themes will be explored according to the order they first arise in the Pastoral Epistles.

---

[1]This discussion will assume Pauline authorship of the Pastoral Epistles, although this is not critical for applying the letters to the workplace. For a thorough discussion of this perspective on authorship, see William D. Mounce, *Pastoral Epistles*, vol. 4, *Word Biblical Commentary* (Nashville: Thomas Nelson, 2000), lxxxiii–cxxix.

True Belief Leads to a Sound Organization
(1 Timothy 1:1–11, 18–20; 3:14–16)

One of the repeated and stressed themes in 1 Timothy is the tight connection between belief and behavior, or teaching and practice. Sound, or "healthy," teaching leads to godliness while false teaching is unproductive at best and damning at worst. From the onset of the letter, Paul charges Timothy to "instruct certain people not to teach any different doctrine" (1 Tim. 1:3) because this different doctrine, along with myths and genealogies, does not promote "the divine training that is known by faith" (1 Tim. 1:4).

Paul is speaking of the importance of sound doctrine in the church, but his words apply just as well to the workplace. W. Edwards Deming, one of the founders of continuous quality improvement, called his methods a "system of profound knowledge." He said, "Once the individual understands the system of profound knowledge, he will apply its principles in every kind of relationship with other people. He will have a basis for judgment of his own decisions and for transformation of the organizations that he belongs to."[2] Knowledge of the deepest truth is essential in any organization.

Luke Timothy Johnson has translated 1 Timothy 1:4 more transparently as "God's way of ordering reality as it is apprehended by faith."[3] The church is—or should be—ordered according to God's way. Few would dispute that. But should other organizations also be ordered according to God's way? The first-century Greco-Roman world believed that society should be ordered according to "nature." Thus if nature is the creation of God, then God's way of ordering creation should be reflected in the way society is ordered as well. As Johnson observes, "There is no radical discontinuity between the will of God and the structures of society. The structures of the *oikos* (household) and the

---

[2] W. Edwards Deming, *The New Economics for Industry, Government, Education,* 2nd ed. (Cambridge, MA: MIT Press, 2000), 92.

[3] Luke Timothy Johnson, *The First and Second Letters to Timothy: A New Translation with Introduction and Commentary, The Anchor Yale Bible Commentaries* (New York: Doubleday, 2001), 149.

ekklēsia (church) are not only continuous with each other, but both are parts of the dispensation [administration] of God in the world."[4] Workplaces, households, and churches all reflect the one and only ordering of creation.

A true understanding of God's ways is essential in all workplaces. For example, a prominent theme in Creation is that human beings were created good. Later we fell into sin, and a central Christian truth is that Jesus came to redeem sinners. Workers are therefore human beings who sin, yet who may experience redemption and become good as God always intended. The truth about goodness, sin, and redemption needs to be factored into organizational practices. Neither churches nor workplaces can function properly if they assume that people are good only and not sinners. Accounts need to be audited and harassment needs to be stopped. Customer service needs to be rewarded. Priests and pastors, employees and executives need to be supervised. Similarly, neither churches nor workplaces can assume that people who err or sin should be discarded automatically. The offer of redemption—and practical help to make the transformation—needs to be made. In churches, the focus is on spiritual and eternal redemption. Nonchurch workplaces are focused on a more limited redemption related to the mission of the organization. Probation, performance improvement plans, retraining, reassignment to a different position, mentoring, and employee assistance programs—as opposed to immediate firing—are examples of redemptive practices in certain workplaces, especially in the West. The particulars of what is actually redemptive will vary considerably of course depending on the type of organization, its mission, the surrounding cultural, legal, and economic environment, and other factors.

If Christians in the marketplace are to understand how God would have them and those around them act (cf. 1 Tim. 3:15), they must understand God's revelation in the Bible and believe in it. Truth leads to love (1 Tim. 1:5), while false doctrine promotes "speculations" (1 Tim. 1:4), "controversy" (1 Tim. 6:4), and spiritual destruction (1 Tim. 1:19). Knowledge of God's ways as revealed in his word cannot be the domain of Bible scholars alone, nor is biblical understanding relevant

---

[4] Johnson, *The First and Second Letters to Timothy*, 149.

only within the church. Christian workers must also be biblically informed so that they can operate in the world according to God's will and for his glory.

All Christians have a leadership role, regardless of their place in the organization. Executives usually have the greatest opportunity to shape the strategy and structure of an organization. All workers have continual opportunities to develop good relationships, produce excellent products and services, act with integrity, help others develop their abilities, and shape the culture of their immediate work groups. Everyone has a sphere of influence at work. Paul advised Timothy not to let his perceived lack of status prevent him from trying to make a difference. "Let no one despise your youth, but set the believers an example in speech and conduct, in love, in faith, in purity" (1 Tim. 4:12).

It is interesting to note that some of this reality is already perceived in contemporary workplaces. Many organizations have "mission statements" and "core values." These words mean roughly the same thing to secular organizations as "beliefs" or "doctrine" mean to churches. Organizations, like churches, pay close attention to culture. This is further evidence that what workers believe or what an organization teaches affects how people behave. Christians in the workplace should be at the forefront of shaping the values, mission, and culture of the organizations in which we participate, to the degree we are able.

Prayer, Peace, and Order are Needed at Work as in Church (1 Timothy 2:1–15)

Paul begins this chapter by urging that "supplications, prayers, intercessions, and thanksgivings be made for everyone, for kings and all who are in high positions" (1 Tim. 2:1–2). The aim of this prayer is that Christians "may lead a quiet and peaceable life in all godliness and dignity" (1 Tim. 2:2). Presumably, these first-century rulers had the power to make life difficult and disruptive for Christians. So Paul urges Christians to pray for their civic rulers. Prayer, peace, and order are Christians' first instruments of engagement with the secular world.

Again we see that Paul's instructions are grounded in the oneness of God, the singularity of Christ as mediator, Christ's universal ransom, and God's universal desire for all to be saved (1 Tim. 2: 3–7). Christ is the Lord of creation and the Savior of the world. His realm includes every workplace. Christians should be praying for all of those who are in their particular workplace, especially those who have supervisory roles "in high positions." Christians should strive to do their jobs without disrupting the work of others, without calling undue attention to themselves, and without constantly challenging authority—in other words, working "in all godliness and dignity" (1 Tim. 2:2). For Christians, this kind of peaceable and submissive behavior is not motivated by fear, people-pleasing, or social conformity, but by a healthy appreciation for the order God has established and by a desire for others to "come to the knowledge of the truth" (1 Tim. 2:4). As Paul says elsewhere, "God is a God not of disorder but of peace" (1 Cor. 14:33).

Does this conflict with the duty to be at the forefront of shaping the mission and core values of our workplaces? Some Christians try to shape missions and values through confrontation around controversial issues, such as same-sex partner benefits, health insurance exclusion for abortion and/or contraceptives, union organizing, display of religious symbols and the like. If successful, this approach may help shape the mission and value of the organization. But it often disrupts others' work, breaks the peace, and disrespects supervisors' authority.

What is needed instead is a more personal, deeper, and more respectful engagement of organizational culture. Rather than clashing over health benefits, could Christians invest in friendships with co-workers and become a source of counseling or wisdom for those facing major life decisions? Instead of pushing the boundary between freedom of speech and harassment, could Christians do their assigned work with such excellence that co-workers ask *them* to explain the source of their strength? Instead of arguing about peripheral issues such as holiday decorations, could Christians help improve the core activities of their workplaces, such as job performance, customer service, and product design, and so earn the respect of those around them? In answering such questions, we can remember that Paul's advice to Timothy is balanced, not self-contradictory. Live in peace and cooperation with those around us. Seek to influence others by serving them, not trying to lord it over them. Isn't that what the King of kings did?

Integrity and Relational Ability are Key Leadership Qualities (1 Timothy 3:1–13; Titus 1:5–9)

First Timothy 3:1–13 is well known and finds a parallel in Titus 1:5–9. Both 1 Timothy 3:1–7 and Titus 1:5–9 lay out qualifications for elders and overseers,[5] whereas 1 Timothy 3:8–13 describes qualifications for deacons including, possibly, women deacons. A variety of qualifications is given, but the common thread seems to be moral integrity and ability to relate well to people. Competence to teach, though mentioned as a qualification for elders (1 Tim. 3:2; Titus 1:9), doesn't receive the same emphasis overall. In these lists, we again observe the connection between the household and the church: managing one's family well is viewed as requisite experience for managing God's household (1 Tim. 3:4–5, 12; Titus 3:6; cf. 1 Tim. 3:15). We will reflect on this connection more in a subsequent section.

As noted earlier, different organizations have different missions. Therefore, the qualifications for leadership are different. It would be a misapplication of this passage to use it as a general qualifications list for workplaces. "Serious" may not be the right qualification for a tour guide, for example. But what about the priority given to moral integrity and relational ability? Moral qualities such as "above reproach," "clear conscience," "faithful [or trustworthy] in all things," and relational qualities such as "hospitable," "not quarrelsome," and "temperate" are much more prominent than specific skills and experience.

If this is true for church leadership, does it also apply for workplace leadership? The well-publicized moral and relational failings of a few prominent business and government leaders in recent years have made integrity, character, and relationships more important than ever in most workplaces. It is no less important to properly develop and select leaders in workplaces than it is in churches. But as we prepare for jobs and careers, do we put a fraction of as much effort into developing ethical character and relational abilities as into developing specialized skills and accumulating credentials?

---

[5] See Philip H. Towner, *The Letters to Timothy and Titus*, New International Commentary on the New Testament (Grand Rapids: Eerdmans, 2006), 246–47, for a brief discussion of the terms "elder" (Greek *presbyteros*) and "overseer" (*episkopos*).

Interestingly, many of the early church leaders were also workplace leaders. Lydia was a dealer in the valuable commodity of purple dye (Acts 16:14, 40). Dorcas was a garment maker (Acts 9:26–41). Aquila and Priscilla were tentmakers (or leatherworkers) who became business partners with Paul (Acts 18:2–3). These leaders were effective in the church after having already proven effective in the workplace and gaining the respect of the wider community. Perhaps the basic qualifications of leadership in church, work, and civic spheres have much in common.

God's Creation Is Good (1 Timothy 4:1–5)

First Timothy affirms "God's way of ordering reality" and that this divine ordering has implications for how Christians should behave in their households, churches, and—by an extension of the text's logic—in their workplaces. The clearest affirmation of God's creation order comes in 1 Timothy 4:1–5. In 1 Timothy 4:4 Paul plainly declares, "Everything created by God is good." This is a clear echo of Genesis 1:31, "God saw everything that he had made, and indeed, it was very good." Within the context of the letter, this sweepingly positive appraisal of creation is used to combat false teachers who are forbidding marriage and certain foods (1 Tim. 4:3). Paul counters their teaching by asserting that these things ought to be received with thanksgiving (1 Tim. 4:3, 4). Food, and anything else in God's creation, is "sanctified" by God's word and by prayer (1 Tim. 4:5). This does not mean that God's word and prayer *make* God's creation good when it isn't good already. Rather, in thankfully acknowledging God as the creator and provider of all things, a Christian sets apart created things such as food for a holy and God-honoring purpose. As a Christian, it is possible even to eat and drink to the glory of God (1 Cor. 10:31).

This affirmation of creation means there is no created material that is inherently evil to work with, and no job engaged with creation that is unacceptable for Christians to do if it doesn't violate God's will. In other words, a Christian can dig wells, design computer chips, scrub toilets, walk on the moon, fix cell phones, plant crops, or harvest trees to the glory of God. None of these jobs or materials is inherently evil. Indeed, each job can please God. This may seem intuitive to those in the modern

Western world who don't struggle much with asceticism, as the ancient Greek and Roman world did. But 1 Timothy 4:4 reminds even us not to view the material realm as something neutral in moral value or to view something such as technology, for example, as inherently evil. The goodness of all of God's creation allows us to live and work in joyful freedom, receiving all things as from God's hands.

Good Relationships Arise from Genuine Respect (1 Timothy 5:1–6:2; Titus 2:1–10)

First Timothy 4:6–16 is full of specific directives Paul gives to Timothy. It would be helpful for Christian workers to remember that training in godliness is a crucial component of professional development (cf. 1 Tim. 4:8). We quickly move from this section, however, to the next, which runs from 1 Timothy 5:1–6:2. Again, this section is similar to a section of Titus 2:1–10. Being a member of the church should not lead us to exploit others within the church (cf. 1 Tim. 5:16; 6:2), but rather should lead us to work harder to bless them. This applies also at work.

In particular, these two passages describe how men and women, old and young, masters and slaves, ought to behave within the family of God. The first two verses of this section in 1 Timothy are important ones. "Do not speak harshly to an older man, but speak to him as to a father, to younger men as brothers, to older women as mothers, to younger women as sisters—with absolute purity." This command does not flatten any distinction between families and the church (as 1 Tim. 5:4, 8 makes clear), but it does suggest that the kindness, compassion, loyalty, and purity that should characterize our most intimate family relationships should also characterize our relationships with those in God's family, the church.

Paul's exhortation to "absolute purity" reminds us that violations of sexual boundaries do occur in families and churches, as well as in workplaces. Sexual harassment can go unchallenged—even unnoticed by those not being harassed—in workplaces. We can bring a blessing to every kind of workplace by paying deeper attention to how men and women are treated, and by raising a challenge to inappropriate and abusive words and actions.

Is it right to think of a workplace as a family? No and yes. No, it is not truly a family, for the reasons portrayed so amusingly in the television series *The Office*. Membership in a workplace is conditional on fulfilling a role adequately. Unlike family members, employees who no longer meet the approval of management are subject to dismissal. Employment is not permanent, not "something you somehow haven't to deserve."[6] It would be naive—possibly even abusive—to pretend that a workplace is a family.

Yet in certain senses, a workplace can be *like* a family, if that term is used to describe the respect, commitment, open communication, and care that family members should show toward one another. If Christians were known for treating co-workers likewise, it could be a great point of the church's redemptive service to the world. Mentoring, for example, is an extremely valuable service that experienced workers can offer to newer colleagues. It resembles the investment that parents make in their children. And just as we protect family members from abuse and exploitation, Christ's love impels us to do the same for people in our workplaces. Certainly we should never engage in abuse or exploitation of others at work, because we imagine we owe them less respect or care than we do to family (or church) members. Rather, we should strive to love all our neighbors, including those in the workplace, as our family and as ourselves.

Godliness with Contentment Is Great Gain (1 Timothy 6:3–10, 17–19)

The last section of 1 Timothy is packed with powerful exhortations and warnings for rich Christians. (We will skip over Paul's charges to Timothy in verses 11–16 and 20, which are directed to Timothy in his particular situation.) First Timothy 6:3–10 and 17–19 have direct workplace applications. In reading and applying these passages, however, we must avoid two common mistakes.

First, this passage does not teach that there is no "gain" to be had by being godly. When Paul writes that those who are "depraved in mind and

---

[6] Robert Frost, "The Death of the Hired Man," line 125, in *North of Boston* (New York: Henry Holt, 1915).

bereft of the truth" imagine that "godliness is a means of gain" (1 Tim. 6:5), what he is denouncing is the mind-set that godliness necessarily leads to financial gain in this life or that godliness should be pursued for the sake of immediate, financial gain. The folly of this thinking is threefold:

1. God often calls his saints to suffer material want in this life and, therefore, God's people should not set their hope on the "uncertainty of riches" (1 Tim. 6:17).

2. Even if someone were to gain great riches in this life, the gain is short-lived because, as John Piper puts it, "There are no U-Hauls behind hearses" (1 Tim. 6:7).[7]

3. Craving wealth leads to evil, apostasy, ruin, and destruction (1 Tim. 6:9–10).

Note carefully, however, that Paul encourages his readers to know that there is *great gain* in godliness when it is combined with contentment in the basic necessities of life (1 Tim. 6:6, 8). Our God is a God "who richly provides us with everything for our enjoyment" (1 Tim. 6:17). Paul commands the righteous rich "to do good, to be rich in good works, generous, and ready to share" (1 Tim. 6:18)—not to sell everything they have and become poor. They are to be rich in good works *so that* they might store up for themselves "the treasure of a good foundation for the future, so that they may take hold of the life that really is life" (1 Tim. 6:19). In other words, godliness *is* a means of gain as long as that gain is understood as life and blessings in the presence of God and not only more money now. Paul's exhortation in 1 Timothy 6:18–19 is similar to Jesus' teaching, "Store up for yourselves treasures in heaven, where neither moth nor rust consumes and where thieves do not break in and steal" (Matt. 6:20; cf. Matt. 19:21; Luke 12:33).

The second mistake to avoid is thinking that this passage and its condemnation of a love for money means that no Christian worker should

---

[7] John Piper, *Desiring God: Meditations of a Christian Hedonist*, rev. and exp. ed. (Colorado Springs: Multnomah, 2003), 188.

ever seek a raise or promotion or that no Christian business should try to make a profit. There are many reasons why someone could want more money; some of them could be bad but others could be good. If someone wanted more money for the status, luxury, or ego boost it would provide, then this would indeed fall under the rebuke of this section of Scripture. But if someone wanted to earn more money in order to provide adequately for dependents, to give more to Christ-honoring causes, or to invest in creating goods and services that allow the community to thrive, then it would not be evil to want more money.[8] To reject the love of money is not to oppose every desire to be successful or profitable in the workplace.

2 Timothy: Encouragement for a Faithful Worker

The letter of 2 Timothy, like 1 Timothy, is addressed from the Apostle Paul to his younger co-worker and is perhaps the last written letter we have from Paul. Unlike 1 Timothy, however, 2 Timothy appears to be more of a personal letter in which Paul encourages Timothy and gives him a solemn charge to remain faithful even after Paul has departed. The very fact that 2 Timothy has been preserved and included in the Christian canon of Scripture indicates, however, that this personal letter has significance beyond its original, particular context.

Cultures Can Persist for Generations (2 Timothy 1:1–2:13; 3:10–17)

One of the striking features of 2 Timothy is the theme of generational faithfulness. Toward the beginning of the letter Paul reminds Timothy of the faith that lived in his grandmother, his mother, and then in Timothy himself (2 Tim. 1:5). This progression suggests that the faithful witness and example of Timothy's grandmother and his mother were among the means God used to bring Timothy to faith. This understanding is confirmed later in the letter when Paul encourages Timothy to "continue

---

[8] See Wayne Grudem's important book, *Business for the Glory of God: The Bible's Teaching on the Moral Goodness of Business* (Wheaton, IL: Crossway, 2003), for a more detailed account of this assertion.

in what you have learned and firmly believed, knowing from whom you learned it, and how from childhood you have known the sacred writings" (2 Tim. 3:14–15a). Paul too, as a member of an older generation, is a model for Timothy to follow. Paul writes, "Join with me in suffering for the gospel" (2 Tim. 1:8), "Hold to the standard of sound teaching that you have heard from me" (2 Tim. 1:13), and "You have observed my teaching, my conduct, my aim in life, my faith, my patience, my love, my steadfastness, my persecutions" (2 Tim. 3:10–11a).

Not only has Timothy received teaching from previous generations, but Paul intends for him to pass on what he has learned to succeeding generations as well: "What you have heard from me through many witnesses entrust to faithful people who will be able to teach others as well" (2 Tim. 2:2). This theme challenges Christian workers to consider what kind of legacy they want to leave behind at their places of employment and in their industry. The first step toward leaving a positive legacy is to do your job faithfully and to the best of your ability. A further step would be to train your successor, so that whoever is going to replace you one day is prepared to do your job well. A Christian worker should be humble enough to learn from others and compassionate enough to teach patiently. Yet in the end, Christian workers must ask themselves whether they left a legacy of redemption in words and deeds.

The generational aspect of 2 Timothy applies not just to individuals, but to all kinds of corporations, both for-profit and not-for-profit. The corporate form was created so that organizations could outlive the individuals who comprise them, without the need to reform the entity at each transition. One of the basic principles of financial audits is that the corporation must be a "going concern," meaning that it must be operating in a sustainable manner.[9] When an organization's pay practices, debt burden, risk management, financial control, quality control, or any other factor become seriously detrimental to its sustainability, its leaders have a duty to call for change.

---

[9] *AG ISA (NZ) 570 The Auditor-General's Statement On Going Concern*, The Auditor-General's Auditing Standards, Controller and Auditor-General, http://www.oag.govt.nz.

This does not mean that corporations should never merge, disband, or otherwise go out of existence. Sometimes an organization's mission has been fulfilled, its purpose becomes obsolete, or it ceases to provide significant value. Then its existence may need to end. But even so, its leaders have a responsibility for the legacy the corporation will leave in society after it is dissolved. For example, a number of companies expose their retirees to the risk of poverty because they have not adequately funded their pension liabilities. Municipal and state governments are even more prone to this failing. Organizations have a duty—from both a biblical and a civic perspective—to ask whether their operations are shifting liabilities to future generations.

Likewise, 2 Timothy suggests organizations must operate in an environmentally and socially sustainable way. To depend for success on unsustainable resource extraction or environmental pollution is a violation of the generational principle. To deplete the community's "social capital"—meaning the educational, cultural, legal, and other social investments that provide the educated workforce, means of transactions, peaceable society, and other factors that workplace organizations depend on—would also be unsustainable. To a certain degree, workplaces invest in environmental and social capital by paying taxes to support governments' environmental and social programs. But perhaps they would have more reliable access to environmental and social capital if they did more to create sustainable systems on their own initiative.

Guard the Tongue (2 Timothy 2:14–26)

In the next section, Paul counsels Timothy with a number of exhortations that could directly apply to the workplace. Paul repeatedly warns Timothy to avoid "wrangling over words" (2 Tim. 2:14), "profane chatter" (2 Tim. 2:16), and "stupid and senseless controversies" (2 Tim. 2:23). This is a good reminder for Christian workers that not all talk at the water cooler is profitable, even if it is not downright evil. Are the conversations we engage in and the ways we speak helpful to those around us? Do our words serve as ambassadors of reconciliation and redemption (2 Cor. 5:20)? Unhelpful conversations can spread like gangrene

(2 Tim. 2:17), lead to ruin and impiety (2 Tim. 2:14, 16), and breed quarrels (2 Tim. 2:23). One thinks of similar warnings in James (cf. James 3:2–12) about the destructive potential of words.

In fact, the most important form of witness to Jesus is the way Christians talk with co-workers when we're not talking about Jesus. Three words of gossip may destroy three thousand words of praise and piety. But Christians who consistently encourage, appreciate, respect, and demonstrate care by their words are a powerful witness for Jesus, even if their words are seldom directly about him. Humility and strictly avoiding judgmentalism are the surest ways to avoid stupid and senseless controversies.

Paul also urges Timothy to "shun youthful passions and pursue righteousness" (2 Tim. 2:22). This may remind us that employees bring their personal difficulties with them to work. Alcohol and drug abuse affect virtually every workplace, and "fully one quarter of employees who use the Internet visit porn sites during the workday . . . and hits are highest during office hours than at any other time of day."[10] Another exhortation that can be applied to Christian workers is that "the Lord's servant must not be quarrelsome but kindly to everyone, an apt teacher, patient, correcting opponents with gentleness" (2 Tim. 2:24–25a). Indeed, much of the portrait Paul sketches of Timothy in this letter could be held up as something for Christian workers to strive toward. Paul, writing a letter to Timothy, becomes a support network for him. We might ask what kinds of support networks today's organizations would do well to provide for workers.

The Time of Difficulty Is Now (2 Timothy 3:1–9)

The fourth and final chapter of 2 Timothy consists mainly of Paul's charge to Timothy, Paul's reflections on his life, and specific instructions and greetings. There is no doubt that some of this material could apply indirectly to work. However, we will examine just one more paragraph in the letter—2 Timothy 3:1–9.

The first verse gives the main point of the paragraph. "In the last days distressing times will come" (2 Tim. 3:1). What the description that

---

[10] Anna Kuchment, "The Tangled Web of Porn in the Office," *Newsweek* (December 8, 2008), http://www.newsweek.com/2008/11/28/the-tangled-web -of-porn-in-the-office.

follows makes clear, however, is that Timothy is living in these last days already (cf. 2 Tim. 3:2, 5). That the "last days" are already upon all of us is the clear and consistent witness of the New Testament (see Acts 2:17; Heb. 1:2; James 5:3; 2 Pet. 3:3). Christians need to be prepared for the hardship and suffering associated with these last days. Paul later warns, "Indeed, all who want to live a godly life in Christ Jesus will be persecuted" (2 Tim. 3:12).

This is a sobering reminder to those Christians who work in environments that may be difficult but are far less threatening than the social realities of the first century or of many places in the world today. As Christians, we should expect mistreatment at work, injustice, prejudice, opposition, and mockery. If we experience few of these things, we have cause for rejoicing, but we should not allow our present benevolent working conditions to lull us to sleep. The days may be coming when being faithful to Christ at work results in more than strange looks and jokes behind our backs. Indeed, workers at any time might find themselves pressured to act unethically or contrary to God's word. At that time it will be seen more clearly whether we have more than a mere "outward form of godliness" (2 Tim. 3:5). If we do, we know that God will stand by us and give us strength (2 Tim. 4:17).

Titus: Working for Good Deeds

Paul's letter to Titus is the final Pastoral Epistle and has many similarities to 1 and 2 Timothy. (For Titus 1:5–9, see 1 Timothy 3:1–13 above. For Titus 2:1–10, see 1 Timothy 5:1–6:2 above.) In this letter, Paul reminds Titus that he had left him in Crete to "put in *order* what remained to be done" (Titus 1:5). Like Timothy, Titus needed to combat false teaching, install proper leadership, and ensure that the people were devoted to good works (Titus 3:8, 14).

Be Zealous for Good Works (Titus 2:11–3:11)

We have already considered the leadership qualifications described in Titus 1:5–9 and the church family relationships described in Titus

2:1–10 in previous sections of this chapter. Much of the rest of this letter can be summarized by Paul's vision of God's people being zealous
for good works. This vision certainly applies to Christian workers—they
should be devoted to good works at their place of employment. Good
works, of course, means work done in such a way as to please God, more
than self or anyone else. Good works carry out the purposes of God seen
in his creation of the world. They make the world a better place. They
help redeem the brokenness of the world and reconcile people to one another and to God. Devotion to this kind of work drives Christian workers
more than a passion to do their jobs well for the sake of money or performance reviews. Yet for Christians to have this godly passion for good
works, we must understand what makes these good works possible and
why we are doing them. The letter to Titus addresses both of these issues.

First, it is critical for Christians to remember that God "saved us, not
because of any works of righteousness that we had done, but according
to his mercy" (Titus 3:5). Our conduct in the workplace, at home, or anywhere else does not establish our relationship with God. We cannot "earn"
his mercy. Nevertheless, the letter to Titus teaches unambiguously that
God's grace not only forgives our sins but also trains us to "renounce impiety and worldly passions, and in the present age to live lives that are self-
controlled, upright, and godly" (Titus 2:12). Jesus gave himself so that he
might both "redeem us from all iniquity" and "purify for himself a people
of his own who are zealous for good deeds" (Titus 2:14). The wonderful
section of Titus 3:3–7 describes God's mercy in conversion and justification as the foundation of the command for believers "to be subject to rulers
and authorities, to be obedient, to be ready for every good work, to speak
evil of no one, to avoid quarreling, to be gentle, and to show every courtesy
to everyone" (Titus 3:1–2). The grace that God grants in salvation results
in a godly (though imperfect) life of obedience and good works. Would
reminding ourselves of this reality throughout the day's activities lead
us to become more effective servants of Christ and stewards of creation?

Second, this section in Titus reminds us of the purposes of good
works. Good works are intended to meet the needs of others and to make
our corner of God's creation productive (Titus 3:14). This hearkens back
to the mandate to till the ground and make it fruitful (Gen. 2:5, 15). Good

works serve God and people, but they are not done primarily to earn favor from God and people. The production of good works is not the opposite of faith but the essential consequence of faith. It is the response we give to God after our "rebirth and renewal by the Holy Spirit" (Titus 3:5). "Having been justified by his grace, we might become heirs according to the hope of eternal life" (Titus 3:7), and as a result we devote ourselves "to good works; these things are excellent and profitable to everyone" (Titus 3:8). Paul is not talking about giving speeches, passing out tracts, or telling people about Jesus. He is talking about good works in the ordinary sense of doing things that others recognize will meet people's needs. In workplace terms, we could say he means something such as helping new co-workers come up to speed on the job, more so than inviting them to join a Bible study.

Moreover, godly behavior is encouraged "so that the word of God may not be discredited" (Titus 2:5) and so that opponents will have nothing evil to say (Titus 2:8). Positively stated, godly behavior is encouraged for Christians, "so that in everything they may be an ornament to the doctrine of God our Savior" (Titus 2:10). Right doctrine leads to good works, and good works make the truth of God attractive to others. That is the aim behind Christian workers' devotion to good works at their jobs—to live out by their actions the truth they proclaim with their lips. This may prove a powerful witness both to defuse antipathy toward Christians and to appeal to nonbelievers to follow Christ themselves.

Throughout the letter Paul gives practical instructions for doing good works. Most of them can be applied to the workplace. We take our cue on this from the letter itself. Nothing about the instructions to older women, for example (be reverent, don't slander, don't become slaves to drink, teach what is good), suggests that *only* older women should follow them, just as nothing about Timothy's instructions suggests they can be applied at church. (On the question of whether instructions to slaves can be applied to modern employees, see Colossians 3:18–4:1 in "Colossians & Philemon and Work.")

Almost any workplace looking for a statement of organizational values and good practices could begin well simply by cutting and pasting from Titus. Paul's advice includes the following:

Respect

- Show respect to everyone (Titus 3:1).

- Be hospitable (Titus 1:8).

- Be kind (Titus 2:5).

- Don't engage in conflict about inconsequential matters (Titus 3:9).

- Don't be arrogant, quick tempered, or obstinate (Titus 1:7, 8).

- Don't use violence as a means of supervision (Titus 1:7). Use gentleness instead (Titus 3:1).

Self-control

- Be self-controlled (Titus 1:8; 2:6).

- Don't be greedy for gain (Titus 1:7).

- Don't become addicted to alcohol (Titus 1:7; 2:3).

- Avoid envy and ill will (Titus 3:3).

Integrity

- Act with integrity (Titus 1:8).

- Love goodness (Titus 1:8).

- Submit to those in authority over you in the workplace (Titus 2:9). Obey the civil authorities (Titus 3:1).

- Respect others' property (Titus 2:10) and manage it faithfully on their behalf if you have a fiduciary duty (Titus 2:5).

Authority and Duty

- Exercise the authority you have been given (Titus 2:15).

- Be prudent (Titus 1:8).

- Silence rebellious people, idle talkers, deceivers, slanderers, and those who intentionally cause personal divisions (Titus 1:10; 2:3; 3:10). Rebuke them sharply (Titus 1:13).

- Train others under your leadership in these same virtues (Titus 2:2–10).

We must be careful not to turn such applications into a simplistic dogma. "Be prudent," therefore, need not mean there is never an appropriate time to take educated risks. "Use gentleness" need not mean never to exercise power. These are applications to modern workplaces from an ancient letter for the church. These items from Titus serve as an excellent source of principles and values well suited to good leadership, both in the church and in the workplace.

Conclusion to the Pastoral Epistles

The Pastoral Epistles focus on organization, relationships, and leadership within the household of God. The household of God begins with the family, extends to the church, and often applies to the workplace. The God who called into being the family and the church is also the God who created work. He established an order for the church that brings peace, prosperity, and stability. The same—or a highly similar—order can bring the same blessings to other workplaces.

The first order of business for any organization is to understand the true nature of God and his creation. Every workplace needs to be founded on the "pillar and bulwark of the truth" (1 Tim. 3:15), if it is to be effective. We begin by recognizing the truth of God's good creation, the fall of humanity, the persistence of God's grace in the world, the mission of Christ and the church to redeem the world and its people, and the promise of the restoration of God's perfect order. We acknowledge that redemption arises solely as God's free gift, resulting in our desire and ability to perform all sorts of good works. We thereby make the world productive and serve the needs of people.

The Pastoral Epistles lay out the implications of this truth for organizing the church, with special concern for leadership and good relationships. The considerations also apply to nonchurch workplaces, as long as the differences between the church and other organizations are respected. Workplace applications of the Pastoral Epistles are not always direct nor obvious, but the truth found in these letters, when prayerfully applied to the workplace, can manifest God's way of ordering reality and thereby bring glory to the one "whom no one has ever seen or can see" (1 Tim. 6:16).

HEBREWS AND WORK

Introduction to Hebrews

The book of Hebrews offers a deep foundation for understanding the value of work in the world. It offers practical help for overcoming evil at work, developing a rhythm of work and rest, serving the people we work among, enduring hardship, bringing peace to our workplaces, persevering over long periods, offering hospitality, cultivating a life-giving attitude toward money, and finding faithfulness and joy in workplaces where Christ's love often seems in short supply.

The book is founded on one essential message: Listen to Jesus! Some believers were feeling pressure to give up on the Messiah and turn back toward the old covenant. Hebrews reminds them that Jesus the King, through whom the world was created, is also the consummate High Priest in the heavenly places, who has initiated a new and better covenant with concrete consequences on earth. He is the ultimate sacrifice for sin, and he is the ultimate intercessor for us in our daily lives. We should look nowhere else for salvation but entrust ourselves to Christ, living in obedience to him until he brings us into the transformed and renewed city of God. There we will find an eternal Sabbath rest, which is not the cessation of work, but the perfection of the cycle of work and rest intended by God in the seven days of creation.

Christ Created and Sustains the World (Hebrews 1:1–2:8)

Critical to the theology in Hebrews is that Christ created and sustains the world. He is the Son "through whom [God] also created the worlds" (Heb. 1:2). Therefore, Hebrews is a book about Christ, the creator, at work in his workplace, the creation. This may be surprising to some who are used to thinking of the Father alone as creator. But Hebrews is consistent with the rest of the New Testament (e.g., John 1:3; Col. 1:15–17) in naming Christ as the Father's agent in creation.[1] Because Christ is fully God, "the reflection of God's glory and the exact imprint of God's very being" (Heb. 1:3), the writer of Hebrews can refer interchangeably to Christ or the Father as the Creator.

How then does Hebrews portray Christ at work in the creation? He is a builder, founding the earth and constructing the heavens. "In the beginning, Lord, you founded the earth, and the heavens are the work of your hands" (Heb. 1:10). Moreover, he sustains the present creation, bearing "all things by his powerful word" (Heb. 1:3). "All things," of course, includes us as well: "For every house is built by someone, but the builder of all things is God . . . and we are his house if we hold firm" (Heb. 3:4, 6). All of creation is built by God through his Son. This strongly affirms the creation as the primary place of God's presence and salvation.

The imagery of God as worker continues throughout Hebrews. He put together or pitched the heavenly tent (Heb. 8:2; by implication, Heb. 9:24), constructed a model or a blueprint for Moses' tabernacle (Heb. 8:5), and designed and built a city (Heb. 11:10, 16; 12:22; 13:14). He is a judge in a court as well as the executioner (Heb. 4:12–13; 9:28; 10:27–31; 12:23). He is a military leader (Heb. 1:13), a parent (Heb. 1:5; 5:8; 8:9; 12:4–11), a master who arranges his household (Heb. 10:5), a farmer (Heb. 6:7–8), a scribe (Heb. 8:10), a paymaster (Heb. 10:35; 11:6), and a physician (Heb. 12:13).[2]

It is true that Hebrews 1:10–12, quoting Psalm 102, does point out a contrast between the Creator and the creation:

> In the beginning, Lord, you founded the earth, and the heavens are the work of your hands; they will perish, but you remain; they will all wear out like clothing; like a cloak you will roll them up, and like clothing they will be changed. But you are the same, and your years will never end.

---

[1] See Sean M. McDonough, *Christ as Creator: Origins of a New Testament Doctrine* (Oxford: Oxford University Press, 2010).

[2] See Robert Banks, *God the Worker: Journeys into the Mind, Heart and Imagination of God* (Sutherland, NSW: Albatross Books, 1992), and R. Paul Stevens, *The Other Six Days* (Grand Rapids: Eerdmans, 2000), 118–23, for a discussion of God's work.

This is very much in keeping with the emphasis on the transitory nature of life in this world, and the need to seek the enduring city of the new heavens and the new earth. Nonetheless, the emphasis of Hebrews 1:10–12 is on the might of the Lord and his deliverance, rather than the fragility of the cosmos.[3] The Lord is at work in the creation.

Human beings are not only *products* of God's creation, we are also sub-creators (or co-creators, if you prefer) with him. Like his Son, we are called to the work of ordering the world. "What are human beings that you are mindful of them, or mortals, that you care for them? You have made them for a little while lower than the angels; you have crowned them with glory and honor, *subjecting all things under their feet*" (Heb. 2:6–8, quoting Ps. 8).[4] If it sounds a bit vain to regard mere humans as participants in the work of creation, Hebrews reminds us, "Jesus is not ashamed to call them brothers and sisters" (Heb. 2:11).

Therefore, our work is meant to resemble God's work. It has undying value. When we make computers, airplanes, and shirts, sell shoes, underwrite loans, harvest coffee, raise children, govern cities, provinces, and nations, or do any kind of creative work, we are working alongside God in his work of creation.

The point is that Jesus is the one supremely in charge of the creation, and only by working in him are we restored to fellowship with God. This alone makes us capable to take our place again as vice-regents of God on earth. Humanity's created destiny is being achieved in Jesus, in whom we find the pattern (Heb. 2:10; 12:1–3), provision (Heb. 2:10–18), end, and hope for all our work. Yet we do so during a time marked by frustration and the menace of death, which threatens our very existence with meaninglessness (Heb. 2:14–15). Hebrews acknowledges that "we do not yet see everything in subjection" to the ways of his kingdom (Heb. 2:8). Evil plays a strong hand at present.

---

[3] Moreover, the citation of Psalm 102 fits in a stream of passages that feature the cosmos as that which was created through the Son and is in the process of being cleansed.

[4] Old Testament quotations in Hebrews are always from the Septuagint, the ancient Greek-language translation of the Hebrew Scriptures. For this reason, they do not always correspond closely to modern translations, which are based on the Hebrew Masoretic text rather than the Septuagint.

All of this is crucial for understanding what Hebrews will later say about heaven and "the coming world" (Heb. 2:5). Hebrews is not contrasting two different worlds—a bad material world with a good spiritual world. Rather, it is acknowledging that God's *good* creation has become subject to evil and is therefore in need of radical restoration in order to become fully good again. *All* of creation—not just human souls—is in the process of being redeemed by Christ. "In subjecting *all things* to them [human beings], God left nothing outside their control" (Heb. 2:8).

The Creation Has Become Subject to Evil (Hebrews 2:14–3:6)

Although Christ created the world entirely good, it has become tainted and subject to "the one who has the power of death, that is, the devil" (Heb. 2:14). The writer of Hebrews says little about how this happened, but he speaks at length about how God is working to "free those who all their lives were held in slavery by the fear of death," namely, "the descendants of Abraham" (Heb. 2:16); this means Abraham's descendants, both through Isaac (the Jews) and Ishmael (the gentiles)—that is to say, everyone. The question asked by Hebrews is, how will God free humanity from evil, death, and the devil? The answer is, through Jesus Christ, the great high priest.

We will explore Jesus' priesthood in greater depth when we turn to the central chapters of the book (Heb. 5–10). For now we simply note that the opening chapters of the book stress that Jesus' creative work and his priestly work are not isolated from one another. Hebrews brings together both: "Lord, you founded the earth, and the heavens are the work of your hands" (Heb. 1:10), and "So that through death he might destroy the one who has the power of death, that is, the devil" (Heb. 2:14). This tells us that Christ is God's agent of both the original creation and the work of *redemption*. Christ's work of creation leads him, after the Fall, to "free those who all their lives were held in slavery" (Heb. 2:5) and to "make a sacrifice of atonement for the sins of the people" (Heb. 2:17).

We know very well how far our workplaces have fallen from God's original intent. Some workplaces exist primarily because we need to restrain the evil that now infests the world. We need police to restrain criminals, diplomats to restore peace, medical professionals to heal disease, evangelists to call people back to God, auto body shops to repair accidents, investigative journalists to uncover corruption, and engineers to rebuild decaying bridges. And every workplace suffers greatly from the Fall. Mismanagement, labor-management disputes, gossip, harassment, discrimination, laziness, greed, insincerity, and a host of other problems large and small, impede our work and our relationships at every turn. God's solution is not to abandon his creation, or to evacuate human beings from it, but to utterly transform it, to re-create it in its essential goodness. To accomplish this, he sends his Son to become incarnate *in* the world, just as he was the creator *of* the world. In our workplaces, we become Christ's "holy partners in a heavenly calling" (Heb. 3:1) to both sustain and restore his creation. This does not replace the creative work that began in the Garden of Eden, but instead tempers it and adds to it. Creative and redemptive works occur side by side and are intertwined until Christ's return and the abolition of evil.

Life in the Wilderness: Journey to the New World (Hebrews 3:7–4:16)

As much as the creation is therefore the good work of God in Christ, there is still a stark contrast between the present broken world and the glorious world to come. In Hebrews 2:5, the author describes his main topic as "the coming world, about which we are speaking." This suggests that the primary focus throughout the book is on creation perfected by God at the consummation of all things. This is borne out by the lengthy discussion of "Sabbath rest" that dominates chapters 3 and 4.

Throughout the book, Hebrews often takes an Old Testament text as its point of departure. In this case, it draws upon the Exodus story to illuminate the idea of Sabbath rest. Like Israel in the Exodus, the people of God are on a pilgrimage toward the promised place of salvation. In Israel's case, it was Canaan. In our case, it is the perfected creation. The Sabbath rest in Hebrews 4:9–10 is not simply a cessation of activity

(Heb. 4:10) but also a Sabbath *celebration* (Heb. 12:22).[5] Continuing with the Old Testament story, Hebrews takes the conquest of the land under Joshua as a further sign pointing toward our ultimate rest in the world to come. Joshua's rest is incomplete and needs fulfillment that comes only through Christ. "For if Joshua had given them rest, God would not speak later about another day" (Heb. 4:8).

At least two crucial things flow from this. First, life in the present world is going to involve difficult work. This is implied by the idea of the *journey*, which is essential to the Exodus story. All who have ever traveled know that any journey involves an immense amount of labor. Hebrews uses the Sabbath motif to depict not only rest but also the work that surrounds it. You work for six days, and then you rest. Likewise, you work hard in Christ during your life journey, and then you rest in Christ when God's kingdom is fulfilled. Of course, Hebrews is not implying you do nothing *but* work—as we will see shortly, there are also times of rest. Nor is it saying that activity ends when Christ's kingdom comes to completion. The point is that Christians have work to do in the here and now. We are not supposed to plop down in the wilderness, put our feet up, and wait for God to show up and make our lives perfect. God is working through Christ to bring this broken world back to what he intended for it in the beginning. We are privileged to be invited to participate in this grand work.

The second point concerns weekly Sabbath rest and worship. It is important to note that the author of Hebrews does not address the question of the weekly Sabbath, either to affirm it or to condemn it. It is likely that he assumed his readers would observe the Sabbath in some way, but we cannot be sure. In Hebrews the value of weekly rest is governed by its consequences for the coming kingdom. Does resting now connect us more deeply to God's promise of future rest? Does it sustain us on the journey of life? Is keeping Sabbath now an act of faith in which we celebrate the joy we know will be fulfilled in eternity? It certainly seems that some sort of Sabbath rest (however that might be worked out in any

---

[5] J. Laansma, *I Will Give You Rest: The Rest Motif in the New Testament with Special Reference to Mt 11 and Heb 3–4*, vol. 98, Wissenschalftliche Untersuchungen zum Neuen Tesament (Tübingen: Mohr Siebeck, 1997).

given community) would be an ideal way to remind us that our labor is not an endless cycle of drudgery leading nowhere, but rather purposeful activity punctuated by worship and rest.

Seen in this light, our weekly work routines—the six days, as much as the one—can become exercises in spiritual awareness. When we feel the bite of the curse on work (Gen. 3:16–19) through economic breakdowns, poor management, gossipy co-workers, unappreciative family members, inadequate pay, and the like, we remind ourselves that God's house has been badly damaged by his human tenants, and we long for its complete restoration. When our work goes well, we remind ourselves that God's creation, and our work in it, is a good thing, and that in some measure our good work is furthering his purposes for the world. And on our Sabbath, we take time for worship and rest.

Our Great High Priest (Hebrews 5:1–10:18)

The central section of Hebrews is dominated by the theme of Jesus as our great high priest. Taking Psalm 110 as his guide, the author of Hebrews argues that the Messiah was destined to be "a priest according to the order of Melchizedek" (Heb. 5:6), and that this priesthood is superior to the Levitical priesthood that supervised the religious life of Israel. According to Hebrews, the old priesthood, under the old covenant, could not genuinely take away sins but could only remind the people of their sins by the endless sacrifices offered by imperfect and mortal priests. Jesus' priesthood offers one definitive sacrifice for all time and offers us a mediator who always lives to intercede for us. We will highlight here the implications of these two themes of *sacrifice* and *intercession* on how we go about our work.

Christ's Sacrifice Makes Possible Our Service (Hebrews 5:1–7:28)

Jesus, through his self-sacrifice, succeeded in taking away human sin forever. "When Christ had offered for all time a single sacrifice for sins, 'he sat down at the right hand of God.' . . . For by a single offering he has perfected for all time those who are sanctified" (Heb. 10:12, 14). "Unlike the other high priests, he has no need to offer sacrifices day after day, first for his own sins, and then for those of the people; this he did once for all when he offered himself" (Heb. 7:27). This complete atonement for sin is often referred to as "the work of Christ."

It may seem that the forgiveness of sins is a purely church or spiritual matter with no implications for our work, but this is far from true. On the contrary, the definitive sacrifice of Jesus promises to liberate Christians to live lives of passionate service to God in every sphere of life. The text highlights the ethical—that is, practical—consequences of forgiveness in Hebrews 10:16, "I will put my laws in their hearts, and I will write them on their minds." In other words, we who are forgiven will desire to do God's will (in our hearts) and will receive the wisdom, vision, and ability to do so (in our minds).

How is this so? Many people regard church activities in roughly the same way as some Israelites regarded the rituals of the old covenant. If we are to get on God's good side, such people reckon, we need to do some religious things, since that seems to be the sort of thing God is interested in. Going to church is a nice, easy way to meet the requirement, although the downside is that we have to keep doing it every week so that the "magic" doesn't wear off. The supposed good news is that once we meet our religious obligations, we are then free to go about our business without too much concern about God. We won't do anything heinous, of course, but we are basically on our own until we refill our buckets with God's favor by attending church again next week.

The book of Hebrews lays waste to such a view of God. While the Levitical system was a part of God's good purposes for his people, it was always meant to point beyond itself to the future, definitive sacrifice of Christ. It was not a magical favor dispensary but a canteen for the journey. Now that Christ has come and offered himself on our behalf, we can experience the genuine forgiveness of sins through God's grace directly. There is no further point in making perpetual ritual cleansings. We have no buckets that need to be—or can be—filled with God's favor by doing religious activities. Trusting in Christ and his sacrifice, we are in the right with God. Hebrews 10:5 puts it as clearly as can be: "When Christ came into the world, he said, 'Sacrifices and offerings you have not desired, but a body you have prepared for me'" (Heb. 10:5).

None of this, of course, means that Christians shouldn't go to church or that rituals have no place in Christian worship. What is crucial, though, is that the consummate sacrifice of Christ means that our worship is not a self-contained religious exercise sealed off from the rest of our lives. Instead, it is a "sacrifice of praise" (Heb. 13:15) that refreshes our connection with our Lord, cleanses our conscience, sanctifies our will, and thus frees us to serve God each day, wherever we are.

We are sanctified for service. "See, God, I have come to do your will, O God," says Christ (Heb. 10:7). Service is the inevitable outcome of forgiveness by God. "How much more will the blood of Christ, who through the eternal Spirit offered himself unblemished to God, cleanse our consciences from acts that lead to death, so that we may serve the living God!" (Heb. 9:14, NIV).[6]

Ironically, then, a focus on Christ's priestly, heavenly work should lead us to be of tremendous practical, earthly service. The sacrifice Christ offered, which leads ultimately to a renewal of heaven as well as earth (Heb. 12:26; see also Rev. 21:1), was enacted here on earth. Likewise, our own service is performed here in the rough and tumble of everyday life. But we walk and work in this world in the confidence that Jesus has gone before us and completed the same journey we are on. This gives us confidence that our labor for him in every area of life will not be in vain.

Christ's Intercession Empowers Our Life and Work (Hebrews 7:1–10:18)

Priests in ancient Israel not only offered sacrifices for the people, but they also offered prayers of intercession. Thus Jesus prays for us before the throne of God (Heb. 7:25). "[Jesus] is able for all time to save those who approach God through him, since he always lives to make intercession for them" (Heb. 7:25). "He entered into heaven itself, now

---

[6] We have used the NIV here because of a quirk in the NRSV translation, which reads "worship" instead of "serve." "Worship" is indeed a possible translation of the Greek *latreuein*, which like the Hebrew *abad* can mean either "worship" or "serve." But in this context, the NRSV is alone among the major translations in translating it as "worship." The NIV, TNIV, NASB, KJV, and others render it here as "serve."

to appear in the presence of God on our behalf" (Heb. 9:24). We need Jesus to be "always" interceding in the presence of God on our behalf because we continue to sin, fall short, and stray away. Our actions speak ill of us before God, but Jesus' words about us are words of love before the throne of God.

To put it in workplace terms, imagine the fear a young engineer might feel when he is called to meet the chief of the state highway department. What will he possibly say to the chief? Recognizing that the project he is working on is running late and over budget makes him more afraid. But then he learns that his supervisor, a beloved mentor, will also be at the meeting. And it turns out his supervisor is great friends with the chief of the highway department from their days back at university. "Don't worry," the mentor assures the engineer, "I'll take care of things." Won't the young engineer have much greater confidence to approach the chief in the presence of the chief's friend?

Hebrews emphasizes that Jesus not only is a high priest but also a high priest in solidarity with us. "For we do not have a high priest who is unable to sympathize with our weaknesses, but we have one who in every respect has been tested as we are, yet without sin" (Heb. 4:15). To return to a verse we discussed earlier, Jesus speaks to God of the "body you have prepared for me" (Heb. 10:5). Christ came in a genuine human body, and he really did embrace life as one of us.

In order to be a faithful high priest, the author reasons, Jesus has to be able to sympathize with the people. He cannot do this if he has not experienced the same things they have experienced. And so he states quite carefully that Jesus *learned* obedience. "Although he was a Son, he learned obedience through what he suffered" (Heb. 5:8). This does not mean, of course, that Jesus had to learn to obey in the way we do—by ceasing to disobey God. It means that he needed to *experience suffering and temptation firsthand* to qualify as a high priest. Other verses make the same point in equally expressive language, that Jesus' sufferings "perfected" him (Heb. 2:10; 5:9; 7:28). The full meaning of "perfect" is not only "flawless" but also "complete." Jesus was already flawless—but *to be qualified as our high priest*, he needed those sufferings to complete him for the job. How else could he genuinely relate to us as we struggle in this world day by day?

What is most encouraging here is that this suffering and learning took place in the setting of Jesus' *work*. He does not come as a kind of a theological anthropologist who "learns" about the world in a detached, clinical way, or as a tourist popping by for a visit. Instead he weaves himself into the fabric of real human life, including real human labor. When we face struggles at work, we can then turn to our sympathetic high priest with the full assurance that he knows firsthand what we are going through.

Realizing the Faith (Hebrews 10–11)

Following Jesus is hard work, and only faith in the eventual fulfillment of his promises can keep us going. "Now faith is the assurance of things hoped for, the conviction of things not seen" (Heb. 11:1). We need faith that the promises God made are true, however unlikely that might seem in the present circumstances. A more precise translation of this verse helps us see the practical importance of faith. "Now faith is the *realization* of things hoped for, the *proving* of things not seen."[7] "Realization" is particularly appropriate here, because the double sense it has in English perfectly captures the nuances of the examples of faith given in Hebrews 11. When we at last see things clearly, that is one form of realization. We finally understand. But the second form of realization is seeing things made real, when what we hoped for has finally come true. The heroes of faith in Hebrews 11 realize things in both ways. Taking up the second half of the verse, they are so convinced of what God has said that they prove it by what they do.

Hebrews gives us the practical examples of Noah, Abraham, Moses, and others from the Old Testament. They were all looking forward to the fulfillment of God's promise for something better than their present experience. Noah had faith in the righteous world beyond the flood, and he

---

[7]W. Bauer, W. F. Arndt, F. W. Gingrich, and F. W. Danker, *Greek-English Lexicon of the New Testament and Other Early Christian Literature*, 3rd ed. (Chicago: University of Chicago Press, 2001), under *pistos*. The King James Version is closer to the Greek than some of the modern translations: "Now faith is the substance of things hoped for, the evidence of things not seen."

realized that faith meant building an ark to save his household (Heb. 11:7). Abraham had faith in the coming kingdom (or "city") of God (Heb. 11:10), and he realized that faith meant setting out on a journey to the land God promised him, even though he did not know where he was going (Heb. 11:8–12). Moses had faith in a life in Christ far surpassing the pleasures he could have claimed as a son of Pharaoh's daughter, and he realized that faith meant "choosing rather to share ill-treatment with the people of God than to enjoy the fleeting pleasures of sin" (Heb. 11:25–26). These hopes and promises were not completely fulfilled in their lifetimes, yet they lived every day as if already experiencing God's power to fulfill them.

Faith like this is not wishful thinking. It is taking seriously God's self-revelation in Scripture (Heb. 8:10–11), combined with a "repentance from dead works" (Heb. 6:1), perseverance in "love and good deeds" (Heb. 10:24), and an ability to see the hand of God at work in the world (Heb. 11:3), despite the evil and brokenness around us. Ultimately, faith is a gift from the Holy Spirit (Heb. 2:4), for we could never hold on to such faith by our own force of will.

This was a crucial message for the audience of Hebrews, who were tempted to throw away their hope in Christ in exchange for a more comfortable life in the here and now. Their eyes were fixed not on future glory, but on present deprivation. The book's word of exhortation is that the promises of God are more enduring, more glorious, and indeed more real than fleeting pleasures in the here and now.

If we are to realize the faith God has given us, we have to work in the midst of the tension between God's promise for the future and the realities of today. On the one hand, we should fully recognize the provisional, finite nature of all that we do. We will not be surprised when things don't work out as we had hoped. "All these, though they were commended for their faith, did not receive what was promised" (Heb. 11:39). Situations arise in which our best efforts to do good work are thwarted not only by circumstance, but also by the deliberate misdeeds of human beings. This may cause us grief, but it will not lead us to despair, because we have our eyes fixed on God's city to come.

Sometimes our work is thwarted by our own weakness. We fall short of the mark. Consider the list of names in Hebrews 11:32. When we read their stories we see clearly their own failures, sometimes significant failures. If we read about Barak's timidity as a general (Judg. 4:8–9) through human eyes, we likely would see no faith at all. Yet God sees their faith through God's eyes and credits their work by his grace, not their accomplishment. We can take heart in this when we also have stumbled. We may have spoken harshly to a co-worker, been impatient with a student, ignored our responsibility to our family, and done our work poorly. But we have faith that God is able to bring about his intent for the world even in the midst of our weakness and failure.

On the other hand, *precisely because* we have our eyes on God's city to come, we seek to live according to the ways of that city to the greatest possible extent in every aspect of daily life and work. The heroes of the faith in Hebrews realized their faith in all kinds of workplaces. They were people "who through faith conquered kingdoms, administered justice, obtained promises, shut the mouths of lions, quenched raging fire, escaped the edge of the sword, won strength out of weakness, became mighty in war, put foreign armies to flight" (Heb. 11:33–34).

Imagine a building contractor, which is a fitting illustration for a book concerned with God's cosmic house building. The contractor has a clear vision of life in God's coming kingdom. He knows it will be characterized by justice, harmonious relationships, and enduring beauty. As a person of faith, he seeks to *realize* this vision in the present. He stewards the earth's raw materials in the construction of the home, creating a home of beauty but not wasteful opulence. He treats his workers with the concern and respect that will be characteristic of God's future city. He shows heavenly love to his clients by listening to their hopes for their earthly homes, trying to realize those hopes within the constraints of money and materials. He perseveres through troubles, when the antique radiator is two inches too long for the bathroom, or when a carpenter cuts an expensive joist two inches too short. He accepts that an earthquake or hurricane could destroy all his labors in minutes, yet he puts his whole self into his work. Amid both the joys and the frustrations, he wants to live out the values of God's city by showing consistent love to others in the quality of his personal relationships and in the quality of the houses he builds. And he trusts that every building, frail and imperfect as it is, is a witness day by day to the great city to come, "whose architect and builder is God" (Heb. 11:10).

Enduring Hardship, Pursuing Peace (Hebrews 12:1–16)

Hebrews moves from providing examples of faithful saints to providing challenges for the people of its own day. Like the rest of the New Testament, Hebrews describes the Christian life as full of hardships. We are to endure these hardships as measures of God's fatherly discipline. Through them, we come to share in Christ's holiness and righteousness. Just as the Son came under discipline and so was perfected (Heb. 5:7–10), God's sons and daughters undergo the same process.

It is the most common thing in the world for us to interpret our hardships as divine punishment. Those who oppose us may even view it as such, hurling our very real sins and faults in our faces. But Hebrews reminds us there is no punishment for those who have been forgiven through the all-sufficient, once-for-all sacrifice of Christ. "Where these have been forgiven, there is no longer any sacrifice for sin" (Heb. 10:18). Our loving Father will discipline us (Heb. 12:4–11), but discipline is not punishment (1 Cor. 11:32). Discipline is hard training, but it is a form of love, "For the Lord disciplines those whom he loves" (Heb. 12:6). Let no one pretend to interpret our hardships as God's punishment. "He disciplines us for our good, in order that we may share his holiness" (Heb. 12:10).

But this discipline is not only for our personal benefit. Hebrews goes on to exhort Jesus' followers to "pursue peace with everyone, and the holiness without which no one will see the Lord." The "peace" of which Hebrews 12:14 speaks is the full notion of the Hebrew *shalom*, which conveys an ultimate state of justice and prosperity, shared among the whole community. It is the final goal of salvation. It is captured in another way later in the chapter with the imagery of the holy, heavenly city of Zion (Heb. 12:22–24).

We know how hard it is to endure hardship and pursue peace in our work. Having received the promises of God, we naturally hope they will immediately make our work more pleasant. We want to be fruitful, multiply our wealth, and gain authority—all good things in God's eyes (Gen. 1:28)—and to enjoy friendships (Gen. 2:18) in and through our work. If instead we encounter hardship, money troubles, lack of power, and hostility from co-workers, endurance may be the last thing on our minds. It may seem much easier to give up, quit, or change jobs—if we have the choice—or to disengage, slack off, or pursue a rough justice of our own making. Or we may grow weary and lose heart, remaining at our work but losing interest in doing it as a service to God. May God give us the grace to endure difficult workplace situations! The hardships we face in our work may be God's means of discipline for us, to grow us into more faithful and useful people. If we cannot maintain integrity, serve others, and pursue reconciliation in the midst of difficult jobs or hostile work environments, how can we become like Jesus, "who endured such hostility against himself from sinners" (Heb. 12:3)?

Shaking Things Up (Hebrews 12:18–29)

One of the widespread misunderstandings of Hebrews is that it pits the heavenly (uncreated) world against the earthly (created) one, that it anticipates an annihilation of the cosmos while heaven remains as God's unshakable kingdom. Such a misunderstanding might seem to find support in texts such as Hebrews 12:26–27.

> At that time his voice shook the earth; but now he has promised, "Yet once more I will shake not only the earth but also the heaven." This phrase, "Yet once more," indicates the removal of what is shaken—that is, created things—so that what cannot be shaken may remain.

But upon closer examination, we see that heaven and earth are not very different from each other. The heavens will be shaken as well as the earth (Heb. 12:26). Hebrews describes the heavenly world as a "creation" just as much as the cosmos (Heb. 8:2; 11:10). It speaks of resurrection (Heb. 6:2, 11:35), which is a reclamation, not an annihilation, of creation. It understands the cosmos (Heb. 1:2–6, 11:3) to be the inheritance of the Son. It proclaims that the offering of Christ was a bodily, in-this-world event of flesh and blood (Heb. 12:24; 13:2; 13:20). Ultimately, "shaking" is the removal of whatever is imperfect or sinful from both heaven and earth, not the destruction of the earth in favor of heaven.

The language here is a reference to Haggai 2, where "shaking" refers to the overthrow of foreign occupiers, so that Israel and its temple can be reconstructed. This reference, and the argument of Hebrews as a whole, indicates that the ultimate result of this shaking will be the filling of God's temple—on earth—with glory. The entire cosmos becomes God's temple, cleansed and reclaimed. In Haggai 2, the shaking of heaven and earth leads to the *realization* of the peace on earth we are exhorted to pursue earlier in Hebrews 12. "'In *this place* I will give prosperity [*shalom*],' says the Lord of Hosts" (Hag. 2:9).

What is transient, then, is not the created world but the imperfection, evil, and strife that infect the world. Pouring our lives into God's kingdom means working through the *creation* and *redemption* that belong to the advancing rule of Christ (Heb. 7:2). No matter whether we are fry cooks, educators, athletes, managers, homemakers, ecologists, senators, firefighters, pastors, or anyone else, the way to participate in Christ's kingdom is not to abandon "worldly" work in favor of "spiritual" work. It is to persevere—with thanksgiving to God (Heb. 12:28)—in all kinds of work under the discipline of Christ.

Hospitality (Hebrews 13:1–3)

Amid the various concluding exhortations in Hebrews 13, two have a special relevance for work. Let us begin with Hebrews 13:2 where it says, "Do not neglect to show hospitality to strangers, for by doing that some have entertained angels without knowing it" (Heb. 13:1–2). The verse alludes to Abraham and Sarah entertaining visitors (Gen. 18:1–15) who turn out to be angels (Gen. 19:1), the very bearers of the promise of a son to Abraham and Sarah (Gen. 18:10), which figures so prominently in this book (Heb. 6:13–15; 11:8–20). These verses also remind us of the many acts of hospitality by Jesus (e.g., Matt. 14:13–21; Mark 6:30–44; Luke 9:10–17; John 2:1–11; 6:1–14; 21:12–13) and those who followed him (e.g., Mark 1:31; Luke 5:9), and parables such as the wedding banquet (Matt. 22:1–4; Luke 14:15–24).

Hospitality may be one of the most underrated forms of work in the world—at least, in the modern Western world. Many people work hard to practice hospitality, even though for most people it is unpaid work. Yet few, if asked what their occupation is, would say, "I offer hospitality." We are more likely to see it as a diversion or a private interest, rather than a service to God. Yet hospitality is a great act of faith—that God's provision will bear the expense of giving away food, drink, entertainment, and shelter; that the risk of damage or theft of property will be bearable; that time spent with strangers will not diminish time with family and friends; and, most of all, that strange people are worth caring about. Even if we have to go out of our way to give it—to prison, for example (Heb. 13:3)—hospitality is one of the most significant acts of work or service that human beings can do (Matt. 25:31–40).

In addition, almost all workers have the opportunity to practice an ethos of hospitality in the course of their jobs. Many people work in hospitality industries. Do we recognize that we are fulfilling Hebrews 13:1–3 when we provide a clean, well-maintained hotel room, or a healthful, delicious dinner, or cater a party or reception? No matter the industry or occupation, every interaction with a co-worker, customer, supplier, client, or stranger in the workplace is a chance to make others feel welcomed and valued. Imagine the witness to God's love if Christians had a reputation for hospitality in the course of ordinary business.

Money Matters (Hebrews 13:5–6)

The second work-related exhortation in chapter 13 concerns the love of money: "Keep your lives free from the love of money, and be content with what you have; for he has said, 'I will never leave you or forsake you'" (Heb. 13:4–5). This command to be free of the love of money suggests that financial pressures were among the special problems faced by the original readers of this book. This was already indicated in Hebrews 10:32–36 and indirectly by Hebrews 11:25–26. Perhaps the emphasis on the future "city" (Heb. 11:10; 12:22; 13:14) was stimulated in part by their experience of economic and social alienation from their present city.

We have full confidence of protection and provision by our God, but in no respect does this guarantee that we will enjoy lives of material prosperity. Jesus never promised us an easy life, and our hard work may not be rewarded in this life with wealth or luxury. The point of Hebrews 13:5–6 is that the Lord will provide all that we need *for a life founded on faith*. Of course, plenty of faithful believers have experienced severe financial hardship, and many have even died from exposure, thirst, hunger, disease, and worse. They died that way *through* faith, not for a *lack* of it. The author of Hebrews is perfectly aware of this, having recounted Christians who suffered torture, mocking, flogging, imprisonment, stoning, being sawn in two, death by the sword, destitution, persecution, torment, and wandering across mountains, deserts, in caves and holes in the ground (Heb. 11:35–38)! Ultimately God's promises and our prayers are fulfilled just as they were for his Son—through resurrection from the dead (Heb. 5:7–10). This book operates with a transformed economic vision, that our needs are met in the advance of God's kingdom, rather than in our personal prosperity. Therefore, if we have nothing, we do not despair; if we have enough, we are content; and if we have much, we sacrifice it for the sake of others.

The warning against the love of money does not stem from a discovery that God's kingdom in creation, the material world, is somehow less spiritual than God's kingdom in heaven. It stems, rather, from the startling awareness that in a fallen world, the love of money creates an attachment to the present order that stands in the way of our working toward the transformation of the world. If money is the chief reason we take a job, start a company, run for office, join a church, choose our friends, invest our resources, spend our time, or find a mate, then we are not living by faith.

Working Outside the Camp (Hebrews 13:11–25)

The third work-related exhortation in chapter 13 is to "go to [Jesus] outside the camp and bear the abuse he endured" (Heb. 13:13). According to Hebrews 13:11–13, "The bodies of those animals whose blood is brought into the sanctuary by the high priest as a sacrifice for sin are burned outside the camp," outside the realm of the holy, in the place of the unclean. "Jesus also suffered outside the city gate," outside the camp, in the realm of the unholy, "to sanctify the people by his own blood."

Hebrews thus draws the lesson that we should also journey outside the camp and join Jesus there.

Many Christians work in places "outside the camp" of holiness, that is, in workplaces where hostility, ethical challenges, and suffering are regular occurrences. Sometimes we feel that to follow Christ well, we need to find holier workplaces. But this passage from Hebrews shows us that the opposite is true. To follow Christ fully is to follow him to the places where his saving help is desperately needed, but not necessarily welcomed. Doing the work of Jesus' kingdom entails suffering along with Jesus. The phrase "bearing his disgrace" echoes the faith of Moses, who chose the "disgrace of Christ" over the honor and treasures of Egypt (Heb. 11:24–26). This "disgrace" was the loss of honor and possessions mentioned earlier in the book. Sometimes, sacrificing our possessions, privileges, and status may be the only way we can help others. Yet helping others is precisely why God sends us to work "outside the camp" in the first place. "Do not neglect to do good and to share what you have, for such sacrifices are pleasing to God" (Heb. 13:16).

Conclusion to Hebrews

Hebrews summons us into the world of God's promise to Abraham—a promise to bring all humanity into the sacred space of his kingdom. It announces the fulfillment of God's will to incorporate all the cosmos into the sphere of his own holiness. As a people on a pilgrimage into God's kingdom, we are called to invest our lives, including our work lives, in the cosmos whose architect and builder is God. The book of Hebrews exhorts us to be content with what God provides and to work for peace (*shalom*) and holiness for all. We are to gladly suffer the loss of honor and possessions for the joy that lies ahead of us. In this journey, we are supplied, emboldened, and encouraged by God's Son, the true priest whose self-sacrifice opens a way for the world to be purified and restored to what God intended from the beginning. Even in the midst of our suffering, thanksgiving is our basic attitude and wellspring of perseverance. Christ calls us to make the values of his kingdom known within the economic, social, and political structures of a fallen world.

This requires escaping the trap of living for money. What we do, and what we refrain from doing, are both predicated on these values. We have one work, whatever our occupation, and one ambition—to "do his will, working among us that which is pleasing in his sight, through Jesus Christ, to whom be glory forever and ever" (Heb. 13:21).

THE GENERAL EPISTLES AND WORK

Introduction to the General Epistles

The seven letters of James, 1 and 2 Peter, 1, 2, and 3 John, and Jude are often called the General (or Catholic) Epistles because they seem to speak to the Christian church in general, rather than to individual churches. They are also united by their interest in practical matters such as organizational leadership, hard work, fairness, good relationships, and effective communication.

The General Epistles reflect the essential challenge Christians faced in the Roman Empire—how to follow Jesus in a tough environment. Early Christians faced problems such as slavery, favoritism, and abuse by the rich and powerful. They dealt with harsh words and conflicts. They dealt with the real tensions between ambition and dependence on God, and the fear that doing things God's way would put them in conflict with those in authority. In general, they felt a sense of alienation living and working in a world that seemed incompatible with following Jesus.

Many of today's Christians experience similar tensions at work. On the one hand, many Christians have more opportunity to serve God in their work than in any other sphere of life. Business, government, educational, nonprofit, and at-home workplaces accomplish a tremendous amount of good in society. On the other hand, most workplaces are generally not dedicated toward God's purposes, such as serving the common good, working for the benefit of others, deepening relationships among people, spreading justice, and developing character. Because workplaces' ultimate aims—generally maximizing profit—are different from Christians' ultimate aims, we should expect to experience tension in our dual roles as followers of Christ and workers in the nonchurch workplace. Although most workplaces are not intentionally evil—just as many parts of the Roman Empire were not actively hostile to Jesus' followers—it can still be challenging for Christians to serve God in their work. Because the General Epistles were written to guide Christians experiencing tensions in the world around them, they can be helpful to workplace Christians today.

These General Epistles address such practical concerns head on. Two major principles underlie the variety of items treated in these letters:

1. We can trust God to provide for us.

2. We must work for the benefit of others in need.

From these two principles, the General Epistles derive instructions that have surprisingly practical applications in the twenty-first-century workplace. But perhaps we should not be surprised. God chose the Roman Empire as the place where God would enter human life in the form of Jesus Christ. God is also choosing today's workplace as a point of his presence.

James: Faith and Work

James brings an action-oriented perspective to the principles that we can trust God to provide for us and that we must work for the benefit of others in need. If faith is real—if we truly trust God—then our faith will lead to all kinds of practical actions for the benefit of others in need. This perspective makes James an eminently practical book.

Perseverance, Wisdom and Spiritual Growth (James 1:1–3)

James begins by emphasizing the deep connection between daily life and spiritual growth. Specifically, God uses the difficulties and challenges of daily life and work to increase our faith. "My brothers and sisters, whenever you face trials of any kind, consider it nothing but joy, because you know that the testing of your faith produces endurance, and let endurance have its full effect, so that you may be mature and complete, lacking in nothing" (James 1:2–4). "Any kind" of trial can be an impetus for growth—including troubles at work—but James is particularly interested in challenges so intense that they result in "the testing of [our] faith."

What kinds of challenges do we face at work that might test our faith in—or faithfulness to—Christ? One kind might be religious hostility. Depending on our situation, faith in Christ could expose us to anything from minor prejudice to limited job opportunities to dismissal or even bodily harm or death in the workplace. Even if others don't put pressure on us, we may tempt ourselves to abandon our faith if we think that being identified as a Christian is holding back our careers.

Another kind of trial could be ethical. We can be tempted to abandon faith—or faithfulness—by committing theft, fraud, dishonesty, unfair dealings, or taking advantage of others in order to enrich ourselves or advance our careers. Another kind of trial arises from failure at work. Some failures can be so traumatic that they shake our faith. For example, getting laid off (made redundant) or dismissed from a job may be so devastating that we question everything we previously relied on, including faith in Christ. Or we may believe that God called us to our work, promised us greatness, or owes us success because we have been faithful to him. Failure at work then seems to mean that God cannot be trusted or does not even exist. Or we may be so gripped by fear that we doubt God will continue to provide for our needs. All of these work-related challenges can test our faith.

What should we do if our faith is tested at work? Endure (James 1:3–4). James tells us that if we can find a way not to give into the temptation to abandon the faith, to act unethically, or to despair, then we will find God with us the whole time. If we don't know how to resist these temptations, James invites us to ask for the wisdom we need to do so (James 1:5). As the crisis passes, we find that our maturity has grown. Instead feeling the lack of whatever we were afraid of losing, we feel the joy of finding God's help.

Depending on God (James 1:5–18)

In speaking about wisdom, James begins to develop the principle that we can trust God to provide for us. "If any of you is lacking in wisdom, ask God, who gives to all generously and ungrudgingly, and it will be given you" (James 1:5). It may seem surprising that we can ask God for wisdom about the tasks of ordinary work—making decisions, assessing opportunities, trusting colleagues or customers, investing resources, and so on—but James tells us to "ask in faith, never doubting" that God will give us the wisdom we need. Our problem is not that we expect too much help from God at work, but that we expect too little (James 1:8).

It is absolutely essential to grasp this. If we doubt that God is the source of all we need, then we are what James calls "double-minded." We have not yet made up our mind whether to follow Christ or not. This makes us "unstable in every way," and we will not be able to accomplish much for the benefit of anyone, or able even to "receive anything from the Lord" on our own behalf (James 1:7). James is under no illusions about how hard it can be to trust God. He knows all too well the trials his audience is already beginning to experience throughout the breadth of the Roman Empire (James 1:1–2). Yet he insists that the Christian life must begin with trusting God to provide.

He immediately applies this to the economic sphere in James 1:9–11. Rich people must not delude themselves that this is due to their own effort. If we depend on our own abilities, we will "wither away" even while we go about our business. Conversely, poor people should not think this is due to God's disfavor. Instead, they should expect to be "raised up" by God. Success or failure comes from many factors beyond ourselves. Those who have ever lost their livelihood due to recession, corporate sale, office relocation, crop failure, discrimination, hurricane damage, or a thousand other factors can testify to that. God does not promise us economic success at work, nor does he doom us to failure, but he uses both success and failure to develop the perseverance needed to overcome evil. If James 2:1–8 invites us to call on God in times of trouble, then verses 9–11 remind us to call on him in times of success as well.

Notice that although James contrasts the goodness of God with the evil of the world, he does not allow us to imagine that we are on the side of angels and those around us on the side of devils. Instead, the divide between good and evil runs down the middle of every Christian's heart. "One is tempted by one's own desire, being lured and enticed by it" (James 1:14). He is speaking to church members. This should make us slow to identify church as good and workplace as bad. There is evil in both spheres—as church scandals and business frauds alike remind us—yet by God's grace we may bring goodness to both.

In fact, the Christian community is one of the means God uses to raise up the poor. God's promise to provide for the poor is fulfilled—in part—by the generosity of his people, and their generosity is a direct result of God's generosity to them. "Every generous act of giving, with every perfect gift, is from above, coming down from the Father of lights" (James 1:17). This affirms both that God is the ultimate source of provision and that believers are responsible to do all they can to bring God's provision to those in need.

Listening, Taking Action, and Avoiding Anger (James 1:19–21)

James continues his practical guidance with words about listening. Christians need to listen well both to people (James 1:19) and to God (James 1:22–25). "Be quick to listen, slow to speak, slow to anger" (James 1:19). We listen, not as a technique to influence anyone else, but as a way to let God's word "rid [ourselves] of all sordidness and rank growth of wickedness" (James 1:21). Interestingly, James suggests that listening to others—and not just listening to God's word—is a means of ridding ourselves of wickedness. He does not say that other people speak God's word to us. Instead, he says that listening to others removes the anger and arrogance that keep us from doing God's word spoken in Scripture. "Your anger does not produce God's righteousness. . . . Welcome with meekness the implanted word that has the power to save your souls" (James 1:20–21). When others speak words that we do not welcome—words of disagreement, criticism, dismissal—it is easy to respond in anger, especially in high-pressure situations at work. But doing so usually makes our position worse, and always discredits our witness as Christ's servants. How much better to trust God to defend our position, rather than defending ourselves by angry, hasty speech.

This advice applies to all kinds of work and workplaces. Listening is well established in business literature as a crucial leadership skill.[1]

---

[1] To give one example, the first result on the Harvard Business School Publications website www.harvardbusiness.org on Sept. 18, 2009, browsing under the topic "Interpersonal Skills," is "Listening to People."

Businesses must listen carefully to their customers, employees, investors, communities, and other stakeholders. In order to meet people's true needs, organizations need to listen to the people whose needs they hope to meet. This reminds us that the workplace can be fertile soil for God's work, just as the Roman Empire was, hardship and persecution notwithstanding.

Working for the Benefit of Others in Need (James 1:22–28)

This brings us to the second principle of faithful work—working for the benefit of others in need. "Be doers of the word, and not merely hearers who deceive themselves" (James 1:22). This principle follows naturally from the principle of trusting God to provide for our needs. If we trust God to provide for our needs, then it frees us to work for the benefit of others. On the other hand, if our trust in God does not lead us to act for the benefit of others in need, then James suggests that we don't really trust God. As James puts it, "Religion that is pure and undefiled before God the Father is this: to care for orphans and widows in their distress" (James 1:27). Belief means trust, and trust leads to action.

The source of James's insight seems to be Jesus himself, especially his teachings about the poor and the practical care he showed to a variety of marginalized people. This can be seen, for example, in James's allusions to Jesus' teachings regarding the special place of the poor in God's kingdom (James 2:5; Luke 6:20), along with Jesus' warnings about rotting treasures "on the earth" (James 5: 1–5; Matt. 6:19).

This has direct application to work because meeting needs is the number one mark of a successful workplace, whether in business, education, health care, government work, the professions, nonprofits, or others. A successful organization meets the needs of its customers, employees, investors, citizens, students, clients, and other stakeholders. This is not James's primary focus—he is focused particularly on the needs of people who are poor or powerless—but it nonetheless applies. Whenever an organization meets people's true needs, it is doing God's work.

This application is not limited to serving customers in established businesses. It requires even greater creativity—and demonstrates God's provision even more—when Christians meet the needs of people who are too poor to be customers of established businesses. For example, a group of Christians started a furniture factory in Vietnam to provide jobs for people at the lowest level of the socioeconomic spectrum there. Through the factory, God provides for the needs of both overseas customers needing furniture and local workers who were previously unemployed.[2] Similarly, TriLink Global, an investment firm led by Gloria Nelund, helps start businesses in the developing world as a means to meeting the needs of poor and marginalized people.[3]

Christians' duty does not end with serving the poor and needy through individual workplaces. Social structures and political-economic systems strongly affect whether the needs of the poor are met. To the degree that Christians can influence these structures and systems, we have a responsibility to ensure that they meet the needs of poor and needy people, as well as the needs of rich and powerful people.

Discriminating Against the Poor and Currying Favor with the Rich (James 2:1–13)

James applies both of his underlying principles as a warning against favoritism toward the rich and powerful. He begins with the second principle—working for the benefit of others in need. "You do well if you really fulfill the royal law according to the scripture, 'You shall love your neighbor as yourself.' But if you show partiality, you commit sin" (James 2:8–9). The sin is that when we favor the rich and powerful, we are serving ourselves rather than others. This is because the rich and powerful have the potential to bestow a bit of their riches and power on us. The poor can do nothing for us. But they are the people in need. James illustrates the point by depicting the special treatment that a wealthy, well-dressed person might be given in church, while a poor, shabby person is treated with contempt. Even in something as simple as coming to church, the poor are in need of a word of welcome. The rich—being welcomed everywhere—are not in need.

---

[2] Interview by William Messenger on July 29, 2010, in Hong Kong. Name of source withheld by request.

[3] Al Erisman, "Gloria Nelund: Defining Success in the Financial World," *Ethix* 80 (March/April 2012), available at http://ethix.org/category/archives/issue-80.

James draws on Leviticus 19:18—"Love your neighbor as yourself"—to indicate that showing favoritism toward the rich and excluding or slighting the poor is no less an offense against God's law than murder or adultery (James 2:8–12). Doing this means that either we are not treating our neighbors as ourselves, or we are failing even to recognize that a poor person is our neighbor.

Although James is talking about church gatherings, there are workplace applications. At work, we can pay attention to people who can help us or to people who need our help. In a healthy workplace, this might be merely a matter of emphasis. In a dysfunctional workplace—where people are pitted against each other in a struggle for power—it takes courage to stand on the side of the powerless. Refusing to play favorites is especially dangerous when we are faced with socially entrenched favoritism such as ethnic discrimination, gender stereotyping, or religious bigotry.

Although James couches his argument in terms of working to benefit others in need, this application implicitly raises the principle of trusting in God. If we truly trusted God for our provision, then we wouldn't be tempted to favor the rich and powerful so much. We wouldn't be afraid to associate ourselves with the unpopular crowd at work or school. James is not exhorting us to do good works *despite* lacking faith in Christ and trusting God's provision. James is demonstrating how good works *are made possible* by faith in Christ. Ironically, the poor themselves already live this truth on a daily basis. "Has not God chosen the poor in the world to be rich in faith and to be heirs of the kingdom that he has promised to those who love him?" (James 2:5). This is likely an allusion to Jesus' words in the Sermon on the Mount or Plain (Matt. 5:3; Luke 6:20). The poor are not inheriting the kingdom because they are better people than the rich, but because they put their trust in God. Lacking the means to depend on themselves, or to curry favor with the rich, they have learned to depend on God.

Faith and Work(s) (James 2:14–26)

James takes up the topic of work in detail in the second part of chapter 2. When discussing work, he invariably uses the plural "works" (Greek *erga*) rather than the singular "work" (Greek *ergon*). This leads some to suppose that James uses "works" to mean something different from "work." However, *erga* and *ergon* are simply plural and singular forms of the same word.[4] James is describing any kind of work, from works of kindness, such as giving food to someone who is hungry, to on-the-job work, such as increasing the sustainable yield of rice paddies. His use of the plural shows that he expects Christians' work to be continual.

James's focus on work has led to deep controversy about the letter. Luther famously disliked James because he read James 2:24 ("You see that a person is justified by works and not by faith alone") to be a contradiction of Galatians 2:16 ("A person is justified not by the works of the law but through faith in Jesus Christ"). Other leaders of the Protestant Reformation did not share this view, but Luther's objection came to dominate the Protestant reading of James.[5] Although we cannot go into the long debate about Luther and the book of James here, we can inquire briefly whether James's emphasis on work is at odds with the Protestant rejection of "justification by works."

What does James himself say? James 2:14 is arguably the centerpiece of his argument, so we will consider this section before moving on to James 2:1–13: "What good is it, my brothers and sisters, if you say you have faith but do not have works?" James bluntly answers his own question by stating, "So faith by itself, if it has no works, is dead" (James 2:17)—as dead (as he notes in a carefully chosen example) as someone in desperate need of food who receives only empty words of well-wishing from his neighbor (James 2:15–16). James takes it for granted that believing in Christ (trusting in God) will move you to feel compassion for— and act to help—someone in need.

We have opportunities every day to meet the needs of people we work for and among. It can be as simple as making sure a confused customer finds the right item for their need or noticing that a new co-worker needs help but is afraid to ask. James urges us to take special concern for those

---

[4] See Gk. #2041 in James Strong, *Enhanced Strong's Lexicon* (Ontario: Woodside Bible Fellowship, 1995), and #2240 in Gerhard Kittle, Gerhard Friedrich, and Geoffrey William Bromiley, eds., *Theological Dictionary of the New Testament* (Grand Rapids: Eerdmans, 1985), 6:635.

[5] Luke Timothy Johnson, "The Letter of James," vol. 12, *The New Interpreter's Bible* (Nashville: Abingdon Press, 1998), 177.

who are vulnerable or marginalized, and we may need to practice noticing who these people are at our places of work.

This is the heart of the book of James. James does not imagine that
work is at odds with faith. There can be no "justification by works" because there can be no good works unless there is already faith (trust) in
God. James doesn't mean that faith can exist without works yet be insuf-
ficient for salvation. He means that any "faith" that doesn't lead to works
is dead; in other words, it is no faith at all. "As the body without the spirit
is dead, so faith without works is also dead" (James 2:26). James doesn't
command Christians to work for the benefit of others in need *instead of*
placing faith in Christ, or even *in addition* to placing faith in Christ. He
expects that Christians will work for the benefit of others in need *as a
result of* placing faith in Christ.[6]

The insight that Christian faith always leads to practical action is
in itself a lesson for the workplace. We cannot divide the world into
spiritual and practical, for the spiritual *is* the practical. "You see that
[Abraham's] faith was active along with his works," James says (James
2:22). Therefore we can never say, "I believe in Jesus and I go to church,
but I keep my personal faith out of my work." That kind of faith is dead.
James's words "You see that a person is justified by works and not by
faith alone" (James 2:24) challenge us to work out our commitment to
Christ in our daily activities.

The rest of the letter gives practical applications of the two underlying principles of trust in God and working to benefit others in need.
Given our assessment of James 2:14–26, we will proceed with the perspective that these applications are outworkings of faith in Christ, valid
in James's day and instructive in ours.

Taming the Tongue (James 3:1–12)

James follows up his practical guidance about listening (see James
1:19–21) with similar advice about speaking. Here he employs some of
the fiercest language in the book. "The tongue is a fire. The tongue is

---

[6]For a discussion of how this understanding of faith squares with that of
Paul, see Douglas Moo, *The Letter of James* (Grand Rapids: Eerdmans, 2000),
37–43, 118–44.

placed among our members as a world of iniquity; it stains the whole body, sets on fire the cycle of nature, and is itself set on fire by hell. . . . It is a restless evil, full of deadly poison" (James 3:6, 8). James is no doubt well aware of the Old Testament proverbs that speak about the life-giving power of the tongue (e.g., Prov. 12:18, "Rash words are like sword thrusts, but the tongue of the wise brings healing"), but he is also aware of the tongue's death-dealing powers. Many Christians rightly take care not to harm others through harsh speech at church. Shouldn't we be just as careful at work not to "curse those who are made in the likeness of God"? (James 3:9, referring to Gen. 1:26–27). Water-cooler gossip, slander, harassment, disparagement of competitors—who has never been injured by harsh words in the workplace, and who has never injured others?

Selfish Ambition and Submission to God (James 3:13–4:12)

James 3:14–4:12 also employs the paired principles of dependence on God and service to others in need. As usual, James puts them in reverse order, discussing service first and trust later. In this case, James starts with an admonition against selfish ambition, followed by an exhortation to submit to God.

Selfish Ambition Is the Impediment to Peacemaking (James 3:16–4:11)

Selfish ambition is the opposite of serving the needs of others. The passage is aptly summarized by James 3:16: "For where there is envy and selfish ambition, there will also be disorder and wickedness of every kind." James highlights a particular practice that overcomes selfish ambition: peacemaking.[7] "A harvest of righteousness is sown in peace for those who make peace" (James 3:18). In typical fashion, he alludes to a workplace—grain harvesting in this case—to make his point. He names several elements of peacemaking: grieving for the harm we do others (James 4:9), humbling ourselves (James 4:10), refraining from slander, accusation, and judgment (James 4:11), and mercy and sincerity (James 3:17). All of these can and should be employed by Christians in the workplace.

---

[7] Again echoing the Sermon on the Mount (Matt. 5:9).

Selfish Ambition Is Overcome by Submission to God (James 4:2–5)

Selfish ambition causes quarrels and fights within the Christian community, and James says the underlying cause is their failure to depend on God. "You covet something and cannot obtain it; so you engage in disputes and conflicts. You do not have, because you do not ask. You ask and do not receive, because you ask wrongly, in order to spend what you get on your pleasures" (James 4:2–3). We fail to depend on God when we don't even ask him for what we need. Interestingly, the reason we don't depend on God is because we want to serve our own pleasures rather than serving others. This wraps the two principles into an integral unit. James states this metaphorically as an adulterous love affair with the world, by which he means the wealth and pleasure we are tempted to believe we can find in the world without God (James 4:4–5).[8]

Investing in Others (James 4:1–12)

Although James uses the metaphor of adultery, he is talking about selfish ambition in general. In the workplace, one temptation is to use others as stepping stones to our own success. When we steal the credit for a subordinate's or co-worker's work, when we withhold information from a rival for promotion, when we shift the blame to someone not present to defend themselves, when we take advantage of someone in a difficult situation, we are guilty of selfish ambition. James is right that this is a chief source of quarrels. Ironically, selfish ambition may impede success rather than promote it. The higher our position in an organization, the more we depend on others for success. It can be as simple as delegating work to subordinates, or as complex as coordinating an international project team. But if we have a reputation for stepping on other people to get ahead, how can we expect others to trust and follow our leadership?

The remedy lies in submitting to God, who created all people in his image (Gen. 1:27) and who sent his Son to die for all (2 Cor. 5:14). We submit to God whenever we put our ambition in the service of others

---

[8] James borrows the metaphor of adultery from the Old Testament prophets, who frequently used it to depict the pursuit of wealth and pleasure as substitutes for God.

ahead of ourselves. Do we want to rise to a position of authority and excellence? Good, then we should begin by helping *other* workers increase their authority and excellence. Does success motivate us? Good, then we should invest in the success of those around us. Ironically, investing in others' success may also turn out to be the best thing we can do for ourselves. According to economists Elizabeth Dunn of the University of British Columbia and Michael Norton of Harvard Business School, investing in other people makes us happier than spending money on ourselves.[9]

Business Forecasting (James 4:13–17)

James moves to a new application in giving a warning specifically about business forecasting.[10] Somewhat unusually, he focuses first on the principle of trusting God. He opens with sobering words: "Come now, you who say, 'Today or tomorrow we will go to such and such a town and spend a year there, doing business and making money.' Yet you do not even know what tomorrow will bring. What is your life? For you are a mist that appears for a little while and then vanishes" (James 4:13–14). It might seem that James is condemning even short-term business planning. Planning ahead, however, is not his concern. Imagining that we are in control of what happens is the problem.

The following verse helps us see James's real point: "Instead, you ought to say, 'If the Lord wishes, we will live and do this or that'" (James 4:15). The problem is not planning; it is planning as if the future lies in our hands. We are responsible to use wisely the resources, abilities, connections, and time that God gives us. But we are not in control of the outcomes. Most businesses are well aware how unpredictable outcomes are, despite the best planning and execution that money can buy. The annual report of any publicly traded corporation will feature a detailed section

---

[9] Elizabeth Dunn and Michael Norton, *Happy Money: The Science of Smarter Spending* (New York: Simon & Schuster, 2013).

[10] These warnings seem to echo both Jesus' teaching and the Old Testament prophets. See, for example, Ezekiel 34:3; Amos 2:6–7; 5:12; Micah 2:2; 6:12–16; Matthew 6:19; Luke 6:24–25; 12:13–21; 32–34; 16:19–31; 18:18–30. Note also that James 1:1–18 focuses on understanding past and present success and failure, while this section focuses on forecasting the future.

on risks the company faces, often running ten or twenty pages. Statements such as "Our stock price may fluctuate based on factors beyond our control" make it clear that secular corporations are highly attuned to the unpredictability James is talking about.

Why then does James have to remind believers of what ordinary businesses know so well? Perhaps believers sometimes delude themselves that following Christ will make them immune to the unpredictability of life and work. This is a mistake. Instead, James's words should make Christians more aware of the need to continually reassess, adapt, and adjust. Our plans should be flexible and our execution responsive to changing conditions. In one sense, this is simply good business practice. Yet in a deeper sense, it is a spiritual matter, for we need to respond not only to market conditions but also to God's leading in our work. This brings us back to James's exhortation to listen with deep attention. Christian leadership consists not in forcing others to comply with our plans and actions, but in adapting ourselves to God's word and God's unfolding guidance in our lives.

Oppression of Workers (James 5:1–6)

James returns to the principle that work must serve the needs of others. His words in the beginning of chapter 5 are scathing. He warns "the rich" to "weep and wail for the miseries that are coming to you" (James 5:1). While the gold in their vaults and the robes in their closets may look as shiny as ever, James is so certain of their coming judgment that he can speak as if their riches were already decomposing: "Your riches have rotted, and your clothes are moth-eaten. Your gold and silver have rusted" (James 5:2–3). Their self-indulgence has succeeded only in "fattening" them "for the day of slaughter" (James 5:5). The day of slaughter seems to be a reference to the day in which God judges those whom he called to lead and care for his people, but who preyed on them instead (Zech. 11:4–7).

These rich people are doomed both for how they acquired their wealth and for what they did (or didn't do) with it once they had it. James echoes the Old Testament as he excoriates them for their unjust business practices: "Listen! The wages of the laborers who mowed your fields, which you kept back by fraud, cry out, and the cries of the har-vesters have reached the ears of the Lord of hosts" (James 5:4; cf. Lev. 19:13).[11] Money that should be in the hands of laborers sits instead in the treasuries of the landowners. And there it stays—they hoard their wealth and ignore the needy around them (James 5:3).

Business leaders must be especially diligent about paying their work-ers fairly. An analysis of what constitutes fair pay is beyond the scope of this discussion,[12] but James's words "the wages you have kept back by fraud" (James 5:4) are an accusation of abuse of power on the part of these particular wealthy landowners. The workers were owed wages, but the rich and powerful found a way out of paying them without incurring punishment by the legal system. The rich and powerful often have means to subvert the judiciary, and it's astonishingly easy to exercise unfair power without even recognizing it. Abuses of power include misclas-sifying employees as independent contractors, inaccurately registering workers in a lower skill code, paying women or minorities less for doing the same job as others, and using children for jobs so dangerous that adults refuse to do them. Misuse of power can never be excused just because it is a so-called standard practice.

James also condemns those who "have lived on the earth in luxury and in pleasure" (James 5:5). The question of what constitutes living in luxury and in pleasure is also complex, but it confronts many Chris-tians in one way or another. James's chief concern in this passage is the well-being of the poor, so the most relevant question may be, "Does the way I live enhance or diminish the lives of poor people? Does what I do with money help lift people out of poverty or does it help keep people impoverished?"

Waiting for the Harvest (James 5:7–20)

James concludes his letter with a variety of exhortations on patience, truthfulness, prayer, confession, and healing. As always, these appeal

---

[11] Leviticus 19 is one of James's favorite Old Testament passages; see Luke Timothy Johnson, *Brother of Jesus, Friend of God* (Grand Rapids: Eerdmans, 2004), 123ff.

[12] See, however, "Pay" at www.theologyofwork.org.

either to the principle that faithful works must benefit others or that it must be done in dependence on God, or both. And as usual, James makes direct applications to the workplace.

Patience

James begins with a workplace example to illustrate the looming return of Christ: "Be patient, therefore, beloved, until the coming of the Lord. The farmer waits for the precious crop from the earth, being patient with it until it receives the early and the late rains. You also must be patient. Strengthen your hearts, for the coming of the Lord is near" (James 5:7–8). He then echoes these words as he draws to a close: "Elijah was a human being like us, and he prayed fervently that it might not rain, and for three years and six months it did not rain on the earth. Then he prayed again, and the heaven gave rain and the earth yielded its harvest" (James 5:17–18).

Patience at work is a form of dependence on God. But patience is hard in the workplace. Work is done to obtain a result—otherwise it wouldn't be work—and there is always the temptation to grasp for the result without actually doing the work. If we're investing to make money, wouldn't we like to get rich quick rather than slow? That mentality leads to insider trading, Ponzi schemes, and gambling away the grocery money at the slot machines. If we're working to get promoted, shouldn't we position ourselves better in our supervisor's eyes by any means available? That leads to backstabbing, stealing credit, gossip, and team disintegration. If we're working to meet a quota, couldn't we meet it faster by doing lower-quality work and passing off the problems to the next person in the production chain? And these are not only problems of personal morality. A production system that rewards poor quality is as bad or worse than the worker who takes advantage of it.

Truthfulness

"Above all, my beloved, do not swear, either by heaven or by earth or by any other oath, but let your 'Yes' be yes and your 'No' be no, so that you may not fall under condemnation" (James 5:12). Imagine a workplace in which people always told the truth—not simply avoiding lying but always saying whatever would give the hearer the most accurate understanding of the way things really are. There would be no need for oaths and swearing, no retroactive clarifications, no need for contract provisions defining who gets what in the case of misstatements or fraud. Imagine if sellers always provided maximally informative data about their products, contracts were always clear to all parties, and bosses always gave accurate credit to their subordinates. Imagine if *we* always gave answers that communicated as accurate a picture as possible, rather than subtly concealing unflattering information about our work. Could we succeed in our present jobs or careers? Could we succeed if everyone became maximally truthful? Do we need to change our definition of success?[13]

Prayer

James returns to the principle of dependence on God in his discussion of prayer. "Are any among you suffering? They should pray" (James 5:13). "If any of you is lacking in wisdom, ask God" (James 1:5). James is inviting us to get specific with God. "God, I don't know how to handle this production failure, and I need your help before I go talk to my boss." God is able to accomplish what we need, though he does not guarantee to answer every prayer exactly as we expect. Many Christians seem strangely reluctant to pray about the specific issues, situations, persons, needs, fears, and questions we encounter every day at work. We forget James's exhortation to ask for specific guidance and even particular outcomes. Have faith, says James, and God will answer us in the real situations of life. "Ask God, who gives to all generously and ungrudgingly, and it will be given you" (James 1:5).

Confession and Healing

James exhorts us to confess our sins to one another, so that we may be healed (James 5:16). The most interesting words for the workplace are "to one another." The assumption is that people sin against each other, not just against God, and at work that is certainly the case. We face daily pressure to produce and perform, and we have limited time

---

[13] For more on this topic, see "Truth and Deception" at www.theologyof work.org.

to act, so we often act without listening, marginalize those who disagree, compete unfairly, hog resources, leave a mess for the next person to clean up, and take out our frustrations on co-workers. We wound and get wounded. The only way to be healed is to confess our sins *to one another*. If someone just shot down a co-worker's promotion by inaccurately criticizing that person's performance, the wrongdoer needs to confess it to the one wronged at work, not just to God in private prayer time. The wrongdoer may have to confess it to the rest of the department too, if he or she is really going to heal the damage.

What is our motivation for confession and healing? So that we may serve the needs of others. "Whoever brings back a sinner from wandering will *save the sinner's soul from death*" (James 5:20; emphasis added). Saving someone from death is serving a very deep need! And perhaps—since we are all sinners—someone else will save us from death by turning us from the error of our ways.

1 Peter: Serving the World as Resident Alien Priests

Writing to a group of Christians who are being slandered, falsely accused, and perhaps even physically abused because of their allegiance to Jesus (1 Pet. 2:12, 18–20; 3:13–17; 4:4, 14, 19), Peter explains how Christians are called to transform their suffering into service to the world. Christ has called us to follow him in a world that does not recognize him. We are resident aliens in this strange land, which is not yet our true home. Therefore, we are bound to experience "various trials" (1 Pet. 1:6). Yet we are not victims of the world, but servants to the world—"a holy priesthood" as Peter puts it (1 Pet. 2:5)—bringing God's blessings to the world. The job of the Christian, then, is to live in this alien land, blessing it until Christ returns and restores the territory to his kingdom.

Resident Aliens and Priests (1 Peter 1:1–2:12)

In the opening line of his letter, Peter addresses his readers as "exiles . . . who have been chosen" (1 Pet. 1:1), a phrase that foreshadows Peter's entire message. This phrase has two parts, "exiles" and "chosen."

If you are a citizen of Christ's kingdom, you are an exile, because at present the world around you is not under Christ's rule. You are living under foreign rule. While you await Christ's return, your true citizenship in his kingdom is "kept in heaven for you" (1 Pet. 1:4). Like exiles in any country, you do not necessarily enjoy the favor of the rulers of the land where you live. Christ came to this land himself but was "rejected by mortals" (1 Pet. 2:4), and all citizens of his kingdom should expect the same treatment. Nonetheless, God has called us to stay here, to reside in this alien land while conducting the work of Christ (1 Pet. 1:15–17).

Although couched in a political metaphor, Peter's discussion rings with workplace terminology: "deeds" (1 Pet. 1:17), "silver or gold" (1 Pet. 1:18), "tested by fire" (1 Pet. 1:7), "purified" (1 Pet. 1:22), and "built into a . . . house" (1 Pet. 2:5). Peter's workplace terms remind us that we live in a world of work, and we have to find a way of following Christ in the midst of the working world around us.

Having described what it means to be "exiles," Peter takes up the other term from 1 Peter 1:1—"chosen." If you're a Christian, you have been chosen by God. For what purpose? To be one of God's priests in the foreign country you inhabit. "Like living stones, let yourselves be built into a spiritual house, to be a holy priesthood, to offer spiritual sacrifices acceptable to God through Jesus Christ" (1 Pet. 2:5). The title of priest, or "royal priesthood," is repeated in 1 Peter 2:9.

Priests in Ancient Israel Offer Sacrifices and Blessings for Israel

Before continuing, we must understand what it meant to be a priest in ancient Israel. Priests performed two chief functions: offering sacrifices in the Temple in Jerusalem, and pronouncing the priestly blessing.[14] In order to perform their duty of offering sacrifices, priests had to be able to enter the inner portions of the temple and—once a year, in the case of the high priest—to stand in the Holy of Holies before the divine presence. In order to say the priestly blessing, priests had to speak for God

---

[14]The priestly blessing was commanded by God to be offered by priests in Numbers 6:23–24 and consists of the words in Numbers 6:24–26, "The Lord bless you and keep you; the Lord make his face shine upon you and be gracious to you; the Lord lift up his countenance upon you and give you peace."

himself. Both of these duties required priests to enter God's presence. This in turn required exceptional purity or holiness, since God's presence cannot abide anything impure or polluted.[15] Yet priests served part time according to a rotation system (Luke 1:8) and had ordinary jobs as their chief means of livelihood. They could not sequester themselves from daily life but had to maintain purity despite the dirt and corruption of the world.

Christians as Priests Offer Self-Sacrifice and Blessings for Others in Need

So for Peter to call Christians "a holy priesthood" (1 Pet. 2:5) and "a royal priesthood" (1 Pet. 2:9) does *not* mean that all Christians should think of themselves as professional pastors. It does not mean that becoming an evangelist or missionary is the highest way of fulfilling God's call to be chosen people. It means that Christians are to live lives of exceptional purity in the midst of whatever our livelihoods are. Only so can we offer sacrifices to God and blessings from God on behalf of the people around us.

Peter states this directly: "Beloved, I urge you as aliens and exiles to abstain from the desires of the flesh that wage war against the soul. Conduct yourselves honorably among the Gentiles, so that, though they malign you as evildoers, they may see your honorable deeds and glorify God when he comes to judge" (1 Pet. 2:11–12). (Notice the concern to glorify God's presence "when he comes to judge.")

Of course, Christians do not perform the same sacrifice as Jewish priests (we do not slaughter animals). Instead, we perform the kind of sacrifice our Lord did: self-sacrifice for the benefit of others in need. "To this you have been called," Peter says, "because Christ also suffered for you, leaving you an example, so that you should follow in his steps" (1 Pet. 2:21). This is not to be taken over-literally as death on a cross, but is to be understood as "spiritual sacrifices" (1 Pet. 2:5)—

---

[15] For God's holiness and the consequent need for human holiness in his presence, see Leviticus 11:44–45. For the extensive cleansing and consecration process of the high priest on the Day of Atonement, see Leviticus 11:44–45. For the extensive cleansing and consecration process of the high priest on the Day of Atonement, see Leviticus 16.

meaning acts performed at the expense of self for the benefit of others in need (1 Pet. 4:10). Our workplaces offer daily opportunities for self-sacrifices—small or large.

This brief survey of 1 Peter 1:3–2:10 fills out the picture Peter paints when he calls his readers "exiles . . . who have been chosen." The term "exiles" means that we live out this vocation as resident aliens in a land that is yet to be our home—a place currently characterized by systemic injustice and corruption. The term "chosen" affirms that followers of Jesus—a "royal priesthood"—have the priest's vocation to be a blessing to the world, especially through self-sacrifice.

Suffering under the World's Authorities (1 Peter 2:13–4:19)

What might it look like for Christians to exercise our calling as resident aliens and priests in the work environment? Peter addresses this directly in instructions to his readers as foreigners and slaves. As foreigners, we are to honor and submit to the civil rule of whatever country we find ourselves in (1 Pet. 2:13–14), even though our citizenship in God's kingdom entitles us to live as "free people" (1 Pet. 2:16). As slaves—which apparently constituted a large segment of Peter's readers, since he does not address any other class of workers—we should submit ourselves to our masters, whether they treat us justly or unjustly (1 Pet. 2:18–19). In fact, unjust treatment is to be expected (1 Pet. 4:12), and it offers us an opportunity to follow in Christ's footsteps by suffering without retaliating (1 Pet. 2:21). Notice that Peter is talking about suffering unjustly, not suffering from the consequences of your own incompetence, arrogance, or ignorance. Of course, you need to suffer obediently when receiving just punishment.

In practical terms, you are not free to disobey those in authority even in order to get what you think is rightfully yours. You will surely find yourself in situations where you don't get what you deserve—a promotion, a raise, an office with a window, a decent health care plan. You may even find your employer actively cheating you, forcing you to work off the clock, punishing you for your boss's errors. It might seem ethical to cheat your employer just enough to make up what you were cheated out of—calling in sick when you're not, charging personal items to the company, stealing office supplies or goofing off on company time. But no, "It is better to suffer for doing good, if suffering should be God's will, than to suffer for doing evil" (1 Pet. 3:17). God does not give you the option to take back what was wrongfully taken from you. The fact that you lied to or cheated someone to make up for how they lied to or cheated you does not make your action less evil. Your call is to do right, even in a hostile work environment (1 Pet. 2:20). "Do not repay evil with evil or insult with insult" (1 Pet. 3:9). Instead, Christians should treat those in authority—even harsh and unjust masters—with respect and honor.

Why? Because our vocation as priests is to bless people, and we can't do that while defending ourselves, just as Christ could not die for the salvation of the world while defending himself (1 Pet. 2:21–25). Christ, of course, was not afraid to exercise power and challenge authority in certain circumstances, and Peter is not claiming to recapitulate the entire gospel here. Other parts of the Bible—especially the Prophets—emphasize God's call to resist oppressive and illegitimate authority. And submission doesn't always mean obedience. We can submit to authority by disobeying openly and accepting the consequences, as Jesus himself did. Here and throughout the epistle, Peter draws us almost exclusively to the self-sacrifice of Christ as a model.

Instructions for Leaders and Followers (1 Peter 5)

Peter now gives instructions for church leaders, termed "elders" ("presbyters" and "bishops" in the Anglicized Greek derivations used in many churches today). The advice is good for workplace leaders, too. It focuses on serving others. "Tend the flock of God . . . willingly [and] eagerly" (1 Pet. 5:2). Don't be greedy for money (1 Pet. 5:2). Don't lord it over others, but be an example for others to emulate (1 Pet. 5:3). Peter advises humility to the young—in fact, to everyone—when he quotes Proverbs 3:34, "God opposes the proud, but gives grace to the humble" (1 Pet. 5:5). These are not unique to 1 Peter, and we will not expand on them here. It is enough to remember that the concept of servant-leadership, circulating widely in today's workplace, is well known to Peter. How could it be otherwise, since Jesus is the servant-leader par excellence (1 Pet. 4:1–2, 6)?

2 Peter: Work and New Creation

Second Peter reinforces many of the themes we saw in James and 1 Peter concerning the need for holy living and endurance in suffering. We will not repeat these, but instead discuss only chapter 3, which raises a profound challenge to a theology of work. If "the present heavens and earth have been reserved for fire, being kept until the day of judgment and destruction of the godless" (2 Pet. 3:7), what is the value of our work in the present day? To borrow the title of Darrell Cosden's important book, what is the heavenly good of earthly work?[16]

The End of the World and the End of Work? (2 Peter 3:1–18)

Does our earthly work matter to God? Darrell Cosden has given a resounding "yes" to that question. Central to his argument is the bodily resurrection of Jesus, which (1) affirms the goodness of the material world, (2) demonstrates that there is continuity between the present world and new creation,[17] and (3) is a sign that new creation, while not fully realized, has been initiated. Our work is ultimately valuable because the fruits of our labor, having been redeemed and transformed, will have a home in heaven. But chapter 3 seems to call into question two integral aspects of Cosden's theology of work: (1) the inherent goodness of created matter, and (2) the continuity between this present world and the world to come, the new creation.

Peter is responding here to lawless scoffers who claimed that God would not intervene in history to judge evil (2 Pet. 3:3–4). He appears to describe a future that lacks all continuity with the present world; instead, it looks like the annihilation of the cosmos:

---

[16] Darrell Cosden, *The Heavenly Good of Earthly Work* (Peabody, MA: Hendrickson Publishers, 2006).

[17] "Jesus' nail-scarred hands and feet are the prototype for the coming new creation. What we find true in his body, we also find true in this vision. What we have done—although it is ambivalent at best on its own—once redeemed and transformed, does find a home in the new creation." Cosden, 76.

1. "The present heavens and earth have been reserved for fire, being kept until the day of judgment and destruction of the godless." (2 Pet. 3:7)

2. "The heavens will pass away with a loud noise, and the elements will be dissolved with fire, and the earth and everything that is done on it will be disclosed." (2 Pet. 3:10)

3. "All these things are to be dissolved." (2 Pet. 3:11)

4. "The heavens will be set ablaze and dissolved, and the elements will melt with fire." (2 Pet. 3:12)

5. But we should not be too quick to assume that annihilation is really in view here.[18] Peter is using the end-times imagery commonly found in Old Testament prophetic oracles to assure his readers of God's impending judgment. The Old Testament prophets and Second Temple Jewish literature regularly employed fire imagery metaphorically to refer to both the purging of the righteous and the destruction of all evil.[19]

A reading of 2 Peter 2:7, 10 and 2 Peter 3:12 in keeping with the conventions of apocalyptic literature, would understand the fire and melting imagery as a metaphor for the process in which God separates good from evil.[20] This is how Peter uses fire imagery in his first letter,

---

[18] See Richard J. Bauckham, *Jude, 2 Peter,* ed. Bruce M. Metzger, David A. Hubbard, and Glenn W, Barker, vol. 50, *Word Biblical Commentary* (Dallas: Word, 1983); and John Dennis, "Cosmology in the Petrine Literature and Jude," in *Cosmology and New Testament Theology,* ed. Jonathan Pennington and Sean McDonough (London: Continuum, 2008), 157–77, for thorough discussions of this complex passage.

[19] See, for example, Isaiah 30:30; 66:15–16; Nahum 1:6; Zephaniah 1:18; 3:8; Zechariah 13:7–9; Malachi 3:2–3; 4:1–2; Sirach 2; Wisdom of Solomon 3. The New Testament uses fire imagery this way as well: 1 Corinthians 3:10–15; 1 Peter 1:5–7; 4:12–13, etc.

[20] Douglas Moo, "Nature in the New Creation: New Testament Eschatology and the Environment," *Journal of the Evangelical Theological Society* 49, no. 3 (2006), 468. See also Al Wolters, who argues that the fire imagery refers to the

reminding his readers that, like gold, they too will be tested through fire; those who make it through the fire will be praised and honored by God (1 Pet. 1:5–7). These passages stress not that the heavens and the earth will be literally annihilated, but rather that all evil will be utterly consumed. Likewise, Peter carefully describes the world in terms of transformation and testing: "dissolved," "melt with fire," "judgment," "reserved for fire." Douglas Moo points out that the word Peter uses for "dissolved" in 2 Peter 3:10–12, *luō*, does not connote annihilation, but instead speaks to radical transformation. He suggests that an alternate translation might be "undone."[21]

Peter's reference to the flood of Noah's time (2 Pet. 3:5–6) should caution us against reading "deluged" to mean total annihilation. The world did not cease to exist, but was purified of all humanity's wickedness. Humanity's goodness—limited to Noah, his family, their possessions, and their work of tending the animals on board—was preserved, and life resumed on the physical earth.

Finally, Peter's positive vision of the ultimate future describes a renewal of the material order: "But, in accordance with his promise, we wait for new heavens and a new earth, where righteousness is at home" (2 Pet. 3:13). This is no thin, disembodied netherworld, but a new cosmos that contains both a "heaven" and an "earth." In 2 Peter 3:10 we read that "the earth and everything that is done on it will be disclosed." Disclosed, not destroyed. Thus even after the burning, "works" will remain.

This is not to say that 2 Peter is the chief source for the theology of the eternal value of present work, but only that 2 Peter is consistent with such a theology. While we may not receive as much detail as we would want, clearly for Peter there is some sort of continuity between what we do on earth now and what we will experience in the future. All evil will be utterly consumed, but all that is righteous will find a permanent home in the new creation. Fire not only consumes, it purges. The dissolution does not signal the end of work. Rather, work done for God finds its true end in the new heavens and new earth.

---

process of God refining the world. Al Wolters, "Worldview and Textual Criticism in 2 Peter 3:10," *Westminster Theological Journal* 49 (1987), 405–13.

[21] Moo, "Nature in the New Creation," 468–69.

1 John: Walking in the Light

Although written under greatly different circumstances than James,[22] 1 John also challenges the notion that faith can live without "works," that is, acts of obedience toward God. In chapter 2, John states that genuine knowledge of God is manifested by transformed character and behavior, epitomized in obedience to God:

> Now by this we may be sure that we know him, if we obey his commandments. Whoever says, "I have come to know him," but does not obey his commandments, is a liar, and in such a person the truth does not exist; but whoever obeys his word, truly in this person the love of God has reached perfection. By this we may be sure that we are in him: whoever says, "I abide in him," ought to walk just as he walked. (1 John 2:3–6)

Again in keeping with James, 1 John regards caring for those in need as one expression of genuine knowledge of God. "How does God's love abide in anyone who has the world's goods and sees a brother or sister in need and yet refuses help?" (1 John 3:17). First John takes us one step further in understanding the relationship between faith and works or, to use John's terms, between knowledge of God and obedience.

Using a variety of images, John explains that our obedience to God indicates, and is the result of, a prior reality variously described as passing from darkness to light (1 John 2:8–11), being loved by God (1 John 3:16; 4:7–10, 16, 19–20), being born of God or made children of God (1 John 2:29; 3:1–2, 8–9), or passing from death to life (1 John 3:14). According to John, right living is first and foremost a result and response to God's love toward us:

> Everyone who loves is born of God and knows God. Whoever does not love does not know God, for God is love. God's love was revealed among us in this way: God sent his only Son into the world so that we might live through him. In this is love, not that we loved God but that he loved us and sent his Son to be the atoning sacrifice for our sins. (1 John 4:7–10)

---

[22] Colin G. Kruse, *The Letters of John* (Grand Rapids: Eerdmans, 2000), 14–28.

John describes the result of this process as the ability to "walk in the light as he himself is in the light" (1 John 1:7). God's love through Jesus' atoning sacrifice brings us into a qualitatively different kind of existence, whereby we are able to see and walk in keeping with God's will for our lives. We don't merely turn on the light once in a while. We walk in the light continually, as a new way of life.

This has immediate significance to workplace ethics. In recent years, there has been increasing attention to "virtue ethics" after a long history of neglect in Protestant thought and practice.[23] Virtue ethics focuses on the long-term formation of moral character, rather than on formulating rules and calculating consequences of immediate decisions. Not that rules or commands are irrelevant—"For the love of God is this, that we obey his commandments" (1 John 5:3)—but that long-term moral formation underlies obedience to the rules. A full discussion is beyond the scope of this discussion,[24] but John's concept of walking in the light as a way of life certainly commends the virtue approach. What we do (our "works") springs inevitably from who we are becoming (our virtues). "We love because he first loved us" (1 John 4:19), and we are becoming like him (1 John 3:2).

One specific application of the light metaphor is that we should be open and transparent in our workplace actions. We should welcome scrutiny of our actions, rather than trying to hide our actions from the light of day. We could never defraud investors, falsify quality records, gossip about co-workers, or extort bribes while walking in the light. In this sense, 1 John 1:7 echoes the Gospel of John 3:20–21, "All who do evil hate the light and do not come to the light, so that their deeds may not be exposed. But those who do what is true come to the light, so that it may be clearly seen that their deeds have been done in God."[25]

For example, Rob Smith heads a business-in-mission organization in Africa that builds boats for use on Lake Victoria. He says he is

---

[23] See the introduction to Stanley Hauerwas, *Character and the Christian Life* (Notre Dame: University of Notre Dame Press, 2001).

[24] See Alistair Mackenzie and Wayne Kirkland, "Ethics," at www.theology ofwork.org./key-topics/ethics.

[25] For a fuller discussion, see "John and Work" in *The Theology of Work Bible Commentary*, vol. 4 or at www.theologyofwork.org.

frequently approached by local officials who want him to pay a bribe. The request is always made in secret. It is not a documented, open payment, as is a tip or an expediting fee for faster service. There are no receipts and the transaction is not recorded anywhere. He has used John 3:20–21 as an inspiration to draw these requests into the light. He will say to the official requesting the bribe, "I don't know much about these kinds of payments. I would like to bring in the ambassador, or the management, to get this documented." He has found this to be a helpful strategy to dealing with bribery. Although it is widely believed that bribery is an effective—albeit unethical—means of increasing market share and profit, research by George Serafeim at Harvard Business School indicates that paying bribes actually decreases a company's financial performance in the long term.[26]

In a related manner, 1 John underscores that we don't need full-time jobs in ministry to do meaningful work in God's kingdom. While most Christians don't have jobs in which they get paid to do the so-called "spiritual" tasks of preaching and evangelism, all Christians can walk in the light by obeying God in their actions (1 John 3:18–19, 24). All such actions come from God's prior love, and therefore are deeply spiritual and meaningful. Thus nonchurch work has value, not only because it is a place where you may get a chance to evangelize, or because the wages you earn can go toward funding missions, but because it is a place where you can embody fellowship with Christ by serving others around you. Work is a highly practical way of loving your neighbor, because work is where you create products and services that meet the needs of people nearby and far away. Work is a spiritual calling.

In this sense, 1 John brings us full circle back to James. Both stress that acts of obedience are integral to the Christian life, and indicate how this factors into a theology of work. We are able to obey God, at work and elsewhere, because we are becoming like Christ, who laid down his life for the benefit of others in need.

---

[26] George Serafeim, "The Real Cost of Bribery," *Harvard Business School Working Knowledge,* November 4, 2013, http://hbswk.hbs.edu/item/7325.html.

2 John and Work

The Second Letter of John fits into the overall framework of the General Epistles, while offering its own insights about life and work in Christ. It is short, but full of practical instruction.

Truthfulness (2 John 1–11)

Truth and Love at Work (2 John 1–6)

Each of John's letters is notable for bringing the concepts "truth" and "love" together into a single idea (1 John 3:18; 2 John 1, 3; 3 John 3). Here in 2 John, we find the most extended development of this idea.

> Grace, mercy, and peace will be with us from God the Father and from Jesus Christ, the Father's Son, in truth and love. I was overjoyed to find some of your children walking in the truth, just as we have been commanded by the Father. But now, dear lady, I ask you, not as though I were writing you a new commandment, but one we have had from the beginning, let us love one another. (2 John 3–5)

According to John, love plus truth equals an environment in which "grace, mercy and peace will be with us."

Regrettably, we often act as though grace, mercy, and peace depend on love *minus* truth. We may hide or shade uncomfortable truths in our communications with others at work in the misguided belief that telling the truth would not be loving. Or we may fear that telling the truth will lead to conflict or ill will, rather than grace or peace. Thinking we are being merciful, we fail to tell the truth.

But love must always begin with the truth. Love comes to us through Christ, and Christ is the perfect embodiment of the truth of God. That is to say, God knows the way things really are, and he wraps his knowledge in love and brings it to us through his Son. So if we are ever to love as God loves, we must begin with the truth, not with falsity, evasion, or fairytales. It is true that telling the truth may lead to conflict or upset feelings—ours or others'. But genuine grace, mercy, and peace come from facing reality and working through difficulties to genuine resolutions.

Jack Welch, a former CEO of General Electric (USA), was a controversial figure due in part to his practice of giving truthful, candid performance reviews. He let employees know on a monthly basis how well they were meeting expectations. Once a year he told them whether they were top performers, middle performers who needed to improve in specific areas, or bottom performers who were in danger of losing their jobs.[27] Some may regard this as harsh, but Welch regarded it as loving:

> I've come to learn that the worst kind of manager is the one who practices false kindness. I tell people, You think you're a nice manager, that you're a kind manager? Well, guess what? You won't be there someday. You'll be promoted. Or you'll retire. And a new manager will come in and look at the employee and say, "Hey, you're not that good." And all of a sudden, this employee is now fifty-three or fifty-five, with many fewer options in life. And now you're gonna tell him, "Go home"? How is that kind? You're the cruelest kind of manager.[28]

The Cost of Truthfulness (2 John 7–11)

"Many deceivers have gone out into the world," John reminds us (2 John 7), and telling the truth can bring us into conflict with those who benefit from deception. Do we choose to tell the truth despite opposition, or do we participate in the deception? If we choose deception, we had better at least admit that we are no longer honest people. (See "You Shall Not Bear False Witness Against Your Neighbor" in Deuteronomy 5:20; Exodus 20:16 at www.theologyofworkorg for more on this topic.)

Ed Moy, later to become the head of the U.S. Mint, tells the story of his first job out of college. When he started the job, he had to fill out an expense report for his use of the company car, identifying his personal use of the car and separating this from his company use. The practice in the office had been had been to list personal use only for the travel from

---

[27] "Should I Rank My Employees?" *Wall Street Journal*, April 7, 2009, http://guides.wsj.com/management/recruiting-hiring-and-firing/should -i-rank-my-employees.

[28] Jack Welch, in "What I've Learned: Jack Welch" *Esquire*, December 31, 2006, http://www.esquire.com/features/what-ive-learned/wi10104jackwelch #ixzz2nkRA41TP.

home to work, claiming the rest as company use even if the purpose of the trip was personal. When Ed honestly broke out his personal use, his boss almost fired him, explaining, "We are underpaid, and this is our way to gain more income. Your report will make the rest of us look bad." Ed respectfully said, "You can fire me if that is what you need to do. But would you really want someone working for you who would lie over such a small thing? How could you trust that person when the stakes were higher?" Ed kept his job, though the transition was a bit difficult![29]

What are we to do about relationships with deceitful people and false teachers? Ed's example suggests that breaking off contact is not necessarily the best solution. We may be able to do more for the cause of truth and love by remaining engaged and telling the truth in the midst of deception than by leaving the scene. Besides, if we broke contact with everyone who ever practiced deception, would anyone be left, even ourselves?

The Value of In-Person Communications (2 John 12–13)

John ends the letter by saying that he wants to continue the conversation in person. "Although I have much to write to you, I would rather not use paper and ink; instead I hope to come to you and talk with you face to face" (2 John 12). Perhaps he realizes that whatever else he has to communicate could be misunderstood if presented in the impersonal medium of writing a letter. This gives us a valuable insight about sensitive communications—some things are better said in person, even if distance makes it difficult to see one another face to face.

In twenty-first-century workplaces we find even more complex challenges to personal communication. Remote communication choices today include video conferencing, telephone, texting, letter, e-mail, social media, and many other variations. But effective communication still requires matching the medium to the nature of the message. E-mail might be the most effective medium for placing an order, for example, but probably not for communicating a performance review. The more

---

[29] Ed Moy, "Faith and Work: Spiritual Insights from a Career in Business & Public Service," at *Kiros*, Seattle, October 11, 2013. Audio recording available at http://kiros.btexpo.ws/media.

complicated or emotionally challenging the message, the more immediate and personal the medium needs to be. Pat Gelsinger, former senior vice president at Intel Corporation, says,

> I have a personal rule. If I go back and forth with somebody in email more than four or five times on the same topic, I stop. No more. We get on the phone, or we get together face to face. I have learned that if you don't resolve something quickly, by the time you get together one of you is mad at the other person. You think they are incompetent since they could not understand the most straightforward thing that you were describing. But it is because of the medium, and it is important to account for this.[30]

The wrong medium for a particular communication can easily lead to misunderstanding, which is failure to transmit the truth. And the wrong medium can also get in the way of showing love. So choosing the right medium for communication is an essential aspect of communicating truth and showing love to people with whom we work. We need to communicate with respect and compassion, even in difficult conversations, and especially when we communicate with people we don't like very much. Sometimes this means meeting face to face, even if it is inconvenient or uncomfortable.

3 John and Work

Like 2 John, 3 John is so short that is not divided into chapters. Nonetheless, it contains two passages applicable to work.

Gossip (3 John 1–12)

John addresses the letter to a "co-worker" (2 John 8) named Gaius. John demonstrates a personal touch when he says, "I pray that all may go well with you, and that you may be in good health, just as it is well with your soul" (3 John 2). He pays attention to his co-worker's body (health)

---

[30] Pat Gelsinger, "Faster Chips, More Opportunity?" interview in *Ethix* 57 (January/February 2008), http://ethix.org/2008/02/01/faster-chips-more-opportunity.

and soul. By itself, this is an important lesson for the workplace—not to see colleagues merely as workers but as whole people.

John then offers himself as an example of someone who is not being treated well in his work. A member of the congregation named Diotrephes has been trying to undermine "our authority," John says, by "spreading false charges against us" (3 John 10). In all three of his letters, John's primary concern has been bringing together truth and love (3 John 1). Diotrephes is doing the complete opposite—speaking falsely in hate. You can almost feel John's pain as he says—to use the more dramatic translation of the New International Version—"I will call attention to what he is doing, gossiping maliciously about us" (3 John 10, NIV).

It is doubly painful that Diotrephes is a believer. This reminds us that being a Christian does not by itself make us perfect. No doubt Diotrephes thinks of himself in the right. What we recognize as false gossip, he may well consider simply warning others so they can protect themselves.

When we give our opinion of others in our places of work, do we ever make unfavorable impressions about ourselves or others? One simple test would help us see ourselves as others see us. Would we talk about people the same way if they were in the room? If not, we are very likely giving a false impression of those we're speaking about, as well as giving a bad impression about ourselves. John, while he has a complaint about Diotrephes, is not gossiping. He knows that his letter will be read aloud in the church, so his complaint will be in the open for Diotrephes to hear and respond to.

Giving his opponent an opportunity to respond to his complaint is an essential element of John's combining of truth and love. He believes that his complaint against Diotrephes is true, yet he recognizes that his opponent deserves an opportunity to explain or defend himself. How different from the kind of trial-by-press campaigns conducted by many public figures today, in which insinuations are spread through the mass media, where there is no opportunity to respond on the same scale.

This principle applies not only to how we speak of individuals but also groups. To collectively denigrate others is as bad as, if not worse than, gossiping or slandering an individual. Virtually every kind of unjust treatment of people at work begins by casting them as members of an inferior or dangerous group. Whenever we hear this happening, it signals our opportunity to speak out against prejudice and guilt by association and in favor of finding the truth of the specific situation.

John's commendation of Demetrius, the brother carrying the letter, is also interesting. John uses his influence as a leader in the church to raise up Demetrius to Gaius and his church. John commends Demetrius for both his life of truth and the respect given him by fellow believers. Leaders in the workplace can use their power and influence effectively toward the end of truth, justice, love, and mercy, even when the gospel is not outwardly acknowledged.

Greet People by Name (3 John 13–15)

The letter ends with the same thought that concludes 2 John. John has things to communicate that would be better said face to face than in pen and ink (3 John 13–14). But there is a twist in 3 John that offers another insight for our daily work. At the very end, John adds, "Greet the friends there, each by name." Speaking a person's name adds further to the personal touch that John recognizes is needed in communication.

Many of us come face to face with hundreds of people in the course of our work. To some degree, we need to communicate with each of them, even if only to avoid knocking into each other in the hallway. How many of them do we know well enough to greet by name? Do you know your boss's boss's boss's name? Probably. Do you know the name of the person who empties the trash in your workplace? Do you greet people by name when you are in conflict with them? Do you learn the names of newcomers to the organization who may need your help at some point? The names you bother to learn and those you don't can reveal a lot about your level of respect and compassion for people. John cares enough to greet "each" person by name.

Jude

The brief letter of Jude paints a startling picture of one very dysfunctional workplace—a church blighted by ungodly leaders. Some of the problems are unique to churches, such as denying Jesus Christ (Jude 4) and heresy ("Korah's rebellion," Jude 8). Others could occur in a secular workplace: rejection of authority, slander (Jude 8), violence ("the way of Cain"), and greed ("Balaam's error," Jude 8).[31] The worst abuses are perpetrated by leaders who gorge themselves at the expense of their flocks. "They feast with you without fear. They are shepherds who care only for themselves" (Jude 12, NRSV alt. reading). Jude's words apply equally to church leaders misappropriating church funds for their own pleasures, executives plundering a corporate pension fund to prop up reported profits (and thus their bonuses), or employees surfing the web on company time.

In the face of this malfeasance, Jude gives a command as surprising in the workplace as in the church: Have mercy. "Have mercy on some who are wavering; save others by snatching them out of the fire; and have mercy on still others with fear, hating even the tunic defiled by their bodies" (Jude 22–23). Jude is not afraid to take strong action against evil. His mercy is not soft or weak, as his images of fire, fear, and defiled bodies indicate. Jude's mercy is severe. But it is mercy nonetheless, for its hope is not merely to punish the offenders but to save them.

This severe mercy may be what some workplace situations require. Someone who commits fraud, harasses other workers, or lies to customers cannot be let off lightly. That leads only to greater evil. But discipline cannot turn into mere revenge. In Christ's eyes, no person is beyond hope. The godly leader treats each person with respect and tries to discern what kind of discipline might lead them back into the fold.

Conclusion to the General Epistles

The General Epistles begin with the twin principles that following Christ makes us able to trust God for our provision, and that trusting God for our provision leads us to work for the benefit of others in need. These principles underlie a variety of practical instructions for life at work (especially in James) and theological insights for understanding the place of work in the life of faith. This raises two questions for us:

---

[31] Bauckham, *Jude, 2 Peter.*

(1) Do we believe these principles? and (2) Are we in fact applying them in our work lives?

Do We Believe the Two Principles?

We see countless situations in our workplaces. Some cast doubt on whether God can be trusted for our provision. Others affirm it. We all know people who seemed to trust God but didn't get what they needed. People lose jobs, houses, retirement savings, even life itself. On the other hand, we receive good things we could never have expected and never have caused to happen ourselves. A new opportunity arises, a small thing we did leads to a big success, an investment works out well, a stranger provides for our needs. Is it true that we can trust God to provide what we truly need? The General Epistles call us to wrestle with this deep question until we have a firm answer. This could mean wrestling with it for a lifetime. Yet that would be better than ignoring it.

The principle that we should work primarily for the benefit of others in need is likewise questionable. It is at odds with the basic assumption of economics—that all workers act primarily to increase their own wealth. It clashes with society's prevailing attitude about work—"Look out for Number One." We demand proof (if we have the power to do so) that we are being paid adequately. Do we equally demand proof that our work benefits others adequately?

Are We Applying the Two Principles in Our Work?

We can assess our level of trust in God's provision by examining the things we do to provide for ourselves. Do we hoard knowledge to make ourselves indispensable? Do we require employment contracts or golden parachutes to feel secure in our future? Do we come to work in fear of being laid off? Do we obsess over work and neglect our families and communities? Do we hold on to an ill-fitting job, despite humiliation, anger, poor performance, and even health problems, because we are afraid there may be nothing else for us? There are no rigid rules, and some or all of these actions may be wise and appropriate in certain situations (obsession excepted). But what does the pattern of what we do at work say about our degree of trust in God for our provision?

The most powerful measure of our trust in God, however, is not what we do for ourselves but what we do for others. Do we help others around us to do well at work, even thought they might get ahead of us? Do we risk our positions to stand up for our co-workers, customers, suppliers, and others who are powerless or in need? Do we choose—within whatever scope of choice we may have—to work in ways that benefit others in need, as much as ways that benefit ourselves?

We need to hold ourselves and others highly accountable for applying these principles to work every day, as the letter of Jude reminds us. Obeying God's word is not a matter of religious sensibilities but of flesh-and-bone consequences for ourselves and those affected by our work. Yet accountability leads us not toward judgmentalism but toward a merciful heart.

The General Epistles challenge us to re-conceptualize our notion not only of work but of who it is we're working for. If we trust God to provide for our needs, then we can work for him and not for ourselves. When we work for God, we serve others. When we serve others, we bring God's blessing into a world in which we live as members of society, yet citizens of another kingdom. God's blessings brought into the world through our work become God's next steps in transforming the world to become our true home. Therefore, as we work "in accordance with his promise, we wait for new heavens and a new earth, where righteousness is at home" (2 Pet. 3:13).

REVELATION AND WORK

Introduction to Revelation

The book of Revelation provides some of the keenest insights in Scripture concerning the "big picture" of work. Yet it is a tough nut to crack, not only because of its intrinsic difficulty but because of the myriad interpretations that have grown up around the book. We cannot hope to solve these problems here, but we may (perhaps) find enough common ground to glean insights from the final book of the Bible.

Perhaps the greatest gap in interpretation is between those who see the book as primarily future, addressing the absolute end of history from chapter 6 on, and those who see most of the book as relating to events around the time John wrote (generally seen as the late first century AD). The good news is that responsible interpreters who hold the "futurist" view acknowledge that the events in the future are modeled on God's work in the past, most notably in Creation and the Exodus from Egypt. Likewise, even those who interpret the book primarily from the standpoint of the first century acknowledge that it does talk about the ultimate future (e.g., the New Jerusalem). For this reason, no one should object to finding *enduring spiritual truths* in the images of the book, nor in seeing a significant future orientation in the promises contained within it.

The Time of God's Kingdom (Revelation 1)

Before the book of Revelation is even a few verses old, John says something that might seem to undercut a robust theology of work: "The time is near!" Some take this to mean that John thought Jesus was coming right away in his lifetime and that he got it wrong; others believe it means that once the end-time events start happening, they will move quickly. Neither of these fit well with the rest of the New Testament, since it is clear that, in some sense, the "end times" begin with the death and resurrection of Jesus (see Heb. 1:1; 1 Cor. 10:11; Acts 2:17). So it is best to take "The time is near" to mean "God's kingdom is in your face!" with the implicit question, "How then are you going to live?" The apparent certainties of everyday life must be seen against the kingdom of God, which is already breaking into the world.

This has profound consequences for our view of work. While there is much in Scripture to commend work, nothing in the present state of affairs should be viewed as absolute. As we will see, work done faithfully for God's glory has enduring value, but God must always be allowed the first and final word. Living in light of his values is critical; there can be no compromise with the world system and its idolatrous ways.

Messages to the Churches (Revelation 2 and 3)

The messages to the seven churches emphasize the importance of works in the Christian life, and thus indirectly contribute to a proper understanding of work in general. The messages to several churches begin, "I know your works . . ." Ephesus is rebuked for not doing the works they did at first (Rev. 2:5), and Sardis likewise has not completed the work it ought to have done for Jesus (Rev. 3:2).

It bears repeating that "works" are not a bad thing in the Bible. They are rather the concrete expression of our love for God. The myth that God only cares about our heart and our feelings is a major reason work in general has been given short shrift in some Protestant circles.

There is evidence that the notorious worldliness of the Laodicean church was evident in its outlook on work and economics. When Jesus counsels these believers to buy from him gold refined in the fire, white garments to hide their nakedness, and salve to heal their eyes, he is likely playing off three of the major industries in Laodicea: banking, wool, and ophthalmology. It seems likely that the Laodiceans assumed that the resources available to them from their culture were all they needed in life. Churches, especially in prosperous countries, must recognize that material abundance can often mask spiritual poverty. Success in our work should never lead us to a sense of self-sufficiency.

The Throne Room of God (Revelation 4 and 5)

John's vision in chapters 4 and 5 is at the heart of Revelation. It is in essence a visualization of the Lord's Prayer: "Thy kingdom come, thy will be done, on earth as it is in heaven." Through Jesus' faithful witness and sacrificial death, God's kingdom will come.

We may highlight from chapter 4 that God is praised precisely as Creator of all things (esp. Rev. 4:11; cf. Rev. 14:7, where the essence of the "good news" is to worship "the one who made heaven and earth, the sea and the springs of water"). The visible world is not an afterthought, or a mere prelude to heaven, but an expression of God's glory and the basis upon which his creatures may praise him. This again is foundational for a proper understanding of work. If the world is simply an illusion separating us from the real life of heaven, work in the world will necessarily be seen as more or less a complete waste of time. If, by contrast, the world is the good creation of God, the prospects for meaningful work become more hopeful. While we must remember the world is always contingent upon God, and that the present world order is subject to considerable shaking up, it is equally important to remember that the world as God's creation stands meaningfully in his presence and is designed for his praise. In chapter 5, it is worth noting in this regard that the redemption secured by Christ, which permits God's kingdom to move forward, is precipitated by Christ's work in the visible creation. As Jacques Ellul notes, Jesus' reception of the kingdom is based on his work on earth: "The terrestrial event provokes the celestial event. . . . What happens in the divine world is defined, determined, provoked by the venture of Jesus upon the earth."[1]

The Strange Way Forward (Revelation 6–16)

God's plan to advance his kingdom, however, takes a surprising turn: before deliverance comes disaster. Yet it is perhaps not so surprising as all that. Chapters 6–16 are most reminiscent of the paradigmatic episode

---

[1] Jacques Ellul, *Apocalypse*, trans. G. W. Schreiner (New York: Seabury, 1977), 47–48.

of God's deliverance of his people, the Exodus from Egypt. Water turning to blood, locust plagues, darkening of the heavenly bodies—all these mark out that God is bringing about the end-times exodus of his people from the latter-day Pharaohs who oppress them. Again, whether we imagine this as largely in John's day or at some point in the future does not take away the basic point. God's ways are consistent from age to age; the patterns of history repeat as God works his way toward the new heavens and new earth.[2]

The importance of this for the workplace is profound. Let us take the well-known four horsemen of the Apocalypse (Rev. 6). It is generally agreed that they represent War and its devastating consequences of death, famine, and plague.[3] Especially of interest for us is the notice in 6:6, "I heard what seemed to be a voice in the midst of the four living creatures saying, 'A quart of wheat for a day's pay, and three quarts of barley for a day's pay, but do not damage the olive oil and the wine!'" While the notice about the oil and wine is obscure (it may signify that the judgment is only partial[4]), the prices of the wheat and barley are clearly inflated (Aune says it is eight times the normal price of wheat and five and one-thirds times the normal price of barley).[5]

While this could be referring to some future devastation, the cycle is all too familiar to every generation—humanity's inability to get along peaceably leads to horrific economic consequences. Since Christians are caught up in these sufferings (see the fifth seal, Rev. 6:9–11), we must

---

[2] If we take Revelation as primarily focused on John's day, the "exodus" theme might refer in the first instance to the fact that those who maintain their faithful witness will "go out" to God's presence upon their death. A futurist view would lay emphasis on the literal overthrow of the wicked kingdoms and the entry of God's people in the millennial kingdom (which may or may not be conceived of as centered in Israel). In any case, in both scenarios, the ultimate fulfillment of the exodus motif is the entry of God's people into the New Jerusalem (see below).

[3] See, e.g., Ben Witherington, *Revelation* (Cambridge: Cambridge University Press, 2003), 132–34; Grant R. Osborne, *Revelation*, vol. 27, *Baker Exegetical Commentary on the New Testament* (Grand Rapids: Baker Academic, 2002), 274; G. K. Beale, *Revelation* (Grand Rapids: Eerdmans, 1999), 370–71.

[4] For authors favoring this view, see the discussion in Osborne, 281.

[5] See the extensive discussion in David E. Aune, "Rev. 6–16," vol. 52b, *Word Biblical Commentary* (Dallas: Word, 1998), 397–400.

face the fact that our work and workplaces are often subjected to forces beyond our control. As awful as these forces may be, however, another message of Revelation 6 is that they are under God's control. To the extent that we are able, we must strive to create workplaces where justice is upheld and where people can experience the blessing of developing the gifts God has given them. But we must also recognize that God's providence permits catastrophes to enter our lives as well. Revelation encourages us to look to the ultimate destination of the New Jerusalem in the midst of an often bumpy road.

There is also perhaps an implicit challenge in 6:6 to avoid exploiting the vulnerable in the time of need. Economic realities may require price hikes in a crisis, but that is no excuse for making a tidy profit from the misery of others.

The bowl judgments in chapters 8 and 9 teach a similar lesson, though here the emphasis is on environmental disaster. Since the precise mechanics are not mentioned, the ecological devastation could perhaps involve human pollution as well as more overtly supernatural phenomena. The key is that God strikes the world in its capacity as the nurturer of idolatrous humanity. This is done not only to punish but also to wake people up to the fact that the earth is as much God's as heaven is. We cannot engineer our way out of God's presence. We cannot manipulate the environment to serve as a shelter from him.

As Revelation moves on, the emphasis shifts from God's judgments on the world to the faithful witness of his people under the reign of the Beast (who may be a single idolatrous ruler at the very end of history, or the archetype of all such idolatrous rulers). It is (deliberately) ironic that the faithful "conquerors" (Rev. 2–3) are at one level "conquered" by the Beast (Rev. 13:7), though they are ultimately vindicated by God (Rev. 11:11). The suffering of the saints includes economic suffering: those who refuse the notorious "mark of the Beast" are not allowed to "buy or sell" (Rev. 13:17). The analogies with the "mark" of Ezekiel 9 suggest that the mark of the Beast is a symbol for adherence to the idolatrous (Roman?) system ("666" can render "Nero Caesar," the consummate bad emperor). But even if one takes a more literal and futurist view, the spiritual lesson is clear: the refusal to follow the world's system of false worship can sometimes lead to negative economic consequences for the faithful. This can happen in a greater or lesser way in any society.[6] John is not denying that following God's ways can lead to positive economic consequences (as is clearly taught in Proverbs, for example). But in keeping with the rest of Revelation, he is saying that the forces of evil—though ultimately under God's control—can twist things such that what should lead to blessing instead leads to suffering. Christians must always set their mind to do what is right and honoring to God, realizing that this could lead to exclusion from economic opportunity. Judgment on idolaters is certain, and no amount of financial gain is worth throwing one's lot in with those who oppose God. This is why the Beast-followers of chapter 13 are immediately contrasted with the 144,000 of chapter 14, "in whose mouths no lie was found" (Rev. 14:5). They maintain their faithful and true witness to God no matter what.

A Tale of Two Cities (Revelation 17–22)

The most important insights into the big picture of work, however, come in the concluding chapters, where the worldly city Babylon is set against God's city, the New Jerusalem. The introductions of the cities in 17:1 and 21:9 are set in clear parallel:

> "Come, I will show you the judgment of the great whore who is seated on many waters."

> "Come, I will show you the bride, the wife of the lamb."

Babylon represents the dead-end street of humanity's attempt to build their culture apart from God. It has every appearance of being the paradise for which humanity has always longed. It is no coincidence that its gold and jewels recall those of the New Jerusalem (Rev. 17:4). Like the New Jerusalem, Babylon exercises authority over the nations and receives their wealth (note the references to "the merchants of the earth" in Rev. 18:3 and the lament of the sea traders in Rev. 18:15–19).

But it is in fact a counterfeit, doomed to be exposed by God in the final judgment. Especially instructive is the cargo list in Revelation 18:11–13

---

[6] See the judicious comments of Osborne, 518.

(see Bauckham, "Economic Critique,"[7] which describes the luxury goods flowing into Babylon). The list is modeled on Ezekiel 27:12–22 and the fall of Tyre, but it has been updated to include the luxury goods popular in Rome in John's day.

> And the merchants of the earth weep and mourn for her, since no one buys their cargo anymore—cargo of gold, silver, jewels and pearls, fine linen, purple, silk and scarlet, all kinds of scented wood, all articles of ivory, all articles of costly wood, bronze, iron, and marble, cinnamon, spice, incense, myrrh, frankincense, wine, olive oil, choice flour and wheat, cattle and sheep, horses and chariots, slaves—and human lives.

The final note about "human lives" likely relates to the slave trade, and it is the final nail in the coffin of Babylon's exploitative empire: she will stop at nothing, not even trafficking in human flesh, in pursuit of sensual self-indulgence.

The lesson that God would judge a city for its economic practices is a sobering thought. Economics is clearly a moral issue in the book of Revelation. The fact that much of the condemnation appears to stem from its self-indulgence should hit with particular force at modern consumer culture, where the constant search for more and better can lead to a myopic focus on satisfying real or imagined material needs. But the most worrisome thing of all is that Babylon looks *so close* to the New Jerusalem. God did create a good world; we are meant to enjoy life; God does delight in the beautiful things of earth. If the world system were a self-evident cesspool, the temptation for Christians to fall to its allures would be small. It is precisely the genuine benefits of technological advance and extensive trading networks that constitute the danger. Babylon promises all the glories of Eden, without the intrusive presence of God. It slowly but inexorably twists the good gifts of God—economic interchange, agricultural abundance, diligent craftsmanship—into the service of false gods.

At this point, one might feel that any participation in the world economy—or even any local economy—must be so fraught with idolatry that the only solution is to withdraw completely and live alone in the

---

[7] Richard Bauckham, "The Economic Critique of Rome in Revelation 18," in *The Climax of Prophecy: Studies in the Book of Revelation* (Edinburgh: T&T Clark, 1993), 338–83.

wilderness. But Revelation offers an alternative vision of life together: the New Jerusalem. This is "the city that comes down from heaven," and as such it is the consummate representation of God's grace. It stands in stark contrast to the self-made monstrosity that is Babylon.[8]

At one level, the New Jerusalem is a return to Eden—there is a river flowing through its midst, with the tree of life standing by with fruit-laden branches and leaves for the healing of the nations (Rev. 22:2). Humanity can once again walk in peace with God. Indeed, it outstrips Eden, since the glory of the Lord itself provides the illumination for the city (Rev. 22:5).

But the New Jerusalem is not simply a new and better garden: it is a garden-*city*, the urban ideal that forms the counterweight to Babylon. There is, for instance, still meaningful human participation in the life of the celestial city come to earth. Central to this, of course, is the worship people bring to God and the Lamb. But there seems to be more than this in the note that "people will bring into [the New Jerusalem] the glory and honor of the nations" (Rev. 21:24–26). In the ancient world, it was desirable to build a temple with the best materials from all over the world; this is what Solomon did for the temple in Jerusalem. More than that, people would bring gifts from far and wide to adorn the temple after its completion. It is probable that the image of kings bringing their gifts to the New Jerusalem flows from this background. It does not seem too much of a stretch to imagine that these gifts are the products of human culture, devoted now to the glory of God.[9]

We must also consider the implications of Old Testament visions of the future, which see it in meaningful continuity with present-day life. Isaiah 65, for example, is a critical background text for Revelation

---

[8] Richard Bauckham, *The Theology of the Book of Revelation* (Cambridge: Cambridge University Press, 1993), 126–43.

[9] Cf. G. B. Caird, *The Revelation of Saint John* (Peabody, MA: Hendrickson, 1993), 279: "Nothing from the old order which has value in the sight of God is debarred from entry into the new. John's heaven is no world-denying Nirvana, into which men may escape from the incurable ills of sublunary existence, but the seal of affirmation on the goodness of God's creation. The treasure that men find laid up in heaven turns out to be *the treasures and wealth of the nations,* the best they have known and loved on earth redeemed of all imperfections and transfigured by the radiance of God." See also Darrell T. Cosden, *The Heavenly Good* (Peabody, MA: Hendrickson Publishers, 2006), 72–77.

21–22 and provides its foundational teaching, "I am about to create new heavens and a new earth; the former things shall not be remembered or come to mind" (cf. Rev. 21:1). Yet this same chapter says of the future blessings of God's people, "They shall build houses and inhabit them; they shall plant vineyards and eat their fruit. They shall not build and another inhabit; they shall not plant and another eat; for like the days of a tree shall the days of my people be, and my chosen shall long enjoy the work of their hands" (Isa. 65:21–22). We can certainly argue that Isaiah is pointing, in ways suitable to his times, to something much greater than mere agricultural abundance—but he can hardly be pointing to less. Yet *less* is precisely what is typically offered in a vision of "heaven" consisting of nothing more than clouds, harps, and white robes.

Parsing out precisely how this works is not easy. Will there still be farming in the new heavens and new earth? Will a godly computer programmer's 1.0 software be consigned to the flames while version 2.0 enters the heavenly city? The Bible does not answer these types of questions directly, but we may once more look at the big picture. God created humans to exercise dominion over the earth, which entails creativity. Would it be sensible for such a God to then turn and regard work done in faith as useless and cast it aside? On balance, it seems far more likely that he would raise it up and perfect all that is done for his glory. Likewise, the prophetic vision of the future envisions people engaged in meaningful activity in the creation. Since God does not go into detail as to how this transfer of products from the now-world to the new-world works, or what exact things we might be doing in the future state, we can only guess at what this means concretely. But it does mean that we can be "always excelling in the work of the Lord, because [we] know that in the Lord [our] labor is not in vain" (1 Cor. 15:58).[10]

Conclusion to Revelation

What does this all mean for everyday life in the workplace? Revelation does not provide detailed instructions for best workplace practices,

---

[10] See Cosden, passim, and Miroslav Volf, *Work in the Spirit* (Oxford: Oxford University Press, 1991), esp. 88–122.

but it does provide some important guidelines, especially with respect to big picture issues. It is not enough to burrow our heads down and do our jobs and mind our business. We have to have some sense of where things are going, and why we are doing what we are doing.

The greater one's position of authority, the greater one's responsibility is to see that organization is directed toward ends that will glorify God, and that it is practiced in a way that expresses love for neighbor. In contrast to the exploitative nature of Babylon, Christian business should strive for mutual benefit: a fair exchange of goods and services, just treatment of workers, and a view toward the long-term good of the people and societies partnering in the enterprise.

While most workplaces today are not formally or informally affiliated with pagan gods (as they often were in the ancient world), subtler forms of idolatry can creep in unawares. One contemporary analogue to biblical Babylon would be a company that sees its own profit and continuity as the ultimate goals of its existence (with perhaps the CEO on the cosmic throne!). We must always remember that all of life is open to God and subject to his approval or disapproval. The annihilation of Babylon serves as a grim reminder that God is not mocked, and that this goes for our workplace dealings as much as religious concerns.

Ultimately, these loyalties reveal themselves in deeds. Those who commit themselves to the way of Jesus must strive to be above reproach in their ethics. The saints stand in abiding need of the forgiveness available through Jesus' blood, and they are called to imitate his fateful witness in their everyday lives.

But it is appropriate to conclude with the positive vision of the New Jerusalem. While there is necessarily a radical break between the now-world and the new-world, there is also a strong sense of continuity between the two. After all, the New Jerusalem is still the New *Jerusalem*. It shares things in common with the earthly city; indeed, it can be seen at one level as the consummation of all that the earthly Jerusalem aspired to be. In the same way, our future is ultimately a gift of God. Yet in the mysteries of his creative goodness, our deeds follow after us (Rev. 14:13)—certainly our deeds of kindness and our worship to God and the works of our hands as well.

BIBLIOGRAPHY

Agrell, G. *Work, Toil and Sustenance: An Examination of the View of Work in the New Testament, Taking into Consideration Views Found in Old Testament, Intertestamental and Early Rabbinic Writings.* Translated by S. Westerholm and G. Agrell. Lund: Ohlssons, 1976.

Aune, David E. "Rev. 6–16." Vol. 52b, *Word Biblical Commentary.* Dallas: Word, 1998.

———. "Trouble in Thessalonica: An Exegetical Study of 1 Thess. 4.9–12, 5.12–14 and II Thess. 6.6–15 in Light of First-Century Social Conditions." ThM thesis, Regent College, 1989.

Bailey, John A. "Who Wrote II Thessalonians?" *New Testament Studies* 25, no. 2 (1979): 137.

Bakke, Dennis W. *Joy at Work: A Revolutionary Approach to Fun on the Job.* Seattle: PVG, 2005.

Bakke, Raymond, William Hendricks, and Brad Smith. *Joy at Work Bible Study Companion.* Lake Mary, FL: Charisma House, 2005.

Balz, Horst R., and Gerhard Schneider. *Exegetical Dictionary of the New Testament.* Translated by J. W. Medendorp and Douglas W. Scott. Grand Rapids: Eerdmans, 1990–93.

Banks, Robert. *God the Worker: Journeys into the Mind, Heart and Imagination of God.* Sutherland, NSW: Albatross Books, 1992.

Barclay, John. "Conflict in Thessalonica." *Catholic Biblical Quarterly* 55 (1993): 512–30.

Bartchy, S. Scott. *MALLON CHRESAI: First Century Slavery and the Interpretation of 1 Corinthians 7:21.* Society of Biblical Literature Dissertation Series No. 11. Missoula: Scholars Press, University of Montana, 1973. Reprinted by Wipf & Stock, 2003.

Bauckham, Richard J. *The Theology of the Book of Revelation.* Cambridge: Cambridge University Press, 1993.

————. "The Economic Critique of Rome in Revelation 18." *The Climax of Prophecy: Studies in the Book of Revelation*. Edinburgh: T&T Clark, 1993.

————. *Jude, 2 Peter*. Edited by Bruce M. Metzger, David A. Hubbard, and Glenn W. Barker. Vol. 50, *Word Biblical Commentary*. Dallas: Word Books, 1983.

Bauer, W., W. F. Arndt, F. W. Gingrich, and F. W. Danker. *Greek-English Lexicon of the New Testament and Other Early Christian Literature*. 3rd ed. Chicago: University of Chicago Press, 2001.

Beale, G. K. *Revelation*. Grand Rapids: Eerdmans, 1999.

Berding, Kenneth. "Confusing Word and Concept in 'Spiritual Gifts': Have We Forgotten James Barr's Exhortations?" *Journal of the Evangelical Theological Society* 43 (2000): 37–51.

Best, Ernest. *The First and Second Epistles to the Thessalonians*. 2nd ed. British New Testament Conference. London: A & C Black, 1986.

Burke, Trevor J. *Family Matters: A Socio-Historical Study of Kinship Metaphors in 1 Thessalonians*. London: T&T Clark, 2003.

Caird, G. B. *The Revelation of Saint John*. Peabody, MA: Hendrickson, 1993.

Carr, Albert Z. "Is Business Bluffing Ethical?" *Harvard Business Review* 46 (January/February 1968).

Cicero. *Epistulae ad Familiares (The Letters to His Friends)*. Translated by W. Glynn Williams. 3 vols. Loeb Classical Library. Cambridge, MA: Harvard University Press, 1929.

Conzelman, Hans. *1 Corinthians*. Translated by James W. Leitch. Philadelphia: Fortress Press, 1975.

Cosden, Darrell T. *The Heavenly Good of Earthly Work*. Peabody, MA: Hendrickson, 2006.

De La Merced, Michael. "Released from Prison." *New York Times*. December 4, 2013.

Deming, Edwards W. *The New Economics for Industry, Government, Education*. 2nd ed. Cambridge, MA: MIT Press, 2000.

Dennis, John. "Cosmology in the Petrine Literature and Jude." *Cosmology and New Testament Theology*. Edited by Jonathan Pennington and Sean McDonough. London: Continuum, 2008.

Donfried, Karl P. "The Cults of Thessalonica and the Thessalonian Correspondence." *New Testament Studies* 31, no. 3 (1985): 341–42.

Dunn, Elizabeth, and Michael Norton. *Happy Money: The Science of Smarter Spending*. New York: Simon & Schuster, 2013.

Dunn, James D. G. *The Epistles to the Colossians and to Philemon: A Commentary on the Greek Text*. The New International Greek Testament Commentary. Grand Rapids: Eerdmans, 1996.

Ellul, Jacques. *Apocalypse*. Translated by G. W. Schreiner. New York: Seabury, 1977.

Engels, Donald. *Roman Corinth: An Alternative Model for the Classical City*. Chicago: University of Chicago Press, 1990.

Erisman, Al. "Gloria Nelund: Defining Success in the Financial World," interview on *Ethix* 80 (March/April 2012). http://ethix.org/category/archives/issue-80.

Fee, Gordon D. *The First Epistle to the Corinthians*. Grand Rapids: Eerdmans, 1987.

Freedman, David Noel. "Haustafeln" and "Household Codes." *The Anchor Bible Dictionary*. 6 vols. New York: Doubleday, 1992.

Frost, Robert. "The Death of the Hired Man." *North of Boston*. New York: Henry Holt, 1915.

Garland, David E. *1 Corinthians*. Baker Exegetical Commentary on the New Testament. Grand Rapids: Baker, 2003.

Gelsinger, Pat. "Faster Chips, More Opportunity?" interview in *Ethix* 57 (January/February 2008). http://ethix.org/2008/02/01/faster-chips-more-opportunity.

Green, Gene L. *The Letters to the Thessalonians*. Grand Rapids: Eerdmans, 2002.

Grudem, Wayne. *Business of the Glory of God: The Bible's Teaching on the Moral Goodness of Business*. Wheaton, IL: Crossway, 2003.

Harris, Murray J. *The Second Epistle to the Corinthians: A Commentary on the Greek Text*. Grand Rapids: Eerdmans, 2005.

Harrison, Steve. *The Manager's Book of Decencies*. New York: McGraw-Hill, 2007.

Hauerwas, Stanley. *Character and the Christian Life*. Notre Dame: University of Notre Dame Press, 2001.

Hawthorne, Gerald F. *Philippians*. Revised and expanded by Ralph P. Martin. Vol. 43, *Word Biblical Commentary*. Nashville: Thomas Nelson, 2004.

Hawthorne, Gerald F., Ralph P. Martin, and Daniel G. Reid, eds. "Ephesians, Letter to the." *Dictionary of Paul and His Letters*. Downers Grove, IL: InterVarsity Press, 1993.

Hawthorne, Gerald F., Ralph P. Martin, and Daniel G. Reid, eds. "Philippians, Letter to the." *Dictionary of Paul and His Letters*. Downers Grove, IL: InterVarsity Press, 1993.

Hock, Ronald F. *The Social Context of Paul's Ministry: Tentmaking and Apostleship*. Philadelphia: Fortress Press, 1980.

Holtz, Traugott. *Der erste Brief an die Thessalonicher*. Evangelisch-katholischer Kommentar zum Neuen Testament. Zürich: Benziger, 1986.

Jewett, Robert. *Romans: A Commentary*. Minneapolis: Fortress Press, 2007.

Johnson, Luke Timothy. *Brother of Jesus, Friend of God*. Grand Rapids: Eerdmans, 2004.

————. "The Letter of James." Vol. 12, *The New Interpreter's Bible*. Nashville: Abingdon Press, 1998.

————. *The First and Second Letters to Timothy: A New Translation with Introduction and Commentary*. The Anchor Yale Bible Commentaries. New York: Doubleday, 2001.

Kittel, Gerhard, Gerhard Friedrich, and Geoffrey William Bromiley, eds. *Theological Dictionary of the New Testament*. Grand Rapids: Eerdmans, 1985.

Kruse, Colin G. *The Letters of John*. Grand Rapids: Eerdmans, 2000.

Kuchment, Anna. "The Tangled Web of Porn in the Office." *Newsweek*. December 8, 2008. http://www.newsweek.com/2008/11/28/the-tangled-web-of-porn-in-the-office.

Laansma, J. *I Will Give You Rest: The Rest Motif in the New Testament with Special Reference to Mt 11 and Heb 3–4*. Vol. 98, Wissenschalftliche Untersuchungen zum Neuen Testament. Tübingen: Mohr Siebeck, 1997.

Lincoln, Andrew T. *Ephesians*. Vol. 42, *Word Biblical Commentary*. Nashville: Thomas Nelson, 1990.

Linsky, Martin, and Ronald A. Heifetz. *Leadership on the Line: Staying Alive Through the Dangerous Leading*. Boston: Harvard Business Review Press, 2002.

Longenecker, Richard N. *Galatians*. Vol. 41, *Word Biblical Commentary*. Waco, TX: Word, 1990.

Louw, Johannes P., and Eugene A. Nida. *Greek-English Lexicon of the New Testament Based on Semantic Domains*. 2 vols. New York: UBS, 1988.

Mackenzie, Alistair, and Wayne Kirkland. "Ethics." Theology of Work Project. December 1, 2010. http://theologyofwork.org/key-topics/ethics.

Malherbe, Abraham J. *Paul and the Thessalonians: The Philosophic Tradition of Pastoral Care*. Philadelphia: Fortress, 1987.

———. *The Letters to the Thessalonians*. *The Anchor Bible*. New York: Doubleday, 2000.

Marshall, Howard I. *1 and 2 Thessalonians*. New Century Bible Commentary. London: Marshall, Morgan and Scott, 1983.

Marshall, Peter. *Enmity in Corinth: Social Conventions in Paul's Relations with the Corinthians*. Wissenschaftliche Untersuchungen zum Neuen Testament 2.23. Tübingen: Mohr Siebeck, 1987.

Martin, Dale B. *The Corinthian Body*. New Haven: Yale University Press, 1995.

McAdams, Dan P. *The Redemptive Self: Stories Americans Live By*. New York: Oxford University Press, 2005.

McDonough, Sean M. *Christ as Creator: Origins of a New Testament Doctrine*. Oxford: Oxford University Press, 2010.

McFarland, Ian A. *Creation and Humanity: The Sources of Christian Theology*. Louisville: Westminster John Knox Press, 2009.

McKnight, Scot. "Collection for the Saints." *Dictionary of Paul and His Letters*. Edited by Gerald F. Hawthorne et al. Downers Grove, IL: InterVarsity Press, 1993.

Meeks, Wayne A. *The First Urban Christians: The Social World of the Apostle Paul*. 2nd ed. New Haven: Yale University Press, 2003.

Mitchell, Margaret M. *Paul and the Rhetoric of Reconciliation*. Louisville: Westminster John Knox Press, 1993.

Moo, Douglas. "Nature in the New Creation: New Testament Eschatology and the Environment." *Journal of the Evangelical Theological Society* 49, no. 3 (2006): 468–69.

———. *The Letter of James.* Grand Rapids: Eerdmans, 2000.

Mounce, William D. *Pastoral Epistles.* Vol. 4, *Word Biblical Commentary.* Nashville: Thomas Nelson, 2000.

Moy, Ed. "Faith and Work: Spiritual Insights from a Career in Business & Public Service." At *Kiros*, Seattle, October 11, 2013. http://kiros.btexpo.ws/media.

Murphy-O'Connor, Jerome. *Paul: A Critical Life.* Oxford: Clarendon, 1996.

Müller, Peter. *Anfänge der Paulusschule: Dargestellt am zweiten Thessalonicherbrief und am Kolosserbrief.* Abhandlungen zur Theologie des Alten und Neuen Testaments. Zürich: Theologischer, 1988.

Nicholl, Colin R. *From Hope to Despair in Thessalonica: Situating 1 & 2 Thessalonians.* Society for New Testament Studies Monograph Series. Cambridge: Cambridge University Press, 2004.

O'Brien, Peter T. *Introductory Thanksgivings in the Letters of Paul.* Vol. 49, *Novum Testamentum.* Leiden: Brill, 1977.

O'Connor, Flannery. "A Good Man Is Hard to Find." *Collected Works.* New York: Library of America, 1988.

Okorie, A. M. "The Pauline Work Ethic in 1 and 2 Thessalonians." *Deltio Biblikon Meleton* 14 (1994): 63–64.

Olson, Jeannine E. *Calvin and Social Welfare.* Selinsgrove, PA: Susquehanna University Press, 1989.

Osborne, Grant R. *Revelation.* Vol. 27, *Baker Exegetical Commentary on the New Testament.* Grand Rapids: Baker Academic, 2002.

Pace, Peter. "General Peter Pace: The Truth as I Know It." *Ethix* 61 (September/October 2008). http://ethix.org/2008/10/01/the-truth-as-i-know-it.

Piper, John. *Desiring God: Meditations of a Christian Hedonist.* Colorado Springs: Multnomah, 2003.

Polkinghorne, Donald E. *Narrative Knowing and the Human Sciences.* Albany: State University of New York, 1988.

Richard, Earl J. *First and Second Thessalonians.* Sacra Pagina. Collegeville: Michael Glazier, 1995.

Riesner, Rainer. *Die Frühzeit des Apostels Paulus: Stüdien zur Chronologie, Missionstrategie, und Theologie.* Tübingen: Mohr, 1994.

Romanuik, K. "Les Thessaloniciens étaitent-ils des parasseuz?" *Ephemerides Theologicae Lovanienses* 69 (1993): 142–45.

Sanders, E. P. *Judaism: Practice and Belief, 63 BCE-66 CE.* London: SCM Press, 1992.

Serafeim, George. "The Real Cost of Bribery." *Harvard Business School Working Knowledge.* November 4, 2013. http://hbswk.hbs.edu/item/7325.html.

Spicq, Ceslas. "Les Thessalonicien 'inquiets' etaient-ils des parrassuex?" *Studia theologica* 10 (1956): 1–13.

Stevens, R. Paul. *The Other Six Days.* Grand Rapids: Eerdmans, 2000.

Stott, John. *The Grace of Giving: 10 Principles of Christian Giving.* Lausanne Didasko Files. Peabody, MA: Hendrickson Publishers, 2012.

Strabo. *Geographica.* Translated and edited by Horace Leonard Jones. 8 vols. Loeb Classical Library. Cambridge, MA: Harvard University Press, 1930–1965.

Strong, James. *Enhanced Strong's Lexicon.* Ontario: Woodside Bible Fellowship, 1995.

Talbert, Charles H. *Reading Corinthians: A Literary and Theological Commentary on 1 and 2 Corinthians.* New York: Crossroad, 1987.

Thiselton, Anthony C. *The First Epistle to the Corinthians: A Commentary on the Greek Text.* New International Greek Testament Commentary. Grand Rapids: Eerdmans, 2000.

Towner, Philip H. *The Letters to Timothy and Titus.* New International Commentary on the New Testament. Grand Rapids: Eerdmans, 2006.

Volf, Miroslav. *Work in the Spirit.* Oxford: Oxford University Press, 1991.

Welch, Jack. "What I've Learned: Jack Welch." *Esquire.* December 31, 2006. http://www.esquire.com/features/what-ive-learned/wil0104jackwelch#ixzz2nkRA41TP.

Witherington, Ben. *1 and 2 Thessalonians: A Socio-Rhetorical Commentary.* Grand Rapids: Eerdmans, 2006.

———. *Revelation.* Cambridge: Cambridge University Press, 2003.

Wohlenberg, Gustav. *Der erste und zweite Thessalonicherbrief.* Kommentar zum Neuen Testament. Leipzig: Deichert, 1903.

Wolters, Al. "Worldview and Textual Criticism in 2 Peter 3:10." *Westminster Theological Journal* 49 (1987), 405–13.

Wright, N. T. *After You Believe: Why Christian Character Matters.* New York: HarperOne, 2010.

———. *The Resurrection of the Son of God.* Vol. 3, Christian Origins and the Question of God. Minneapolis: Fortress Press, 2003.

———. "The Letter to the Romans." Vol. 10, *The New Interpreter's Bible.* Nashville: Abingdon Press, 1994.

"Inaugural Global Slavery Index Reveals More than 29 Million People Living in Slavery." *Global Slavery Index 2013.* October 4, 2013. http://www.globalslaveryindex.org/category/press-release.

"Poliomyelitis Eradication." *Wikipedia.* http://en.wikipedia.org/wiki/Poliomyelitis_eradication.

"Should I Rank My Employees?" *Wall Street Journal*, April 7, 2009. http://guides.wsj.com/management/recruiting-hiring-and-firing/should-i-rank-my-employees.

CONTRIBUTORS

John Alsdorf resides in New York City and is a member of the Theology of Work Project's steering committee.

Katherine Leary Alsdorf is founder and director emeritus of the Center for Faith and Work at Redeemer Presbyterian Church in New York City. She is a member of the Theology of Work Project's steering committee.

Patricia Anders is editorial director of Hendrickson Publishers in Peabody, Massachusetts. She serves as editorial director for the commentary.

Jill L. Baker is an independent researcher of ancient Near Eastern archaeology and faculty fellow at Florida International University, Honors College, in Miami, Florida. She contributed to the commentary on 1 and 2 Samuel, 1 and 2 Kings, and 1 and 2 Chronicles.

Cara Beed is retired lecturer in sociology in the Department of Social Science, retired graduate advisor for the Faculty of Education, and retired honorary fellow at the Australian Catholic University in Melbourne, Victoria, Australia. She is a writer and researcher with works published in many international journals. She is a member of the Theology of Work Project's steering committee.

Daniel Block is the Gunther H. Knoedler Professor of Old Testament at Wheaton College in Wheaton, Illinois. He contributed to the commentary on Ruth.

Daniel T. Byrd is special assistant to the provost at the University of La Verne in La Verne, California. He served as a member of the Theology of Work Project's steering committee from 2007 to 2009.

Alice Camille is a nationally known Roman Catholic author, religious educator, and retreat leader. She resides in Desert Hot Springs, California. She contributed to the commentary on Joshua and Judges.

Darrell Cosden is professor of theological studies at Judson University in Elgin, Illinois. He served as a member of the Theology of Work Project's steering committee from 2007 to 2010.

Al Erisman is executive in residence at Seattle Pacific University in Seattle, Washington, and former director of technology at the Boeing Company. He serves as co-chair of the Theology of Work Project's steering committee. He contributed to the commentary on 2 John and 3 John.

Nancy S. Erisman volunteers as a board member of KIROS and on the leadership team at Westminster Chapel Women in the Workplace in Bellevue, Washington. She served as a contributing editor to the commentary.

Jarrett Fontenot resides in Baton Rouge, Louisiana. He served as a contributing editor to the commentary.

Larry Fowler resides in Gig Harbor, Washington. He served as a contributing editor to the commentary.

Russell Fuller is professor of Old Testament at Southern Baptist Theological Seminary in Louisville, Kentucky. He contributed to the commentary on Psalms.

Duane A. Garrett is the John R. Sampey Professor of Old Testament Interpretation at Southern Baptist Theological Seminary in Louisville, Kentucky. He contributed to the commentary on Deuteronomy, Ecclesiastes, and Song of Songs, and served as editor for the poetical books.

Mark S. Gignilliat is associate professor of divinity at Beeson Divinity School, Samford University in Birmingham, Alabama. He contributed to the commentary on Isaiah and served as editor for the prophetic books.

Michaiah Healy is youth pastor at the Greater Boston Vineyard in Cambridge, Massachusetts. She served as a contributing editor to the commentary.

Bill Heatley is the former executive director of Dallas Willard Ministries in Oak Park, California, and served as a member of the Theology of Work Project's steering committee. He contributed to the commentary on Colossians and Philemon.

Bill Hendricks is president of the Giftedness Center in Dallas, Texas. He is a member of the Theology of Work Project's steering committee.

Brian Housman is executive pastor at the Vineyard Christian Fellowship of Greater Boston in Cambridge, Massachusetts. He contributed to the commentary on 1 and 2 Samuel, 1 and 2 Kings, and 1 and 2 Chronicles.

L. T. Jeyachandran is former chief engineer (civil) at the Department of Telecommunications for the government of India in Calcutta, India, and former executive director of Ravi Zacharias International Ministries (Asia-Pacific) in Singapore. He is a member of the Theology of Work Project's steering committee.

Timothy Johnson is assistant professor of Old Testament and Hebrew at Nashotah House Theological Seminary in Nashotah, Wisconsin. He contributed to the commentary on Job.

Randy Kilgore is senior writer and workplace chaplain at Desired Haven Ministries/Made to Matter in North Beverly, Massachusetts. He is a member of the Theology of Work Project's steering committee.

Alexander N. Kirk resides in Wilmington, Delaware, and contributed to the commentary on 1 and 2 Timothy and Titus.

Aaron Kuecker is associate professor of theology and director of the Honors College at LeTourneau University in Longview, Texas. He contributed to the commentary on Luke and Acts.

Jon C. Laansma is associate professor of classical languages and New Testament at Wheaton College and Wheaton Graduate School in Wheaton, Illinois. He contributed to the commentary on Hebrews.

Clint Le Bruyns is director and senior lecturer at the Theology and Development Programme at the University of KwaZulu-Natal in Pietermaritzburg, KwaZulu-Natal, South Africa. He is a member of the Theology of Work Project's steering committee.

John G. Lewis is director of Saint Benedict's Workshop and Missioner for Christian Formation at the Episcopal Diocese of West Texas in San Antonio, Texas. He consulted on the commentary on Romans.

Kelly Liebengood is associate professor of biblical studies at LeTourneau University in Longview, Texas. He contributed to the commentary on James, 1 and 2 Peter, 1 John, and Jude.

Kerry E. Luddy is director of community relations and discipleship at Brighton Presbyterian Church in Rochester, New York. She served as a contributing editor to the commentary.

Grant Macaskill is senior lecturer in New Testament studies at the University of Saint Andrews in St. Andrews, Fife, Scotland, United Kingdom. He contributed to the commentary on Mark.

Alistair Mackenzie is senior lecturer at the School of Theology, Mission and Ministry, Laidlaw College in Christchurch, New Zealand. He is a member of the Theology of Work Project's steering committee.

Ryan P. Marshall is minister to students at Redeemer Community Church in Needham, Massachusetts. He served as a contributing editor to the commentary.

Steven D. Mason is associate provost and dean of faculty at LeTourneau University in Longview, Texas. He contributed to the commentary on Ezekiel.

Alice Mathews is the Lois W. Bennett Distinguished Professor Emerita at Gordon-Conwell Theological Seminary in South Hamilton, Massachusetts. She is a member of the Theology of Work Project's steering committee. She contributed to the commentary on Genesis 1–11, Proverbs, 1 and 2 Samuel, 1 and 2 Kings, 1 and 2 Chronicles, Introduction to the Prophets, Isaiah, Jeremiah, Lamentations, and Matthew. She also served as a consulting editor for the commentary.

Kenneth Mathews is professor of divinity at Beeson Divinity School, Samford University, in Birmingham, Alabama. He contributed to the commentary on Daniel.

Sean McDonough is professor of New Testament at Gordon-Conwell Theological Seminary in South Hamilton, Massachusetts. He is a member of the Theology of Work Project's steering committee. He contributed to the commentary on Joshua, Judges, John, and Revelation, and served as editor for biblical studies and the Epistles.

Tim Meadowcroft is senior lecturer in biblical studies at Laidlaw College in Auckland, New Zealand. He contributed to the commentary on Hosea, Joel, Amos, Obadiah, Micah, Nahum, Habakkuk, Zephaniah, Haggai, Zechariah, and Malachi.

William Messenger is executive editor of the Theology of Work Project in Boston, Massachusetts, and adjunct faculty member of

Laidlaw-Carey Graduate School in Auckland, New Zealand. He also serves on the board of directors of ArQule, Inc. He is a member of the Theology of Work Project's steering committee. He contributed to the commentary on Jonah and served as general editor.

Andy Mills is former president and CEO at Thomson Financial and Professional Publishing Group in Boston, Massachusetts. He serves as co-chair of the Theology of Work Project's steering committee.

Joshua Moon resides in Minneapolis, Minnesota. He contributed to the commentary on Jeremiah and Lamentations.

Colin R. Nicholl is an independent researcher and author in Northern Ireland, United Kingdom. He contributed to the commentary on 1 and 2 Thessalonians.

Valerie O'Connell is an independent consultant in Burlington, Massachusetts. She served as a contributing editor to the commentary.

Jane Lancaster Patterson is assistant professor of New Testament at Seminary of the Southwest in Austin, Texas. She consulted on the commentary on Romans.

Jonathan T. Pennington is associate professor of New Testament and director of Ph.D. studies at Southern Baptist Theological Seminary in Louisville, Kentucky. He contributed to the commentary on Matthew and served as editor for the Gospels and Acts.

Gordon Preece is director of Ethos: the Evangelical Alliance Centre for Christianity and Society in Melbourne, Victoria, Australia. He is a member of the Theology of Work Project's steering committee.

Mark D. Roberts is executive director of digital media at the H. E. Butt Family Foundation/The High Calling in Kerrville, Texas. He is a member of the Theology of Work Project's steering committee. He contributed to the commentary on Ezra, Nehemiah, Esther, Galatians, Ephesians, and Philippians.

Haddon Robinson is the Harold John Ockenga Distinguished Professor of Preaching, senior director of the Doctor of Ministry program, and former interim president of Gordon-Conwell Theological Seminary in South Hamilton, Massachusetts. He is president and chair emeritus of the Theology of Work Project.

Justin Schell is on the global leadership and support team with The Lausanne Movement. He served as a contributing editor to the commentary.

Andrew J. Schmutzer is professor of biblical studies at Moody Bible Institute in Chicago, Illinois. He contributed to the commentary on Genesis 1–11.

Bob Stallman is professor of Bible and Hebrew at Northwest University in Kirkland, Washington. He contributed to the commentary on Genesis 12–50, Exodus, Leviticus, and Numbers.

Christine S. Tan is director of marketing and social media at the Theology of Work Project in Boston, Massachusetts. She served as a contributing editor to the commentary.

Hanno van der Bijl resides in Mobile, Alabama. He is web editor at the Theology of Work Project and served as a contributing editor to the commentary.

Bruce Waltke is professor emeritus of biblical studies at Regent College in Vancouver, British Columbia, Canada. He has also held teaching positions at Westminster Theological Seminary in Glenside, Pennsylvania, and Knox Theological Seminary in Fort Lauderdale, Florida, where he is a distinguished professor of Old Testament. He contributed to the commentary on Proverbs and served as editor for the Pentateuch.

Joel White is lecturer in New Testament at Giessen School of Theology in Giessen, Germany. He contributed to the commentary on 1 and 2 Corinthians.

Andy Williams is program manager at HOPE International in Kigali, Rwanda. He served as a contributing editor to the commentary.

David Williamson is director emeritus of Laity Lodge in Kerrville, Texas. He is a member of the Theology of Work Project's steering committee.

Lindsay Wilson is academic dean and senior lecturer in Old Testament at Ridley Melbourne Mission and Ministry College in Melbourne, Victoria, Australia. He contributed to the commentary on Psalms.

INDEX OF NAMES AND SUBJECTS

Note: page numbers in *italics* indicate most significant occurrences.

accountability, 21, 22, *33*, 78–79, *154*

activist, 9

ambition. *See* motivation

anger, *127*, *197–98*

appreciation, 85

assessment (performance), 9, 29, 53, 77, 85, *91–92*, *111–12*, *132–33*, *222*

assessment (self), 77, *111–12*

authority, *36–37*, *105*, 199, *204–5*, *213–14*

bad boss, 28

bakers, 21

balance of life and work. *See* work (life rhythm)

beauty, 18

blame, *13*, 203

blessing (material), *160–61*

blue collar work, 35, *146*

bribery, *219–20*

calling, 4, 47–48, *48–49*, *101–6*, 212

calling (changing jobs), *56*

calling (discerning), 56, *220*

Carr, Albert, *20*

character, 25, *219*

charity (dependence on), *140–43*

commitment, *87*

common good. *See* human flourishing

communication, *197–98*, *202–3*, *223–24*, 226

community, *41–43*

community (Christian), 53, 101, *116*, 148

compassion, 35

competition, *31–32*, 96

conflict, *39–40*, 49, 127

conflict (personality), *128*

conflict (resolving), *49*, *72–73*, 96, *114–15*, *134*, 203, *224*, *225*

cook, 21

corporate social responsibility, *162–64*, *198*, *240*

correction (discipline), 148, *186–87*, *227*

corruption, 219–20

corruption (church), *196–97*, *226–27*

corruption (workplace), *37–38*, 105–6, *196–97*

Cosden, Darrell, *215*

creation, *79–80*, *121*, *122*, *154*, *158–59*, *173–76*, *233*

creativity, 18

creation mandate, *122–23*, 144, *167–68*, *175*

culture (countercultural), *20–21*, *37–38*, *125*, *129*

culture (engaging), *49–50*, *54–55*, *60*, *156*

culture (workplace), *155*, *156*, *168*, *200*, 226

deception, 7, *127–28*, *222*

decision making (Christian), *32–33*

diligence, *144–45*, *178*

discipleship. *See* spiritual growth

discrimination, *225*

discrimination (class), *199–200*

discrimination (ethnic), 200, *207*

discrimination (gender), *159*, 200, *207*

dress code, *40*

Dunn, Elizabeth, *205*

economic development, *198–99*

economics, 88, *234–38*

end times, *215–17*

entrepreneurship, 65

eternity, *18*, 139–40, *217*

ethics, *23, 24*, 35, *36–37, 39–40,
82–83, 96–97, 103–6, 156, 219*

ethics (responding to temptation), 195

evangelism. *See* sharing faith

excellence, 53, *78–79, 87*, 96, 97, 132,
144–45

exploitation, 235, 237

failure, *24–25*, 184–85, 195, *196*, 205–6

fairness, *134, 207, 214*

faith, *13–16*, 78, 139, *183–85, 195–97,
200, 202*

faithfulness (human), *15–16, 28*, 195,
235–36, 240

faithfulness (God's), *11, 18, 28*

farming, *17*, 208

financial planning, *205–6*

forgiveness, 29, *124*, 180

freedom, 96–98

generosity, 34, *64–65, 85–86, 89–91,
197*

gifts, *34*, 48–49, *61–63*, 85–86

God's work, 4–6, *11–13*, 16, *18, 101,
108–9, 121*, 123, *173–76*, 179–80,
233

gossip, 7, 148–49, *164–65*, 203,
224–26

government, *37–38*, 65, 164, 199

grace, 6, *16–18*, 19–20

greed, 7, *127*

grief. *See* sorrow

growth. *See* productivity

healing, 210

Holy Spirit, *61*

homemakers, *157*

honesty, *70–71, 75–76*, 208–9,
209–10, 219, *221–23*

hospitality, *41, 188–89*

hostility, 10–11, 40–41, *166*, 195, *210.*
See also sacrifice, suffering, serving God (consequences of))

human flourishing, 23, 24, *32, 34, 42,
54, 57–58, 60, 61–63*, 65, *87–89*,
97, 102, *114, 164, 198, 199, 207, 240*

humbleness, *30*, 40, *75–76, 109, 113,*
203

idolatry, *7, 8, 126–27, 237–38*

inadequacy (feelings of), 76

integrity, *70–71, 73–74, 157*, 219,
222–23

investing, 161–62

jealousy, 7

Jesus as priest, *181–83*

joy, *71–72*, 195

judging others, *8*, 10–11, *19, 23–24,
39–40*, 84, *91–92*, 203

judgment (God's), *187–88, 215–17*

justice, *10, 11–12*, 24, *36–37*, 92,
206–7, 234–35

justice (economic), *59, 64–65*

justice (resource distribution), *64–65,
87–89, 146–48, 198–99*

kingdom of God, *166–67, 231–32,*
233

kingdom of God (already but not yet),
18, 26–27, 144, 177, *184*, 210, *213*

kingdom of God (redemption of the
world), 4–5, 18, *26*, 79–80, 82,
100, 175–77, 215, 233, *234. See
also* redemptive work

kingdom of God vs. kingdom of the
world, 27, *235–36*

kingdom of God (restoration), *122*

kingdom of God vs. worldly values,
57–58, 161, *176–77*, 211, *237–38,
240*

labor, *178*

lawyer, *22*

laziness, *140–43, 148*

leadership, 34, *53–54, 77–78, 145,* 155, *157,* 197–98, *204–5,* 227, *240*

leadership (servant), 20, *53–54, 77–78, 214*

legacy, *163*

listening, *197–98*

love, *36,* 62–63, 80, 200, *218–22,* 224

Luther, Martin, *201*

lying. *See* deception

management, 9, *19,* 95, 104, *106,* 133, *207, 222*

material blessing. *See* blessing (material)

material world (blessing of), 89–91

material world (spiritual value of), *52–53, 63–64,* 158–59, *175, 187– 88,* 190, *215–17, 233, 238, 239*

meekness, *40*

mentoring, *51–52, 145,* 160, 163

mercy, *28–29,* 203, *227*

military, 30

mission statement, *49,* 155, 164

mistakes (admitting), 12, *24–25, 76*

mistakes (learning from), 29

money, *161–62, 189–90, 206–7. See also* wealth

motivation, *53–54, 57–58, 73–74, 75, 109, 116–17, 132–33,* 161–62, *166–70,* 190, *203, 204–5, 218*

Moy, Ed, *222*

Nelund, Gloria, *199*

nonbelievers (working with), *54–55, 81–85, 156*

Norton, Michael, 205

parenting, 22, 116, 123

patience, 97, 208

pay, *59, 116–17, 206–7*

peer group, *22*

performance assessment. *See* assessment (performance)

persecution. *See* hostility

perseverance, *196*

politics, 88, 147, 199

politician, 9

poverty, 89, *196, 197, 198,* 199–200, 207

power, 124, *204, 207, 213–14*

power of God, 4

prayer, *69, 114,* 130, *155–56, 209*

prophecy, 34

prosperity gospel, *90*

provision from God, 59–60, *89–91, 190, 195–97, 200, 204*

pride, 125–26

purpose, 19, *20,* 24, 42, 49, *57–58, 77,* 96–98, *100, 101–2,* 147–48, *197, 198, 199, 211*

reconciliation, *80. See also* conflict (resolving)

redemptive work, 36–37, 154, 196–97. *See also* kingdom of God (redemption of the world)

relationship with God, *4–5, 123–24,* 175

relationship with God (reconciliation), *4–5,* 6–7, *18*

relationships, 4–6, *11–13, 39–40,* 41, *72–73,* 159

relationships (work), *7, 10–11,* 22–24, 25, *34, 41–42, 68–69, 81–85,* 226. *See also* teamwork

respect, *9–10, 36,* 40, *159,* 214

rest, *178–79*

retirement, 164

risk, *114*

Sabbath, *178–79*

sacred vs. secular, 56, 62, 126–29, *153–54, 158–59, 191,* 196–97, 202, *220,* 233

sacrifice, *32,* 92, *124, 191, 212–13. See also* hostility, suffering

sadness. *See* sorrow

salvation, *4–6,* 27, *180, 202*

self-assessment. *See* assessment (self)
selfishness, *31, 109–13, 199*, 203, *204*
servant leadership. *See* leadership
  (servant)
serving God, 103, *106, 125, 130*, 132,
  166–68, 181
serving God (consequences of),
  103–4, 105, 129, *166, 195, 210*,
  222–23, 235–37
serving others, *23, 31–32, 77*, 96–98,
  112–13, 167–68, 188–89, *198–99*,
  201–2, *204–5*
sexual harassment, *159*
sharing faith, 40–41, 87, 142
sharing faith (work as witness), 30,
  144–45, 155, 156, 168, 220
sin, *18–20, 21–22, 127–28, 154*,
  176–77, 196–97, *209–10*
skills. *See* gifts
slavery, *55–56*, 95, *102–3, 104–6*,
  131–33, 237
Smith, Rob, *219–20*
social capital, *164*
sorrow. *See also* suffering
spiritual forces (evil), *18–19, 196–97*
spiritual gifts, *61–63. See also* gifts
spiritual growth, 19–20, 21, *22, 25*,
  96–97, 127, 154–55, 159, *186*, 195,
  209, *218–20*
status, 41–42, *50–52*, 200
stewardship, *57–58, 64–65*
success, *196*, 205–6
suffering, *16–18, 25*, 28, 76, *77–78*,
  182–83, 186–87, 191, 210, 213–
  14, 234–35. See also hostility,
  sacrifice
supervisor, 9

sustainability (environmental), *164,*
  235

talents. *See* gifts
taxes, *37–38*
teacher, 9, 34
teamwork, *34, 41–42*, 51. *See also*
  relationships (work)
tithe, *64–65*
Tri-Link Global (company), *199*
Tyco International (company), *37*

unemployment, *140–43, 146–48*, 195
unpaid work, *143*, 188–89

value of work, 42, 63–64, *100*, 139–
  43, *175, 215–17, 220*, 232, *233*
Vietnam, *199*
vision, 49
vocation. *See* calling
vocations (multiple), *59, 139, 158, 212*

wealth, 90, *161, 196*, 199–200, *206–7,*
  232
Welch, Jack, *222*
whistleblowing, 105
wisdom, *195–96*
women and work, 41–42, 114–15, 147,
  158
work life rhythm, *178–79*
workplace examples (lists), 6, 9,
  10–11, 21, 22, 23, *25–26, 70*, 97,
  195, 196, 200, *204, 207–8*, 208–9,
  213–14, 219
worship, 146, 178–79, 181, *238*

yoked with Jesus, 79–80, *82*

About the Theology of Work Project

The Theology of Work Project is an independent, international organization dedicated to researching, writing, and distributing materials with a biblical perspective on work. The Project's primary mission is to produce resources covering every book of the Bible plus major topics in today's workplaces. Wherever possible, the Project collaborates with other faith-and-work organizations, churches, universities and seminaries to help equip people for meaningful, productive work of every kind.

Theology of Work Bible Commentary
By the Theology of Work Project

William Messenger, Executive Editor, Theology of Work Project
Sean McDonough, Biblical Editor, Theology of Work Project
Patricia Anders, Editorial Director, Hendrickson Publishers

Contributors to Volume 5:

Theology of Work Steering Committee, with thanks to consultants John Lewis and Jane Patterson, "Romans and Work"
Joel R. White, "1 Corinthians and Work" and "2 Corinthians and Work"
Mark Roberts, "Galatians, Ephesians, Philippians and Work"
Bill Heatley, "Colossians & Philemon and Work"
Colin Nicholl, "1 & 2 Thessalonians and Work"
Alex Kirk, "The Pastoral Epistles and Work"
Jon C. Laansma, "Hebrews and Work"
Kelly Liebengood and Al Erisman, "The General Epistles and Work"
Sean McDonough, "Revelation and Work"